ROSSETTI

DANTE GABRIEL ROSSETTI

1853

From the drawing by William Holman-Hunt
Reproduced by permission of Mrs. Holman-Hunt

[*Frontispiece*

ROSSETTI
His Life and Works

Evelyn Waugh

With an Introduction by
John Bryson

Duckworth

This edition with new Introduction 1975
First edition 1928
Second edition (Duckworth's Georgian Library) 1931
Gerald Duckworth & Co. Ltd
The Old Piano Factory
43 Gloucester Crescent, London NW1

ISBN 0 7156 0772 3

Printed and bound in Great Britain by
REDWOOD BURN LIMITED
Trowbridge & Esher

CONTENTS

LIST OF ILLUSTRATIONS

INTRODUCTION

by John Bryson

During the recent Rossetti exhibition at the Royal Academy young visitors all but out-numbered their elders. They came to see a painter and a school which, long out of fashion, was once again coming into favour. Tired, perhaps, by too much exposure to the austerity of abstract art they were discovering the pleasures of colour and symbolism and of 'literary' painting—just as a few years earlier a revival of Beardsley had attracted them. It is particularly interesting therefore to read Evelyn Waugh's first book: not only for a look at Waugh's beginnings as a writer, but to discover what a clever young man had made of Rossetti half a century ago, at a time when there was little general interest in the Pre-Raphaelites—an interest which the book itself was to help create. When he wrote it in 1928, the centenary of Rossetti's birth, the Pre-Raphaelite revival had not yet begun. For twenty years, Waugh tells us, their painting had ceased to command any authoritative admiration, so all he could do was to write a plain account of Rossetti's life and work. For two reasons he thought this might be worth doing. One reason was Rossetti himself—as a character for a story-book his life was of intense interest. The other reason was that the doctrine of criticism was no longer being preached according to Ruskin but according to Mr Roger Fry. People were learning about 'pure painting' and 'significant form'; they were being told that literary painting was 'out', and that an artist was little affected by the aesthetic value of his subject or his surroundings. For proof let them look at Van Gogh's 'Boots'. It might then be stimulating to turn, if only for a few hours, from 'the pellucid excellencies of Picasso to the turgid and perverse genius of Rossetti'.

Waugh's book remains a stimulating introduction both to Rossetti's life and to his work. It is based on the sources then available—on William Michael Rossetti's various books, on the memoirs and letters of contemporaries, on Marillier's catalogue and study of the paintings and on A. C. Benson's volume in the 'English Men of Letters' series. One other source he had which we may envy him: from Sir Hall Caine, who survived till 1931, he got much valuable information on some of the obscurer passages in Rossetti's history.

This is a young man's book with his provocative prejudices and enthusiasms, and his occasional inaccuracies. There are youthful high-spirits in the writing. Observing Millais' easy desertion of his early Pre-Raphaelite scruples in pursuit of social and sporting success Waugh remarks: 'After all, you can see Nature and all that from the back of a horse just as well as cramped over an easel, and in far better company, what's more.' He tells how he himself spent an exceedingly ungraceful half-hour before his looking-glass trying to get into the anatomically impossible position of the nude youth in Rossetti's *Sphinx* drawing. Waugh had a family interest in the Pre-Raphaelites as he explains briefly and enigmatically—'Thomas Woolner the sculptor married one of three handsome sisters called Waugh. Holman Hunt married both the others.' Not however in double harness but successively, the second marriage taking place in Switzerland to avoid the provisions of the Deceased Sister's Marriage Act. Already in his Oxford scholarship exam, Waugh wrote copiously about the Pre-Raphaelites but was not vivaed on them. He was to find later on that William Morris shared his views about the dons. Morris, he tells us gleefully, had, like many wise people before and after him, found life at Oxford pitiably disappointing —the dons idler than those of today, more widely ignorant and no less tedious. But there were unadmitted compensations in the life there. He had some talent for drawing which he was able to practise at the Ruskin School, and he had a good eye for a picture. Time spent among Thomas

Combe's collection of Pre-Raphaelites in the Ashmolean Museum must have helped to lay the foundation for his book.

Here in the making is the writer who was never afraid to give forcible expression to his likes and dislikes. Benjamin Woodward, architect of the University Museum and the Union Society Library, was the 'archfiend' of Oxford architecture—an opinion that will not please the Victorian revivalists today. 'That idiotic Bell Scott' is a *bête noir*, since he preferred South Kensington art-training which worked up from pyramids and spheres to the 'Dying Gladiator' to Ruskin's method at the Working Men's College. There they were taught to draw from leaves and twigs, and Waugh sensibly points out that it was not Ruskin's aim to train finished artists. Rossetti's early industrial patrons like Leathart, Rae and Plint are invoked to point a moral and adorn the tale. They were, he says, men of simple life and great business acumen, *and* they had a mystical respect for the Arts:

> Nowadays of course this class does not exist. Admitted to the pleasures of the aristocracy, our merchant princes no longer emulate their tastes. Lord Wavertree need not pretend to the aesthetic enthusiasms of the Walkers, to the humility with which these good men approached artists of genius, even when they could not fully understand them.

His gift for a well-turned phrase is already evident and he knows the value of apt comparison and anecdote. The ill-fated Walter Deverell, who discovered Miss Siddal, was a handsome young man 'who looked so much like Phiz's drawings of Steerforth'. Charles Faulkner, mathematics don and a founder member of the Morris firm 'was ploughed in 'Divvers' for including Isaiah among the twelve apostles'.

The young Rossetti is introduced to us as Holman Hunt saw him. Long hair, pushing stride, loud voice, careless in dress, allowing the spots of mud to remain dry on his legs for several days. But even today first impres-

sions sometimes need correction. On approach he proved
to be courteous, gentle and winsome, in every respect a
cultivated gentleman. There we can recognise the young
man portrayed in that most attractive of his self-portraits,
the drawing done when he was nineteen and now in the
National Portrait Gallery. By general consent Rossetti's
watercolours of the early period are his purest and most
graceful work, showing 'a delicate enchantment and
splendour of colour that are very lovable'. Not only his
water-colours but the drawings of Lizzie, described by
Madox Brown as 'wonderful and lovely Guggums one
after another, each one a fresh charm, each one stamped
with immortality'. 'How much more beautifully, perfectly, and tenderly you draw,' Rusking told him, 'when
you are drawing her than when you are drawing anyone
else. She cures you of all your worst faults.' Two of the
water-colours are chosen by Waugh for appreciation and
analysis, *Dante Drawing an Angel* from the Ashmolean
(which Ruskin rightly called 'a thoroughly glorious work')
and *Arthur's Tomb* from a private collection. They are
among Rossetti's finest; they represent two moods and
the two major sources of his inspiration—the *Vita Nuova*
and the *Morte d'Arthur*. Waugh also appreciates the
quality of the elaborate pen drawings which are perhaps
less to our taste today—the *Hamlet and Ophelia* and the
one he calls (with an inaccurate but forgivable recollection
of his title) *Mary at Simon Peter's Door*. He realises that in
these the artist was not attempting plain black-and-white
line drawings but making pen-and-ink pictures with
depth and contrast of tone.

   It was in his earliest period that Rossetti was in closest
touch with Ruskin, and when dealing with the relationship Waugh's sympathies are with the older man. There
was indeed a pedantic element in Ruskin's character that
could irritate, but his encouragement of the younger
artist was genuine, generous, and—it is perceptively
observed—based on his own need for friendship. Rossetti
saw that Ruskin was in the mood to make his fortune;
was this then the thought that lay behind his side of the

friendship? Certainly later references to his patron are not always generous or pleasing.

> I do not see [says Waugh] any reason to laugh at the older and more generous man; if he was partly a prig Rossetti was partly a cad, and it is extraordinary how little there is that is priggish in any of his dealings with Rossetti.

Ruskin was more than kind to Elizabeth Siddal, his 'Princess Ida'. With a simple if naïf charm he invites her to come out from Chatham Place to Denmark Hill to walk in the garden and feel the fresh air, and look at a missal or two. 'She would have the run of the house,' he writes to Rossetti, 'and if she would like an Albert Dürer or a photograph for her bedroom I will get it for her.' He sent her to Oxford and put her under Dr Acland's care for observation of her health. There she was welcomed with academic courtesy, and thanks to her hosts received a good deal of attention 'in somewhat exclusive quarters'. She became friendly with Dr Pusey and his daughter at Christ Church, and perhaps met there a young don occupied with his Maths and not yet busy with his camera. She took carriage exercise with Mrs Combe of the Clarendon Press, and as a special treat she was invited by the Warden of New College to come and look at a drawing of a black beetle by Dürer and compare it with a live one from the college kitchen. A practical application of true Pre-Raphaelite method; but that invitation she did not accept.

The long engagement and the marriage with its tragic end is treated with understanding and sympathy but without sentimentality. It may be an overstatement to say that Rossetti was marrying a dying woman; yet it is true that he was consecrating the past, preserving a remembered and not to be repeated happiness. His memorial tribute, the *Beata Beatrix*, is in Waugh's opinion Rossetti's supreme achievement, but when he calls it 'the most purely devotional and spiritual work of European art since the fall of the Byzantine empire' he is surely letting enthusiasm outrun his judgment.

In the long series of 'female heads with floral adjuncts' (as William Michael neatly described them) two faces now look out from all his canvases: the fair and voluptuous Fanny Cornforth and the pensive Jane Morris as she filled his dream—'her dark beauty growing less human as the years went by'. He did use other models, but as Waugh says 'the fact remains that all the voluptuous figures do bear a most confusing resemblance to Mrs Schott, and all the pensive ones—even those that are designedly portraits of quite other people—to Mrs Morris'. With the little evidence available Waugh wisely does not speculate on the nature of the relationship with Janey. In his criticism of these later pictures Waugh shows that he has a keen eye and a very individual way of indicating their merits and their faults. He admires the sensuous splendour of *Monna Vanna* but notes that the great swirl of the white-and-gold dress stands out as though at some yards from the body 'like the partially deflated envelope of an airship designed by some tipsy Maharajah'. He appreciates the richness of *The Beloved* but notices the doubtful drawing, and he cannot agree with the ever-admiring F. G. Stephens that Rossetti is a great colourist. He feels that the painter loved bright things like a child or a peasant but lacked sensitive feeling for the modification of colour and for its structural value. The economy and the richness of a truly great colourist he demonstrates by apt comparison with a Rubens portrait in the National Gallery. Can we agree with him? Is he right about the late work when he suggests that its monotony is due not so much to failure of imagination as to a grasping desire for money? Rossetti was at heart essentially ramshackle in the ordering of his life and affairs and Waugh sees a lack of what he calls 'moral stability' in the readiness to turn out replicas. Even the *Beata Beatrix* was not spared in the profitable profusion of this activity. It is indeed an aspect of Rossetti that no admirer can afford to overlook, but one must not forget that fine things like *Proserpine* and *The Day Dream* came from the late years too.

Friends and contemporaries fill in the background of the story. The young Hall Caine from Liverpool drifts into his position as house-mate at 16 Cheyne Walk and accompanies Rossetti on that last grim autumn visit to Cumberland, with the inescapable Fanny in attendance. Waugh does not adopt the common view of Theodore Watts as a slightly comic figure who took Swinburne under his care at Putney, nor does he repeat the text of Whistler's mocking telegram when Watts added 'Dunton' to his name—'Theodore, what's Dunton?' He is shown as a sound man of business for whom Rossetti had warm respect and whose friendship was one of the bright features of those last gloomy years. Watts was reluctant to interfere with Nature 'in her clever scheme of the survival of the fittest', and so had his excuse ready for the unkempt state of the garden at Cheyne Walk and for whatever of the pets may have remained. Whistler is there as a neighbour in Tite Street and often with him Charles Augustus Howell who is very well described:

A connoiseur of art, a forger, a liar, the least loyal and most enchanting of friends, Howell passes through his period, the Munchausen of the Pre-Raphaelite circle.

Waugh's hope that someone who had known him would write about Howell was fulfilled by Mrs Angeli, Rossetti's niece and last survivor of the circle, in her charming book of reminiscences *Pre-Raphaelite Twilight*. The ever-watchful Max had, of course, already caught him with his partner Rosa Corder in the very act of perpetuating the touch of the vanished hand. The generous side of Rossetti's nature is seen in the way he came to the aid of James Smetham's family. He promoted the sale of his pictures among his own friends when Smetham, torn between Methodism and mysticism, suffered a permanent mental break-down. Enduring affection for his mother is another attractive trait. It is evident in his letters to her and in the tribute of the Sonnet he designed for her eightieth birthday.

The patrons also appear. There is William Graham

who commissioned the enormous *Dante's Dream* but, finding it too large for his house, ordered a reduced version. Then the solicitor Valpy, 'the Vampire', acquired it, but in the end he too exchanged it for smaller works. It was through Hall Caine's efforts that it eventually found its home in the Liverpool Art Gallery. Constantine Ionides and his sister Aglaia were friends as well as buyers. *The Day Dream*, Rossetti's favourite portrait of Mrs Morris, was painted for him and on his death went with his collection to the Victoria and Albert Museum. Frederick Leyland, ship-owner and collector, was another friend whose quarrel with Whistler over the Peacock Room is better remembered than his friendship with Rossetti.

In conclusion Waugh asks what is wrong with Rossetti. Conscious perhaps of Fry looking over his shoulder he does not ask what is right. Submitting his work to the tests of pure painting and significant form he finds it wanting. To look at a head as so much mass, so much variation of colour, so much light and shade, was alien to Rossetti's thought. He is a literary painter, one who knew no distinction between beauty of picture and beauty of subject. His subject is the beauty of woman and his art is devoted to its exaltation. That this need be no restriction has been shown by greater painters than Rossetti; the question simply is whether the artist's treatment has been worthy of the subject. Waugh finds a spiritual inadequacy, a sense of ill-organisation about all that Rossetti did: for him the work lacks the essential rectitude that underlies the serenity of all great art. The problem, he finds, is that here and there in his life Rossetti transcends this inadequacy and his art in fitful moments flames into the exquisite beauty of *Beata Beatrix*. The object of the book was to state the problem, 'though, alas! not to solve it'.

Now, having looked at Rossetti in the lively company of the young Evelyn Waugh, we may ask ourselves whether *we* are still faced with the problem he failed to solve. Is his judgment too sweeping? Is it in fact a real problem, or have moral and artistic values been confused?

Is the lack of serenity that is so obvious in his life equally present in his art? Is it indeed only in fitful moments that he transcends his weaknesses? If these questions still confront us when looking at Rossetti's later work there remains, Waugh would agree, the serenity of his earlier vision. Serenity achieved in the splendid water-colours, in the many sad and tender drawings of Guggum, and in his poetry.

Editor's Note

This edition is a photographic reprint, with a few corrections, of the 'second edition' published in Duckworth's Georgian Library in 1931. In giving titles of pictures Waugh tended to trust to memory and sometimes the titles given are wrong or incomplete. Thus 'The Wedding of St George and Princess Sabra' appears simply as 'The Marriage of St George'. As these titles are not likely to mislead they have been left as they are. In one case, *Monna Vanna* (facing page 138), Waugh wrongly stated that the portrait was of Fanny Cornforth: this has been corrected to Alexa Wilding. A portrait of Fanny Cornforth has been inserted opposite page 64.

The following books are additions to Rossetti studies since the original publication of Evelyn Waugh's book:

Rosalie Glynn Grylls, *Portrait of Rossetti*, 1964
Oswald Doughty and John Robert Wahl (eds), *The Letters of Dante Gabriel Rossetti*, 4 vols., 1965.
Fredeman, W. E., *Pre-Raphaelitism: a Biocritical Study*, 1965.
John Nicoll, *The Pre-Raphaelites*, 1970.
Virginia Surtees, *The Paintings and Drawings of Dante Gabriel Rossetti: a Catalogue Raisonné*, 1971.
John Bryson (ed.), *Dante Gabriel Rossetti and Jane Morris. Their Correspondence*, 1975.

J.B.

AUTHOR'S NOTE

THE authorities for Rossetti's life are copious and access-
ible; of these the most important are: *Dante Gabriel
Rossetti, Letters and Memoir*, and *Ruskin, Rossetti, Pre-
Raphaelitism*, edited and written by his brother William.
(The Ruskin letters which I have quoted in Chapter III
are taken from the second of these works.) *Pre-Raphael-
itism and the Pre-Raphaelite Brotherhood*, by William
Holman-Hunt; *Recollections of D. G. Rossetti*, by Sir
Hall Caine (from which I have quoted some extracts of
Rossetti's correspondence quoted in Chapter VI); *Auto-
biographical Notes* of William Bell Scott; *Recollections of
D. G. Rossetti and his Circle* by Treffry Dunn, from which
I have quoted two substantial extracts in Chapter IV;
The Truth about Rossetti, an article by Theodore Watts-
Dunton in the *Nineteenth Century* of March 1883;
Ancient Lights, by Ford Madox Hueffer, from which I
have quoted some passages from Ford Madox Brown's
Diaries; *The Life of William Morris*, by J. W. Mackail.

For the dates of Rossetti's pictures I have followed
H. C. Marillier's excellent iconography, *Dante Gabriel
Rossetti*. Of the books written about Rossetti, by far the
best is A. C. Benson's volume in the *English Men of
Letters Series*; there are also useful little lives of him
by Joseph Knight, Mr. Frank Rutter, and Mr. Ford
Madox Hueffer. I have quoted extensively from F. G.
Stephens's monograph, in order to show by example the
critical chaos amidst which Rossetti worked.

I am deeply grateful to Sir Hall Caine for much
valuable information on some of the more obscure
passages in Rossetti's history; and to Mrs. Holman-
Hunt for permission to reproduce as frontispiece the
singularly interesting portrait by her husband.

E. W.

CHRONOLOGICAL TABLE

1828.   May 12th, birth.

1846.   Enters Antique School of Royal Academy.

1848.   Meets Ford Madox Brown.
Meets Millais and Hunt.
Formation of P.R.B.

1849.   *The Girlhood of the Virgin*.

1850.   *Ecce Ancilla Domini*.
Meets Miss Siddal.

1852(?).   Meets Fanny Cornforth (Mrs. Schott).

1853.   Miss Siddal's health causes anxiety.

1854.   January, Holman-Hunt leaves England.
Ruskin takes up Rossetti and Miss Siddal.
Found.

1856.   *The Oxford and Cambridge Magazine*.
Meets Morris, Burne-Jones, etc.

1857.   *The Marriage of St. George*.
Red Lion Square.
The Union frescoes.
Meets Jane Burden (Mrs. Morris).

1860.   Miss Siddal desperately ill.
Marriage.

1861.   Publication of *The Early Italian Poets*.

1862.   February, death of Mrs. D. G. R.
16 Cheyne Walk.

1862–67.   The good years.
Beata Beatrix.
Lady Lilith.
The Beloved.

1867.   Insomnia.

1868–69.   Visits to Penkhill.

1869.   Disinterment of poems.

1870.   Publication of poems.
Chloral.
Kelmscott.

1871.   October, " The Fleshly School."

xvii

1872.   *The Fleshly School* appears as pamphlet.
June, collapse.
Urrard and Stobhall.
Kelmscott.
Meets Watts-Dunton.

1873.   *Proserpine.*

1874.   Publication of *Dante and his Circle.*
Leaves Kelmscott for Cheyne Walk.

1875.   Aldwick Lodge.
Broadlands.

1877.   *Astarte Syriaca.*
Severe illness.   Herne Bay.

1877–81.   Complete reclusion.

1880.   Meets Sir Hall Caine.

1881.   Autumn, Vale of St. John.
Publication of *Poems* and *Ballads and Sonnets.*
Collapse.
Birchington.

1882.   Easter Day, death.

CHAPTER I

ORIGINS

Introduction—The Rossetti family—Childhood of Dante Gabriel Rossetti.

" Among my earliest recollections none is stronger than that of my father standing before the fire when he came home in the London winter evenings, and singing to us in his sweet, generous tones : sometimes ancient English ditties—such songs as one might translate from the birds, and the brooks might set to music ; sometimes those with which foreign travel had familiarised his youth—among them the great tunes that had rung the world's changes since '89. I used to sit on the hearthrug listening to him, and look between his knees into the fire till it burned my face, while the sights swarming up in it seemed changed and changed with the music, till the music and the fire and my heart burned together and I would take paper and pencil and try in some childish way to fix the shapes that rose within me. For my hope, even then, was to be a painter."—D. G. ROSSETTI, *St. Agnes of Intercession.*

" I know that real artists, even if they are destined to paint highly imaginative works and to go mad in the end like Van Gogh, generally begin by making an elaborate study of an old pair of boots or something of that kind."—MR. ROGER FRY, *The Artist and Psycho-Analysis.*

I

BIOGRAPHY, as books about the dead are capriciously catalogued, is still very much in the mode.

It has usurped the place held in recent years by the novel, and before that by poetry, as the regular *métier* of all those young men and women who, in every age, concern themselves with providing the light reading of their more cultured friends. Naturally enough, a new manner has resulted, and, to a great extent, a new method ; and polite literature is the less polite for it.

No doubt the old-fashioned biography will return, and, with the years, we shall once more learn to assist with our fathers' decorum at the lying-in-state of our great men ; we shall see their catafalques heaped with the wreaths of august mourners, their limbs embalmed, robed, uniformed, and emblazoned with orders, their faces serenely composed and cleansed of all the stains of humanity. Meanwhile we must keep our tongue in our cheek, must we not, for fear it should loll out and reveal the idiot ? We have discovered a jollier way of honouring our dead. The corpse has become the marionette. With bells on its fingers and wires on its toes it is jigged about to a " period dance " of our own piping ; and who is not amused ? Unfortunately, there is singularly little fun to be got out of Rossetti.

Perhaps because he was a foreigner, and so far removed from the life of the Court and the governing class, perhaps because he was, in an odd kind of way, so essentially an artist, he alone of the fabulous paladins of the last century was never, to any serious extent, a humbug. During his lifetime his moral reputation made him the bogey of many Victorian drawing-rooms, so that there is little to be gained by blackguarding him. For twenty years his painting has ceased to command any authoritative admiration. Without hope of scandal, then, all that remains is to write a plain account of his life and work. But there are two reasons why such a book may be interesting.

One is Rossetti himself. Taking him simply as a character for a story-book, his life is one of intense interest ; but it is necessary first to clear away the traces of legend that hang about him.

"What a supreme man is Rossetti," wrote Philip Marston, the blind poet. "Why is he not some great exiled king, that we might give our lives in trying to restore him to his kingdom ? "

This sort of homage was offered prodigally by the

little circle at Cheyne Walk, and genially accepted. It became, in fact, the normal attitude of approach even for people as little given to hero-worship as Whistler. But it is misleading to insist too strongly upon this dominant regality of Rossetti's.

" He was master of the moment, of the scene, of the company," wrote A. C. Benson, " the undisputed sovereign of any group in which he found himself."

This sort of reputation can be achieved by anyone who is dogmatic, plausible, and vain ; it is shared by eminent actors and newspaper proprietors.

It is true that when he was already a young painter of distinction he was able to impress and inspire a group of undergraduates, and—what is more important—that to the end of his life he could always command the deepest affection and respect from a certain number of friends, among them some of the acutest intellects and most vigorous personalities of his age. But he seldom " found himself " in any other group. At the time of Philip Marston's aspiration, quoted above, he was living a life of almost unbroken seclusion, surrounded by his little court and never seen except in his own impressive surroundings. It was even thought necessary for him to publicly contradict the story that the Princess Louise had been turned away from his door. He was an autocrat in his own household, like many less-known Victorian husbands ; but it does not do to think of him as too much hedged by divinity. There were so many kings just at that time ; like her Saxon predecessor, Queen Victoria had her ship manned almost exclusively by royalties of one sort or another ; and Rossetti has better claims to our attention.

As one follows the story of his life one leaves behind the benign genius of Theodore Watts-Dunton's *Aylwyn* and finds the baffled and very tragic figure of an artist born into an age devoid of artistic standards ; a man of the South, sensual, indolent, and richly versatile, exiled in the narrow, scrambling, specialised life of a Northern city ; a mystic without a creed ; a Catholic without the discipline or consolation of the Church ; a life between the rocks and the high road, like the scrub of a Southern hillside, sombre, aromatic, and impenetrable.

The second reason is suggested by the two quotations at the head of this chapter—an antithesis typical of the change that has come over the artistic standards of Europe in the last fifty years. Criticism has narrowed and clarified from the time of Ruskin to the time of Mr. Roger Fry ; there is probably less nonsense talked about art than ever before, but it is impossible sometimes to suppress the suspicion that with it all there has been a good deal of impoverishment, and that only a part of the æsthetic problem has been solved. Æsthetics must inevitably be a deductive study, and it gives a stimulating *frisson* to one's æsthetic standards to turn, if only for a few hours, from contemplating the pellucid excellencies of Picasso to the turgid and perverse genius of someone like Rossetti.

2

Gabriel Charles Dante Rossetti, as he was christened —Dante Gabriel, as he afterwards chose to be called— was born on May 12th, 1828, at No. 38 Charlotte Street, Fitzroy Square, the second of four children born in successive years. The family remained in the same house until 1836, when they moved to No. 50 in the same street. It was a curious atmosphere for the upbringing of four highly imaginative children.

First there was their father, Professor Gabriele Rossetti, a venerable and fantastic figure, who would sit long into the night, a vast snuff-box at his elbow, a black shade over his eyes, deep in the forgotten scholarship of gnostics and astrologers ; a textual intriguer of indefatigable ingenuity, for whom no passage of Dante was capable of its natural interpretation, but was a vehicle for concealing under symbols and ciphers the ultimate wisdom of the cabalists. " The highest praise for a book, in Gabriele Rossetti's mouth, was that it was a *libro sommamente mistico.*" A Catholic who had never recovered his faith from the raw

free-thinking of his youth, he had developed a religion
of his own from his readings of Swedenborg and the
sacred books of the Brahmins, which, however much it
may have consoled him in his exile and old age, left his
children very little but a mild and muddled awe with
which to confront a very difficult world. He was a
member of the Italian Freemasons in the days when they
were an active political force. Throughout his long life
he retained an unaffected enthusiasm for any kind of
plot, and he must at one time and another have been
connected with every kind of plot there is.

He was born in 1783 of very humble parentage. His
father, Nicolo, was blacksmith at Vasto, in the Abruzzi
(or, as one of Rossetti's biographers prefers, " connected
with the iron trade of that city "). He and his wife were
both wholly illiterate, but Gabriele soon gave promise of
exceptional ability, drew quite creditably, took an interest
in antiquities, and wrote songs for opera. When he was
twenty-five years old, Napoleon handed over the old
Bourbon kingdom of Naples to Joachim Murat. The
new Court had to make friends where it could, and
Gabriele rose rapidly into favour. He became secretary
in the Department of Public Instruction at Rome and
curator of the bronzes at the Museo Borbonico at Naples.
He was a warm supporter of the Napoleonic regime.

In 1815 all the dispossessed princes crept out of hiding,
and " Bomba " with them. During the years that
followed, Gabriele plotted heartily and wrote inflam-
matory verses. In 1820 he was in the thick of a highly
successful little revolution ; in 1821 " Bomba " came
back with an Austrian army, revoked the constitution,
and made out a list proscribing all the more eminent
liberals, Gabriele among them.

Sir Graham More, an English admiral, was cruising
in the bay at the time when Gabriele's plight became
known. At Lady More's suggestion, a party of blue-
jackets was marched up the street where he lay in hiding.
He had already been supplied with a pair of bell-bottomed
trousers, and, while the sailors marked time outside the

house, he slipped in among them and marched off, an incongruous figure, to Sir Graham's ship—an escapade in the true tradition of British seamanship.

After that he spent three years at Malta teaching Italian, and then moved to London, where in 1826 he married Frances Mary Lavinia Polidori.

By birth Mrs. Rossetti was half Italian and wholly pedagogic. Her father, Gaetano Polidori, was a teacher of Italian, and her mother, a Miss Pierce, was an English governess. Until her marriage Mrs. Rossetti was governess to the family of a Sir Patrick Macgregor ; her sister was governess to the Marquess of Bath ; her brother, resolved on a more exciting career, travelled with Byron as his physician, and committed suicide in 1821. Gaetano Polidori made a certain amount of money, and settled down near Great Missenden with a printing press, from which, at irregular intervals, he produced clumsy little editions of cautionary tales for children.

The mothers of important people seem, as a rule, to give evidence of many generic similarities. Mrs. Rossetti was practical, sympathetic, devoted, an excellent house-wife, pious, possessed of great rectitude and considerable learning, of ample and matronly appearance. How many great men have left the same sort of description of their mothers ? She outlived Dante Gabriele by three years.

The eldest of the children was Maria Francesca, born in 1827. She was the least famous of the four, though by no means inconsiderable. She took her duties as eldest daughter very seriously, was inevitably quite learned about Dante, wrote a little with real delicacy, and entered an Anglican convent at the age of forty-six. William Michael was born in 1829 ; Christina Georgina in 1830.

It was a nursery teeming with temperament, and down-stairs in the dining-room things were even more exciting. Practically every Italian who came to London found himself at some time or another in the Rossetti circle ; scholars, organ grinders, refugee aristocrats met in

Charlotte Street to lament the state of their country and plot feverishly in four languages—Mazzini, proposing an invasion of the Papal States in balloons so that Mrs. Carlyle should not be sea-sick ; Benedetto Sangiovanni, a modeller in clay who, it was said, had once stabbed somebody in Calabria ; Filippo Piotrucci, endlessly engaged in making water-colour drawings of the children because he had no other means of subsistence ; on one occasion Louis Napoleon. When dinner was served, all would be invited to dine. Some would do so ; others would slip away to eat farinacious dishes in shabby restaurants ; others would continue the argument over the fire, declaring stubbornly that they had already dined.

" The tragic passions of the group about the fire did not in the slightest degree involve either the mother, the daughters, or the sons. . . . The guests took it in turn to discourse, and no one had delivered many phrases ere the excitement of speaking made him rise from his chair, advance to the centre of the group, and there gesticulate as I had never seen people do except on the stage," wrote Holman-Hunt. " Each orator evidently found difficulty in expressing his full anger, but, when passion had done its measure in work and gesture, so that I as a stranger felt pained at not being able to join in practical sympathy, the declaimer went back to his chair and, while another was taking up his words of mourning and appeal to the too tardy heavens, the predecessor kept up the refrain of sighs and groans. When it was impossible for me to ignore the distress of the alien company, Gabriel and William shrugged their shoulders, the latter with a languid sign of commiseration, saying ' it was generally so.' "

It is no wonder that, with this background, Rossetti found an English day school intolerably colourless. He was sent to a small private school in Portland Place in 1836, and next year to King's College School, where he spent five years, without making any particular mark. He was dreamy, timid, and bored. With his imagination captured by the richer education of his home, he regarded

Br

his work and play as a tiresome interruption. He learned some Latin and a little Greek. Italian, French, and German he already knew. Mathematics and science were abhorrent to him. He made no friends. His life was lived in and for his home ; listening wide-eyed to his father's friends, reading undirected among his father's books—*Melmoth the Wanderer*, *Hamlet*, Keats— writing verse, fiction, and drama, drawing, competing with William and Christina in *bouts-rimés* sonnets. It was a household in which artistic expression was not a freak or a hobby but a normal activity of man.

In 1842 he left school. At this time his father's health was beginning to fail, and money was short, for Italian was beginning to give place to German in English education. During the next ten years the situation became more' acute. It would have been very easy for his parents to have urged him into some profession or trade ; but neither now nor ten years later, when Mrs. Rossetti was obliged to take up teaching again to keep her home together, did they ask or expect any such sacrifice.

There was once a talk of his becoming a telegraph operator. The story was told by Holman-Hunt at the unveiling of the Rossetti memorial on Chelsea Embankment.

"Without waste of time he asked to be shown the work that would be expected of him. He was assured that it would be the simplest in the world, and this was demonstrated by sight of the instrument at work. There were two dials like clock faces, and to each there was an index. The operator took hold of a handle. Rossetti laughed to hear the thing going ' clock, click, click ' and to see the needle going about in fits. ' There, you see,' said the gentleman, ' that's all.' ' Nothing else ? ' commented Gabriel. ' I am extremely obliged to you. It is really amusing. I won't tax your kindness more. It would be absolutely useless for me to undertake the work. I could not do it."

As soon as he left school he went to Cary's Academy, an institution in Bedford Square known as " Sass's." Here he spent four years of irregular application, often wasting days in fits of idleness, writing a great deal of verse, reading and translating the Italian poets, picking up old prints cheap, visiting art exhibitions, scheming to buy an easel, and between times working hard at the probationary drawing necessary to secure admission to the academy schools.

In 1846 his drawing was approved, and he began his career as a serious student of art in the Antique School at the British Museum.

CHAPTER II

THE PRE-RAPHAELITES

The condition of English painting—Haydon—The new patrons—The
Academy—Madox Brown—The origins of Pre-Raphaelitism—Millais
and Hunt—The Brotherhood—The Academy, 1850—Water-colours—
Elizabeth Siddal—Ruskin rescues the P.R.B.

I

IT was a particularly difficult time in which to take up
painting. There were no masters. Landseer was the
favourite of the public, Dyce of the connoisseurs, Maclise
and the kindly Egg were respectable but scarcely inspiring
figures ; Constable had died in 1837 ; Wilkie in 1841 ;
Turner was seventy-one years old, sinking like one of his
own tremendous sunsets in clouds of obscured glory ;
Etty, an infirm old man, sometimes toiled up with infinite
labour to the life school in Trafalgar Square, but had for
many years now allowed his late-won success to seduce
him from the superb technique which alone excused his
essential vulgarity of taste, and with an unsteady hand he
debauched his incomparable flesh tints with greens and
violets and ultramarine.

The tragic death in 1846 of the last of the great classical
painters seemed to epitomise the barrenness and brutality
of the age. On June 22nd Benjamin Haydon was found
dead, a pistol by his side, and the last entry in his diary :

" God forgive me ! Amen. Finis.—B. R. HAYDON.

" ' Stretch me no longer on the rack of this tough
world.'—*Lear*."

It was a catastrophe to shock and discourage many
young painters, for Haydon had, in his time, been a great
figure.

"There are various tempers or habits of egotism. Benjamin Haydon's was simple vanity, intellectual and personal, which made it impossible for him to regard any other man as of the same species as himself."[1]

An invitation to dinner with Lord Mulgrave and the normal courtesies he met with inflamed him in his later years against an aristocracy which "flattered and fawned on him" during his brief prosperity; he raved against the Academy with maniacal fury when it would not accept him immediately at his own stupendous valuation; he squandered the large sums he frequently received—as much as £1,760 for one picture—with futile prodigality.

"He was unconsciously like a comic hero in a farce as he ascended to a well-filled drawing-room, waiting for dinner. Approaching the door, he turned back his coat collar on either shoulder, inflated his chest, even beat his bosom to raise his spirits, and lifted his head high in the air."

A vain, turbulent, thriftless braggart whom everyone tried to help and none could save; in the years that followed his death there were many uneasy consciences that had to be consoled with the truth of this picture.

"At this Westminster Hall Exhibition, I saw all my acquaintances and among them one to whom it carried the warrant of death.[2] I mean Haydon. . . . He walked about like a man in a dream, now and then waking up, affecting an amused manner, then again collapsing. He, the father and master in this country of high art—not only master indeed, but apostle and martyr —found himself surrounded by works more 'scholastic,' 'academic,' and so forth than his own, executed by dozens of young men who had grown up unknown to him, and to whom he was apparently unknown. The inflation was gone: he was suddenly changed into an aged man. . . . Youth can stand much, it takes a great deal to kill at twenty-five, but this veteran, on that day, was one of the most melancholy of spectacles."

[1] William Bell Scott: *Autobiographical Notes.*   [2] Ibid.

Poor Mr. Toad, deserted by Rat, Badger, and even
Mole, with the stoats and the weazels permanently
established in his inheritance !

But this was the man who had defended the Elgin
Marbles, when Payne Knight and all the fashionable
experts denounced them as the work of provincial masons
and Roman copyists. Who

> When men stared at what was most divine
> With brainless idiotism and o'erwise phlegm

had

> Beheld the full Hesperian shine
> Of their star in the East, and gone to worship them.

He had been the last to preserve the broken tradition
of pupil-apprenticeship ; the first to urge on the Govern-
ment the employment of English artists in the decoration
of the new Houses of Parliament ; the last champion of
the Grand Manner, cramped into studios scarcely big
enough to hold his canvases, unable to afford paint
enough for his vast surfaces, or models enough for his
massive compositions, living on potatoes for weeks at a
time, the sheets from his bed taken for draperies, wearing
himself out from dawn to dusk and then by lamplight
to another dawn.

There was something wrong with a generation which
flocked, 12,000 strong a week, to giggle at General Tom
Thumb, while Haydon was dying of neglected vanity.
Indeed the transition from aristocracy to industrialism
came very near to crushing out English Art altogether ;
the present generation is confronted by the incalculable
consequences of the transition from industrialism to
democracy. Rossetti was fortunate as far as finance is
concerned in growing up with a generation between the
two processes. By the time that he came to maturity, he
found a whole class of wealthy patrons ready to support
him—-Peter Millar of Liverpool, George Rae of Birken-
head, Leathart of Gateshead, Plint of Birmingham ; men
of simple life, great business acumen, and a mystical
respect for the Arts.

" I may notice that Mr. Millar's hospitality is somewhat peculiar in its kind," wrote Ford Madox Brown.
" His dinner, which is at six, is one of joint and vege-
tables *without* pudding. Bottled beer for only drink—
I never saw any wine. His wife dines at another table
with his daughters. . . . The chief things I saw were
chain cables forged, and Hilton's *Crucifixion*, which is
jolly fine. . . . His house is full of pictures even to the
kitchen, which is covered with them. Many he has at
all his friends' houses in Liverpool, and his house in
Bute is filled with his inferior ones."

Nowadays of course this class does not exist. Admitted
to the pleasures of the aristocracy, our merchant princes
no longer emulate their tastes. Lord Wavertree need
not pretend to the æsthetic enthusiasms of the Walkers,
nor to the humility with which these good men approached
artists of genius, even when they could not fully understand them.

To the young artists beginning their careers in the late
'forties, the artistic world was thus rich in opportunity
and poor in leadership.

The Academy held a unique position. Even now,
after seventy years of assault and ridicule by every critic
of repute, it still retains great prominence in the public
attention ; ambitious artists still secretly submit their
works to that austere tribunal and conceal their rebuffs.
In the 'forties it was still practically unchallenged except
by the jealous and the disappointed and the personally
quarrelsome. It had all the position that an academy
should have and none of the discretion. It had inherited
a code of conventions from its founders, and academic
recognition was dependent on submission to this code ;
unfortunately it allowed submission to become the only
requisite for recognition. There were fewer competitors
in those days and more spaces. If one followed the
rules laid down with sufficient industry, success was
fairly easily attainable. One might have one's work
hung so near the floor that only those who stooped low
could see it, or it might be " skied " inaccessibly at the

ceiling, but one could be tolerably sure of having it hung. The result was a series of the dreariest exhibitions ever presented at Burlington House. It only needed a decade of prominent nonentities to show up the inadequacy of the Academic Code.

This code, peculiarly inapplicable to the trivial subject pictures then in vogue, was derived mainly from the Caracci interpreted by Sir Joshua Reynolds, " Sir Sloshua " as the Pre-Raphaelites called him.

The canvas was painted like a door in three smooth, solid layers. First the tone values were laid in, then the half light, then the deep shadows and high lights ; " chiaroscuro " meant that the relation of light to darkness must be constant in any picture, darkness preponderating by the ratio of three to one. The bituminous surface was then " toned " with varnish. Viewed obliquely the design was usually invisible in a sheen of reflected light. At the right angle it achieved a certain mellow harmony that went well with dining-room mahogany and roast mutton.

The composition was entirely two-dimensional and took the form of an S or a triangle. Certain types of beauty and dignity were expected in the models portrayed. Within these limits the painters could indulge their fancy to the full in prettiness and pathos, and it was by means of these qualities that they attempted to attract attention.

2

It was into this world that Rossetti came in search of a master.

" A young man of decidedly foreign aspect, about 5 feet 7¼ inches in height, with long brown hair touching his shoulders, not taking care to walk erect, but rolling carelessly as he slouched along, pouting with parted lips, staring with dreaming eyes—the pupils not reaching the bottom lids—grey eyes, not looking directly at any point, but gazing listlessly ; the openings large and oval, the

lower orbits dark coloured. His nose was aquiline but
delicate, with a depression from the frontal sinus shading
the bridge, the nostrils full, the brow rounded and prominent, and the line of the jaw angular and marked, while
still uncovered with beard. His shoulders were not
square, but yet fairly masculine in shape. The singularity of gait depended upon the width of hip, which was
unusual. Altogether he was a lightly built man, with
delicate hands and feet; although neither weak nor
fragile in constitution, he was nevertheless altogether
unaffected by any athletic exercises. He was careless in
his dress, which then was, as usual with professional men,
black and of evening cut. So superior was he to the
ordinary vanities of young men that he would allow the
spots of mud to remain dry on his legs for several days.
His overcoat was brown, and not put on with ordinary
attention; and, with his pushing stride and loud voice,
a special scrutiny would have been needed to discern
the reserved tenderness that dwelt in the breast of the
apparently careless and defiant youth. But anyone who
approached and addressed him was struck with sudden
surprise to find all his critical impressions dissipated in a
moment; for the language of the painter was refined and
polished, and he proved to be courteous, gentle, and winsome, generous in compliment, rich in interest in the
pursuit of others, and in every respect, so far as could be
shown by manner, a cultivated gentleman."[1]

He did not find what he wanted in the Academy
Antique School. Very little attention was paid to the
students there beyond occasional fragments of sententious
counsel dropped by some great man in his way through
the building. The students were left for hours at a time
to work away on highly elaborate studies of the broken
surfaces of the Parthenon frieze, cross-hatched with the
regularity of engine-turned metal, a dot precisely in the
centre of each interstice. Rossetti for the most part
contented himself with scribbling little drawing of palfreys

[1] W. Holman-Hunt: *Pre-Raphaelitism and the Pre-Raphaelite Brotherhood.*

and dragons and damozels; he soon collected a small court of idlers to whom he presented these sketches as he did them. All the time he hungered for paint.

After two years at the Academy, he wrote:

" Every time I attempt to express my ideas in colour " —the phrase is worth noting: it is not his " ideas about colour " that he wishes to express—" I find myself baffled, not by want of ability—I feel this, and why should I not say it ?—but by ignorance of certain apparently insignificant technicalities which, with the guidance of an experienced artist, might soon be acquired. . . . I have got two men in my eye who, possessing abilities equal to the most celebrated, have by some unaccountable accident not obtained, except among brother artists, that renown which they merited. These therefore would, I should think, be the persons to apply to."

The two painters referred to are Ford Madox Brown and—probably—G. F. Watts.

A month later—in March 1848—he addressed the following letter to Madox Brown[1]:

" SIR,—I am a student in the Antique School of the Royal Academy. Since the first time I ever went to an exhibition (which was several years ago, and when I saw a picture of yours from Byron's " Giaour ") I have always listened with avidity if your name happened to be mentioned, and rushed first of all to your number in the catalogue. The *Parisina, the Study in the manner of the early masters, Our Lady of Saturday Night,* and the other glorious works you have exhibited, have successively raised my admiration, and kept me standing on the same spot for fabulous lengths of time. The outline from your *Abstract Representations of Justice,* which appeared in one of the illustrated papers, constitutes, together with an engraving after that great painter, Von Holst, the sole pictorial adornment of my room. And as for the *Mary Queen of Scots,* if ever I do

---

[1] Some time before this he wrote a letter of the same kind to William Bell Scott which also resulted in a lasting friendship.

anything in the art, it will certainly be attributable in a great degree to the constant study of that work.

" It is not therefore to be wondered at if, wishing to obtain some knowledge of colour (which I have as yet scarcely attempted), the hope suggests itself that you may possibly admit pupils to profit by your invaluable assistance. If, such being the case, you would do me the honour to inform me what your terms would be for six months' instruction, I feel convinced that I should then have some chance in the art.

" I remain, Sir, very truly yours,

" GABRIEL C. ROSSETTI."

Everyone knows the story of how this letter was received. Brown, at the time, was not quite twenty-seven years old. He came of violent seafaring stock and would himself have been a sailor if his father, a veteran of the famous *Arethusa*, had not prejudiced his chances of promotion by " speaking his mind " to Commodore Coffin. Unaccustomed even to the most moderate praise and assuming the letter to be a piece of impertinence, he presented himself at the Rossetti doorstep armed with a bludgeon. No blows were struck, however, and Rossetti did not know until some time later of the danger he had been in as he ran downstairs in eager welcome of his furious visitor. Convinced of his sincerity, Brown agreed to take Rossetti as a pupil, refusing to accept any payment. They started work together a few mornings later in Brown's studio.

In this way began one of the most permanent of Rossetti's friendships but, as an artistic apprenticeship, the arrangement was not a great success. It is doubtful how many lessons he had from Madox Brown ; they were certainly not many. He began by copying Brown's picture of *Angels Watching the Crown of Thorns* ; he seems to have enjoyed this. Later Brown set him to work on a still life of some medicine bottles. Here he showed less than Chardin's enthusiasm. His attendance slackened as it had at the Academy. Soon he was merely dropping in for a talk, but these weeks are important in bringing Rossetti into touch at second hand with the Nazarene school of painting.

This school had arisen many years before among the German colony in Rome. During the Napoleonic period this colony had been distinguished by a number of very gifted students, Peter Von Cornelius of Düsseldorf, Friedrich Overbeck of Lubeck, Philipp Veit of Frankfort, William Schadow of Berlin, Schnow, Korh, Führich, and others. They executed some frescoes at various villas, notably *The History of Joseph* in the Prussian Consul's house on the Pincio, and then scattered, for the most part to take up important civic positions in Germany. Only Overbeck remained with a small following. He fell more and more under the influence of the Italian primitives, exciting the contempt of the critics by the austerity with which he denied himself the advantages of all subsequent discoveries. Veit at Frankfort developed upon similar lines. They taught that the religious faith of the artist and his purity of life were vital factors in his art. Many of their followers adopted a monastic life and monastic clothing. They have much in common with the Dominican movement centring round Mr. Eric Gill today. It was scarcely a movement that could be healthily transplanted into Victorian England. Dyce in a mild and cultured way reflected some of its more graceful characters. Brown, who had met Overbeck in Rome, took to some of his technical methods, particularly in the *Our Lady of Saturday Night* (now in the Tate Gallery under the name of *Our Lady of Good Children*), but his salt-tanned temperament was impervious to his spiritual implications. With Rossetti the Nazarene School made an immediate appeal, and its influence, merging with another quite different Mediævalism, determined the character of his work for the next ten years.

This other Mediævalism was already a luxuriant growth. It had started in the middle of the eighteenth century at Strawberry Hill. *The Castle of Otranto,*

Christabel, and the Waverley Novels mark the development of a fashionable craze into a solid literary school. The French Revolution ended the Rococo. The gay love stories of the *ancien régime* gave place to terrific baronial romances of feuds and tournaments, dungeons, witchcraft, and ruined towers. Even the novelettes of the nursery-maid teemed with historical characters ; the humour of the period was spiced with archaisms ; public houses began to proclaim their antiquity in German " black letter " and a generous use of " ye " and " olde " ; domestic architecture developed vaulted halls and Gothic traceries and castellated parapets as Romance threw up her frail machicolations against the inexorable advance of the industrial system.

While Rossetti was still a child, new force had been leant to this tendency by the Catholic revival in the Church of England. The bric-à-brac of Gothic decoration became enriched with metal work and embroidery and a whole new heraldry of ecclesiastical emblems. Mrs. Rossetti, in spite of a strictly Evangelical upbringing, accepted with zest the new glamour that had arisen about church-going. For her two daughters, as for so many spinsters of modest means and urban surroundings, religion became the one vital thing in life. With Gabriel it remained a part of the broad pageantry in which he lived, merging in a luminous haze with Malory and *Melmoth the Wanderer,* his richly loaded palette and the distant, intimate life of the Italian renaissance. His was a philosopher's stone which turned everything that he touched, high and base metal alike, into a golden mist ; Nazarene, Florentine, and Crusader fused into one shadowy figure, glowing and distorted.

3

In 1848 Rossetti fell under another influence which retains a fictitious importance as the original Pre-Raphaelite Brotherhood.

The movement began, as it ended, with people talking

in Bloomsbury. The first conversations had taken place
in what was then No. 83 Gower Street between William
Holman-Hunt and John Everett Millais.

Millais was from earliest childhood marked out for
success. The exhibition of " Johnny " and his sketches
was always one of the liveliest delights of an evening in
Mrs. Millais's drawing-room. He was admitted to the
Academy School at the preposterous age of ten. He was
a pretty little boy, usually dressed in velvet and lace, with
very long fair curls ; at first he suffered considerably from
the more robust students, who would toss him into the
air, use him as a dumb-bell, and carry him by his heels
all over the British Museum, his hair sweeping the floor.
At length Mrs. Millais invited the most brutal of them
to tea in Gower Street, and from then onwards he was able
to press on to prosperity unmolested. In 1843, at the
age of fourteen, he was awarded the gold medal for
drawing from the Antique. By the time Hunt met him
his hair was cut in a " cockatoo tuft " and his self-
possession was overpowering.

Hunt was at work among the Elgin Marbles. He
was eighteen years old and had had a long struggle against
the best-intentioned discouragement before he had
persuaded his parents, business people of small means
living over their warehouse in the City, to let him take
to drawing. Millais came up behind him and said :

" I say, are you not the fellow doing that good drawing
in No. XIII Room ? You ought to be in the Academy.
You may take my word for it ; I ought to know. I've
been there as a student, you know, five years. I got the
first medal last year in the Antique, and its not the first
medal given me, I can tell you. I'm only fifteen just
struck, but don't be afraid. Why, there are students at
the Academy just fifty and more."[1]

Thus encouraged, Hunt was admitted to the Academy
at the next examination, and a warm friendship grew up
between the two boys. In 1847 Hunt was a regular
visitor at 83 Gower Street ; he was finishing his first big

[1] *Pre-Raphaelitism and the Pre-Raphaelite Brotherhood.*

Academy picture, an illustration to Keats's " Eve of St. Agnes." The year before, his small picture of *Woodstock* had been hung. Millais had exhibited a painting of *Pizzaro seizing the Inca of Peru*. Both these paintings show how thoroughly the two students had mastered all that the Academy School could teach them before they struck out for themselves on a new line.

Millais was chiefly concerned with freeing himself from the too close encumbrances of family life. His father and mother were sweet to him. Mrs. Millais spent long hours in the British Museum Reading-Room hunting up historical details for his pictures ; she had made practically all the fancy dresses for *Pizzaro seizing the Inca of Peru* with her own hands ; she would even read aloud to him while he painted. Mr. Millais in a variety of wigs and whiskers sat as a model for almost any elderly male character. But their son had two things against them : they would call him " Johnny," and they would use his studio as their living-room. Rebellion was in the air in 1848, and one afternoon in early spring Mrs. Millais found the studio door locked against her. Inside, Holman-Hunt was lecturing Millais on the decadence of English painting.

Later in the even the family became reconciled. Hunt and Millais went into the parlour to visit " the old people." Mrs. Millais sat crocheting in the armchair. Her needle clicked intently and the boys' entrance was allowed to pass unnoticed. Millais advanced into the room, swaggering ever so little ; Hunt hung back rather ill at ease.

" Now, we've come to have a nice time with you, mama and papa," he said jauntily.

His mother hardly looked up from her work.

" We do not wish to tax your precious time. We have our own occupations to divert us and engage our attention ! "

But Millais was not easily snubbed, as many people learned later.

" Hoity-toity, what's all this ? " he cried affectionately,

pressing a guitar into his father's hand. " Put down your worsted, mama, I'm going to play back-gammon with you directly."

The table was wheeled up ; the needle was taken from the lady's hands, and, as his father played " The Harmonious Blacksmith " to Holman-Hunt, Millais sat down to back-gammon with his mother in great good humour, beating time to the music with his disengaged hand.

From then onwards Hunt and Millais met undisturbed and discussed the new style of painting to be adopted in their pictures for the next Academy.

4

At this stage Hunt's purely academic *Eve of St. Agnes* won him a devout disciple, on the first day of the Academy. Rossetti, who was only known to Hunt by sight, caused him some embarrassment by addressing him in loud tones and telling him that his picture was by far the finest in the exhibition. What really seems to have pleased Rossetti was that the subject should be taken from a poem by Keats, a poet for whom he had not been able to awake much interest in Madox Brown. What with that and the medicine bottles, he was anxious to transfer his allegiance.

At this time his technical education can hardly be said to have been begun. At the Antique School he had not troubled to learn the few useful things they might have taught him. He knew nothing of perspective and practically nothing of anatomy, a deficiency which he never made up to the end of his life. With Madox Brown he had barely become accustomed to the feel of the brush. He applied to Hunt for tuition. To Professor Rossetti it was all one, and when they met he invariably addressed Hunt with the utmost politeness as " Mr. Brown." Indeed, this is by far the wisest attitude towards the vexed question of Rossetti's apprenticeship ; his early artistic development was implicit in his character and directed inevitably by forces that were, in the period, universal. There was a good deal of squabbling among the followers of Hunt and Brown, and, indeed, between the masters themselves, for the credit of having trained a painter who really owed very little to either of them. The truth seems to be that Hunt taught Rossetti to paint, but exercised only a very brief influence on his real artistic development; Brown remained Rossetti's friend, with occasional violent quarrels, throughout the whole of his career, and Rossetti in later life preferred to attribute his training to him than to Hunt, from whom he was widely estranged.

Another question of similar nature but considerably greater importance attaches to the formation of the Pre-Raphaelite Brotherhood. The circumstances are these.

In the autumn of 1848 Hunt and Rossetti went to live together at No. 7 Cleveland Street, Fitzroy Square, a dismal, ill-lighted studio disturbed by the whippings and scamperings of a school of small boys kept by their landlord on the floor below. With a real pupil to lecture to Hunt became increasingly didactic; there is nothing like teaching for developing one's views. Millais was a constant visitor. Some time during the artistic year between the 1848 and 1849 Academy exhibitions, the vague aspirations and discontents of these three young men took form as a more or less definite code of belief. One evening when they were looking over a book of engravings from the frescoes in the Campo Santo at Pisa at Millais's home they decided to form themselves into a Brotherhood.

It is uncertain how much part Rossetti took in the earlier discussions. At a later date, when he was disposed to claim as much share as Hunt in the foundation of the Pre-Raphaelites, he deliberately destroyed the pages of the journal of the Brotherhood dealing with the subject. Those who fell under the dominance of his later manner were unable to imagine him as anything but leader in any group. Hunt could only remember him as a beginner at the time that he and Millais were professional painters. One consideration that should be borne in mind is that Rossetti had the advantages as well as the disadvantages

CR

of his early idleness. While Millais and Hunt were cross-hatching away in the Academy School, he was reading widely and intelligently in four languages. Hunt describes him as having " perhaps a greater acquaintance with the poetical literature of Europe than any man." This is, of course, a fantastic exaggeration, but Hunt had had very little to do with learned people, and Rossetti's education may well have seemed impressive. He had also practised the technique of verse writing, and could write a correct and tolerably happy sonnet on any subject almost as easily and quickly as he could write fourteen lines of prose, by no means a unique gift but, again, likely to impress Hunt. It seems probable that his desire to balance his literary superiority against his friends' superiority in painting may have been a strong inducement to urge upon them an association in which the two arts should have equal importance.

Besides, there is from the first something unconvincing about the idea of Hunt and Millais forming a Brotherhood. Hunt was a lonely man, a busy man, and to a great extent a self-centred man ; he set himself one task—to paint well—and its accomplishment was the sole interest of his life. Socially he was typical of his race and class ; infinitely removed from the continental artistic life of cafés and coteries and being-in-the-movement. Millais was frankly sceptical. " Are you recruiting a regiment to take the Academy by storm ? " he asked, when Hunt suggested the election of further candidates, a superbly typical comment.

But to Rossetti, reared among secret societies, lured to the guilds and apprenticeships of the Middle Ages, some such organisation seemed the natural embodiment of an artistic impulse ; mystic initials with the enchantment of secrecy and the thrill of betrayal ; the monastic sense of novitiate and initiation ; the very number of the brothers, seven, like his seven cypresses in the *Girlhood of the Virgin*, typifying the seven sorrowful mysteries, all bear the unmistakable mark of Rossetti.

He was also largely responsible for the membership.

His brother William, now a clerk in the Inland Revenue Office, though neither a painter, nor, at this period, a serious writer, was admitted as clerk of the Brotherhood.

Woolner, the sculptor, was introduced by Rossetti. After some disappointments and a dreary excursion to the Antipodes, he became an R.A., and a highly respected old man ; he married one of three handsome sisters called Waugh ; Holman-Hunt married both the others. To the end of his days Woolner was a thorough Pre-Raphaelite.

James Collinson was too preoccupied with religious difficulties to be a very satisfactory brother ; he nearly always fell asleep when Hunt began talking. He too was Rossetti's candidate. He became converted to Roman Catholicism, and so far awoke from his habitual torpor as to paint a picture of a Charity boy which Hunt admitted to be " an honest idea " and Rossetti described more enthusiastically as a " stunner." At the time of the formation of the Pre-Raphaelite Brotherhood he was courting Christina Rossetti. Shy of popery she refused to marry him. In November he became an English Churchman again and was accepted. In May 1850 he was again received into the Church of Rome and Christina broke off the engagement. He nearly became a monk, but remained a painter, abandoning the principles of the Pre-Raphaelites in joining the Society of British Artists.

The seventh member, F. G. Stephens, was a pupil of Hunt's brought in for no very clear reason. Later he became an art critic on the *Athenæum*, where, he says, he found his early artistic training of great value.

Hunt had no very high opinion of Ford Madox Brown, but Rossetti asked him to join. If he had accepted Hunt would very probably have broken up the Brotherhood, but, as might have been expected, Brown refused. No doubt he felt it rather beneath his dignity to ally himself with a group so much his juniors in age ; but he did not approve of coteries, anyhow, and he did not altogether like all the ideas of the Brotherhood.

However one divides the honours, Hunt must certainly

be given the chief credit for the ideas. They were, if he had known it at the time, completely alien from all that Rossetti stood for, and as far as Hunt was concerned, they suffered no single addition or deviation from the conversations behind the locked door in Gower Street until his death in 1910.

Chief of these ideas was a devotion to something which Hunt spoke of as " Nature " :

" Where I could I induced him, while my pupil, to take *natural* objects as his models for these symbols ; the little Gothic screen, the embroidery and draperies of the Holy Virgin were done as far as possible *from Nature.*"[1]

" It is simply *fuller Nature* we want. . . . If you notice, a clean purple is scarcely ever given in these days, and pure green is as much ignored."[2]

" The endeavour held in view throughout the writings on Art will be to encourage and enforce an entire adherence to the *simplicity of Nature.*"[3]

" The landscape was done directly and frankly from *Nature* not merely for the charm of minute finish, but as a means of studying her principles of design the more fully."[4]

" I represented gravelly variations as found in *Nature.*"[5]

" We decided that, wherever possible, one of the marks of our painting should be the inclusion of some *natural* scene."[6]

It may be observed from these quotations that the term was allowed considerable elasticity. Broadly it was used as the antithesis to the Baroque. In Italian seventeenth-century painting, a single theme is taken for the design of each picture and varied and stressed with every discoverable device of emphasis. Separated from the central scheme the component parts are frequently ugly and meaningless. Hunt's aim was to effect a disintegration and diffusion of design, the theme becoming a purely

---

[1] *Pre-Raphaelitism and the Pre-Raphaelite Brotherhood.*
[2] Ibid.   [3] Preface to *The Germ.*
[4] *Pre-Raphaelitism and the Pre-Raphaelite Brotherhood.*
[5] Ibid.   [6] Ibid.

intellectual idea, such as the religious allegory of *The Light of the World*, the moral reflection of *The Awakened Conscience*, etc., and the details of the composition being each a reverent study of the natural principles of substance and growth discernible in physical appearances.

Nothing could have been further from Rossetti's natural inclination.

The other idea to which Hunt constantly refers is the introduction of poetry into painting. Despite the importance which he, and the other Pre-Raphaelites, attached to this, it is hard to define any very clear meaning of their aspiration. Sometimes it meant that in their pictures they chose to illustrate incidents taken from poetic literature ; sometimes the choice of such subjects as might be expected to interest poets ; a vague romanticism of strong appeal for Rossetti. There is one quotation from *Pre-Raphaelitism and the Pre-Raphaelite Brotherhood*, however, which throws a curious light upon Hunt's method of thought.

" I often instanced Woolner's bust of Tennyson as distinctly better than any male head Marochetti had ever done, and no one ever ventured to dispute the point ; but when they asked me what Woolner could show, or what designs could be seen, of a poetic kind, I had to confess that my friend had never had an opportunity of realising female grace and beauty."

There is one much-quoted document which deserves some mention for the light it throws upon the nature of the Pre-Raphaelite creed ; the list of Immortals drawn up about this time mainly by Rossetti and subscribed to by the whole of the Brotherhood.

" We, the undersigned," it ran, " declare that the following list of Immortals constitutes the whole of our creed, and that there exists no other Immortality than what is centred in their names and in the names of their contemporaries, in whom this list is reflected."

Then followed the list—a fantastic compilation—graded into five classes with stars.

Jesus Christ comes first and alone ; His fourth star

was added at the instance of Collinson ; then come
Shakespeare and the author of the Book of Job ; a fairly
extensive third class includes Dante (it is surprising that
Rossetti did not see to it that he was in the class above),
Keats, Chaucer, Leonardo da Vinci, an Alfred—presumably the Alfred who burnt the cakes, since Tennyson
occurs below him—Thackeray, and George Washington.
Longfellow and Raphael, among others, get fourths,
while Isaiah, Phidias, Flaxman, Joan of Arc, Michael
Angelo, Leigh Hunt, Christopher Columbus, Titian,
and Haydon satisfy the examiners. Of course the
admission of " contemporaries " gives a slightly less
certain note—does George III, for instance, get in as the
contemporary of George Washington ?—but one simply
cannot begin to take this list seriously, omitting, as it
does, most of the names obviously consistent with the
Brotherhood's aims, Giotto, Dürer, Cimabue, and all
the Flemish Masters, besides Socrates, Plato, Aristotle,
and Praxiteles. For some time it hung in the studio in
Cleveland Street and all visitors were invited to subscribe
to it.

5

Throughout the next year the monthly meetings of
the Brotherhood were held fairly regularly, each member
in turn entertaining the others. In the meantime the
three founders worked strenuously at their paintings
for the next Academy, where they aimed at revealing for
the first time the new influence they were introducing
into English Art.

Rossetti chose for his subject the " Girlhood of the
Virgin," and under Hunt's direction began upon it
straight away, using the still-life accessories as practice
work before beginning on the figures. All three revived
the unusual method of painting directly on to a white-
primed canvas with clear colour ; this practice was later
developed by Holman-Hunt and Millais independently,
and taken up by their friends, into the use of " wet
grounds," which became a marked characteristic of

Pre-Raphaelite painting. The copper bowl in Ford Madox Brown's *Christ washing Simon Peter's feet* is a remarkable example of the effect that can be obtained in this way. Rossetti used it throughout his life for the more brilliant passages in his painting.[1]

Three paintings were thus being produced for the 1849 Academy, marked by a new spiritual attitude in the artist towards his work, a startling new technical method, and the initials P.R.B. after the artists' names.

Hunt's *Rienzi* is well known ; it is a complete expression of all that he stood for ; as is Millais's admirable *Lorenzo and Isabella.*

The Girlhood of the Virgin caused trouble from the first. Rossetti's ignorance of perspective was almost invincible ; its rules seemed to him unintelligible and their application patently absurd. He was still half in love with the Nazarenes. When one considers how divided his aims were, how immature his taste, and that the painting itself was almost the whole of his training, it is extraordinary to find how successful the picture really is. His method of work was " temperamental " in the extreme and made him a distressing studio companion.

" There were frequent days when he would leave his appointed task to engage himself with some other invention in form or in words that had taken possession of his fancy. When he had once sat down and was engaged in the effort to chase his errant thoughts into an orderly road, and the spectral fancies had all to be kept in his mind's eye, his tongue was hushed, he remained fixed and

---

[1] "The process may be described thus. Select a prepared ground originally for its brightness and renovate it, if necessary, with fresh white when first it comes into the studio, white to be mixed with a very little amber or copal varnish. . . . Upon this surface, complete with exactness the outline of the part in hand. On the morning for the painting . . . with fresh white, spread a fresh coat very evenly with a palette knife . . . of such density that the drawing should faintly show through. . . . Over this wet ground, the colour (transparent and semi-transparent) should be laid with light sable brushes. . . . Painting of this kind cannot be retouched except with an entire loss of luminosity."—*Pre-Raphaelitism and the Pre-Raphaelite Brotherhood.*

inattentive to all that went on about him, he rocked himself to and fro and at times he moaned lowly or hummed for a brief minute, as though telling off some idea. All this while he peered intently before him, looking hungry and eager, and passing by in his regard any who came before him, as if not seen at all. Then he would often get up and walk out of the room without saying a word."[1]

There was considerable doubt, at first, whether he would have his picture ready in time, but, once started, he worked with feverish application. At last it was finished, but when " sending in " day arrived Rossetti did a curious thing. The whole intention of the Brotherhood throughout had been that they should all three appear together at Burlington House ; Rossetti, suddenly taking fright that he might be rejected and probably advised by Ford Madox Brown who nurtured a fanatical hatred of the Academy, sent his picture instead to what was known as the Free Exhibition at Hyde Park Corner. Both public and painters paid for admission to this exhibition ; its freedom lay in the right of the artist who had hired a space to exhibit anything he chose. The exhibition opened a week before the Academy, but we may safely acquit Rossetti of any intention of forestalling his friends ; this charge, however, was naturally brought against him when, later, his supporters claimed his priority of appearance as a sign of leadership.

But however innocent his intentions, his action came as a disagreeable surprise to Hunt and Millais ; there was now no question of " taking the Academy by storm."

The picture thus exhibited attracted favourable attention. The *Athenæum* gave it a long notice, describing it as a " manifestation of true mental power in which Art is made the exponent of some high aim," and an " achievement worthy of an older hand."

Rossetti's aunt, Charlotte Polidori, took the Dowager Marchioness of Bath to see it, and succeeded in persuading the old lady to buy it for eighty guineas.

Hunt and Millais had quite a friendly reception when

[1] *Pre-Raphaelitism and the Pre-Raphaelite Brotherhood.*

the Academy opened the next week. The critics were frankly confused ; such unusual work must obviously be dealt with and they were at a loss for a text upon which to preach. As a body they shirked the real questions at issue and, while commending the abilities and industry of the artists, contented themselves with fragmentary criticisms and vague references to the school of Overbeck. The words " affectation" and "mannerism" do appear, but sparsely and timidly used.

Hunt received a note describing his *Rienzi* as " full of genius and high promise " over the surprising subscription, " Your obliged and admiringly, E. Bulwer Lytton." He sold the picture for the sum of one hundred guineas after the close of the exhibition to a collector to whom he was introduced by Augustus Egg. *Lorenzo and Isabella* was bought by three fashionable tailors for £150 and a suit of clothes.

It had been a pretty good year for the Pre-Raphaelites. In early autumn Holman-Hunt and Rossetti set off for a few weeks of crude and confident observation in France and Belgium. They discerned " sweetness " in Fra Angelico, " coarseness " in Rubens, " power " in Leonardo da Vinci, and " sympathy for sublime sentiment " in Titian—but no doubt they had a good time.

On their return to London they settled themselves to work again, Rossetti now taking a studio by himself in Newman Street. Hunt, in Chelsea, began the elaborate *Christian Priests sheltering from Druid Persecution* which now hangs in the Ashmolean Museum at Oxford. Millais, still in Gower Street, and now, in his new suit, very much cock of the walk, was already at work on his *Christ in the House of His Parents*. Rossetti chose *The Annunciation* for his subject.

Left to himself, he tended to simplicity and sweetness. In after years he spoke of this painting as the " blessed white eyesore." It certainly has a suggestion about it of the elder Miss Fairchild in her party frock compared with the luxurious Lady Augusta Noble of his later work, but it is none the worse for that. The Archangel Gabriel is perhaps not a great success, particularly about the feet, though, true to his teaching, Rossetti kept a little dish of burning spirits of wine flickering before him as he painted the flames, and the lily was done from a woollen model, the nearest approximation to Nature procurable at that time of year.   But there is real tenderness in the shrinking Madonna, drawn from Christina, and a real fragrance about the whole virginal white symphony that have endeared it to the children of many quite sophisticated night-nurseries.

At the meetings of the Brotherhood the production of a magazine was discussed and decided upon.   Here Rossetti seems certainly to have taken the lead.   The available capital was extremely small, and neither Hunt nor Millais wanted to be distracted from their painting by writing or illustrating.   However, the Rossetti brothers—William was now on the staff of the *Spectator*—won their way, and out of a variety of more or less unobjectionable titles *The Germ* was chosen—as A. C. Benson pointed out, one of the rare occasions of Rossetti's *flair* for a sonorous title failing him.   His first sugges-tion—" Thoughts towards Nature "—was regarded as affected.

At this crucial stage, when the Pre-Raphaelite Brother-hood, still unestablished, was developing in the most exuberant way, Rossetti did another curious thing to damp the enthusiasm of his friends.   With the hushed circum-spection of his father's conspirators he revealed to a friend named Munro, in closest confidence, the secret of the initials P.R.B.   Facetious guesses had already been made ;   now the true meaning became common knowledge.

It does not nowadays seem a very terrible secret, but in 1850 the results of Rossetti's betrayal were devastating. The British public, ever more ready to resent than to detect rebellion, rose in a storm of protest.   Where before they had only observed a puzzling respect for detail, an unusual vividness of colour, and a neglect of the expected amenities of composition, they now discovered a conspiracy, and one organised, with every circumstance of stealth, not only to throw down the idols of the past and debauch the taste of the present and future, but to undermine Christian faith and Victorian morals.

The opening of the 1850 Academy was the occasion for an onslaught of vituperation, not uncommon, indeed, in political and religious discussion, but almost unparalleled in the history of art. In the last seventy years much of the wind has dropped from the sails which at this time drove the critics on such swift and tumultuous voyages. They have proved themselves so wrong so often that they have become pathetically cautious of condemning work they cannot understand. It was with supreme confidence that the critics of 1850 tucked up their cuffs, dipped their pens in their inkpots, and settled themselves to befoul the Pre-Raphaelites with every word at their command.

Meanwhile *The Germ*, from the first, was a complete failure. It was intended that it should be a sixpenny monthly magazine. Two numbers appeared—in December 1849 and January 1850—but only about a quarter of the copies printed were sold. Under the name *Art and Poetry ; Being Thoughts towards Nature* two more issues were printed, with still less success. After the March number the enterprise was abandoned. The Rossetti family, Gabriel, William, and Christina, dominated this pathetic little publication. It was the direct successor of the family magazines which they used to bring out as children. The rest of the Brotherhood contributed more or less grudgingly ; already it had ceased to be a close corporate body. Rossetti's other friends dropped in at the meetings when the policy of *The Germ* was discussed ; Madox Brown did an etching for it, Coventry Patmore and Mr. Tupper, the printer, sent a poem and an essay. Rossetti's own contributions include *My Sister's Sleep, Hand and Soul, The Blessed Damozel*, the first draft of *Sea Limits, The Carillon*, and a number of sonnets about famous pictures written during his tour with Hunt. The failure of the magazine and the consequent deficit were a serious blow to the Pre-Raphaelites at a very difficult time.

In the summer the attack of the critics began. The word " Pre-Raphaelite " had given them the cue they wanted. *Ecce Ancilla Domini* was exhibited at the National Institution, the successor of the Free Exhibition. " Absurd, affected, ill drawn, insipid, crotchety, puerile," was the verdict of the *Athenæum*, " a work evidently thrust by the artist into the eye of the spectator more with the presumption of a teacher than in the modesty of a hopeful and true aspiration after excellence." But Hunt and Millais, at the Academy, suffered the more for their greater prominence.

The attack was mainly upon three counts. (*a*) The Pre-Raphaelites were presumptuous. They were very young men, daring to set themselves up as superior to the artistic standards of their age. They thought themselves cleverer than Raphael. They wanted to teach their grandmothers to suck eggs. What would now be called the " inferiority complex " of the British public was given a disagreeable jolt. (*b*) They were incompetent. They just didn't know how to draw or paint. Their anatomy and perspective were all wrong. Here, of course, the critics had strayed on to ground of demonstrable fact. Hunt challenged them to prove a single fault in his perspective. The critics answered with louder gibes. The truth, of course, is that the ordinary observer does not perceive correct perspective. The actual optical image is continually corrected by reason. One knows from previous observations that all the legs of a table are the same length, and one does not take one's visual impression seriously when it tells one that they are not. Amateur photography has done a lot to shake the popular respect for perspective. It is a science that must be kept very much under control. It takes some time for the brain to accustom itself to a single phase of its application. Any new departure, however accurate, seems topsy-turvy. As, for instance, when people begin painting still life with the picture plane inclined from the vertical.

The same limitation applies, to a much smaller extent, to anatomy. People had become accustomed to certain poses in pictures, and were shocked by a change. The new poses seemed ungainly, and were taken to be incorrect. There were, as a matter of fact, many more faults of anatomy under the draperies of most of the accepted academicians. It was all a matter of what the public were used to. (c) Arising out of this, the Pre-Raphaelites were morbid and affected. They liked deformity and contortion. The subjects they chose were unseemly. The only explanation could be the desire for self-advertisement or some disease of taste.

"We have already come into contact," wrote the *Athenæum*, " with the doings of a school of artists whose younger members unconsciously write its condemnation in the very title which they adopt (that of Pre-Raphaelite). . . . It is difficult, in the present day of improved taste and information, to apprehend any large worship of an art idol set up with visible deformity as its attributes, but it is always well to guard against the influence of ostentatious example and the fascination of paradox. . . . Their ambition is an unhealthy thirst which seeks notoriety by means of mere conceit. Abruptness, singularity, uncouthness, are the counters by which they play for game. Their trick is to defy the principle of beauty and the recognised axioms of taste. Again, these young artists are mistaken if they imagine that they have reverted to any period of art for their type of pictorial expression. . . . In all these painters (i.e. the primitives) the absence of structural knowledge never resulted in positive deformity. The disgusting incidents of unwashed bodies were not presented in loathsome reality, and the flesh, with its accidents of putridity, was not made the affected medium of religious sentiment in tasteless revelation. . . . Let us conjure these young gentlemen to believe that Raphael may be received as no mean authority for soundness of view and excellence of practice."

It is difficult to be sure of what " affected medium of religious sentiment in tasteless revelation " means, but the rest is pretty plain speaking.

Of the three, Millais came off the worst. He is described as using " a circumstantial art language from which we recoil with loathing and disgust. There are many to whom his work will seem a pictorial blasphemy."

The Times, occupied with political events, was brief but no less certain. " *Christ in the House of His Parents* is, to speak plainly, revolting ; it is disgusting."

" Pre-Raphaelitism is spreading, I am glad to see," wrote Lord Macaulay, " glad, because it is by spreading that such affectations perish."

" The only possible method of fulfilling the Pre-Raphaelite ideal would be to set a petrified Cyclops to paint his petrified brother," wrote Charles Kingsley in *Two Years Ago*.

But, as was fitting, it was left for Charles Dickens to voice the full frenzy of his age. Describing Millais's picture in *Household Words*, he writes, " In the foreground of the carpenter's shop is a hideous, wry-necked, blubbering, red-haired boy in a nightgown, who appears to have received a poke playing in an adjacent gutter, and to be holding it up for the contemplation of a kneeling woman, so horrible in her ugliness that (supposing it were possible for any human creature to exist for a moment with that dislocated throat) she would stand out from the rest of the company as a monster in the vilest cabaret in France or the lowest gin-shop in England."

" I declare the article has the essence of malice," said Mrs. Millais to Holman-Hunt. " The pity is that Jack ever altered his style ; he would never have provoked this outrageous malice had he not changed ; his manner was admired by everyone. I wish he had never had anything to do with *that* Rossetti. . . . I don't like the look of him ; he's a sly Italian, and his forestalling you by sending his first picture to an exhibition, where it was seen with your joint initials on it, a week before the picture by you and Jack would appear, was quite un-English and unpardonable, when you had taught him and treated him with great generosity.

" I don't admire his behaviour," said Mrs. Millais ;

" he loudly indulges in insulting denunciation of persons who have a right to be treated with respect, and asserts himself generally so as to offend people quite unnecessarily. . . . But there's one question I would ask : what is the purpose of the Pre-Raphaelite Brotherhood ? I thought there were to be seven of you ; why should the fight be left only to you and Jack ? Rossetti's picture of *The Annunciation*, whatever critics may say, is undoubtedly very dainty and chaste, but the principle he carries out is not Pre-Raphaelitism as you and Jack started it. His is church traditional work, gilt aureoles and the conventionalism of early priesthood, which we did away with at the Reformation. . . . Rossetti provokes the common sense of the world." [1]

The immediate and most disquieting result of the critics' attack was the failure of the Pre-Raphaelites to sell their pictures. To Millais this was disagreeable but not disastrous. He had his home to live in, and was always able to afford the necessaries of his art. He had a placid and insensitive self-esteem, very different from the vanity of Haydon, which rendered him invulnerable to abuse. At the same time he began to reconsider the position he had taken up. He was a young man with his way to make in the world, and he had gone rather too far. He fully intended to climb just as high as he could ; the more independent he appeared at first, the greater, probably, his eventual eminence. Soon, he knew, the Academy would have to accept Pre-Raphaelitism, or, at any rate, some semblance of it ; it was important that he should do nothing to make their approval harder.

Hunt was in desperate difficulty, and seriously considered emigrating to the colonies. He had, in fact, practically decided on this when Millais managed to sell the Druid picture for him to a heavy-drinking old gentleman in Oxford. With the 160 guineas thus earned he settled down once more with indomitable perseverance to a painting for the next Academy.

For Rossetti, though he had suffered less than Hunt or

[1] *Pre-Raphaelitism and the Pre-Raphaelite Brotherhood.*

Millais, the storm of abuse was profoundly unsettling. His family were worse off than ever, and were obliged, early in 1851, to move to Mornington Crescent, where Christina and her mother made pathetic efforts to open a dame school. Maria Francesca reverted to the family trade of governess. What little money they got came from William, who, besides his salary at the Revenue Office, was getting a little work on the *Spectator*. Aunt Charlotte was still fairly comfortable at Longleat, and it was mainly through her that Gabriel was able to live through the next three years. At the time when the immediate production of saleable pictures was essential he could do practically nothing.

It is part of the Rossetti legend that he now resolved never again to expose his work to vulgar criticism, whatever this proud gesture might cost him. Unfortunately, there is proof that he had every intention of exhibiting next year. It was not like the " sly Italian " to choose retirement while he was still obscure ; that came later, when his fame had reached just that pitch when only withdrawal or greater achievement could advance it. The truth is that discouragement brought out all that was worst in him of indolence and instability. He could get nothing done.

He went off to Sevenoaks to join Hunt in painting landscape, but the discomfort of outdoor work grew more and more irksome. He would sit for hours fretting before some spray of foliage that would not keep still. Then, throwing down his brushes, he would drift away to the inn, leaving his picture to be collected at evening by a farm hand with a wheelbarrow.

He began writing and re-writing verses, a process far from tranquil throughout his life. " I lie on the couch, the racked and tortured medium," he wrote later, " never permitted an instant's surcease of agony until the thing on hand is finished." Physical prostration was the almost invariable consequence of composition.

He began studies for other pictures and destroyed them. Finally he returned empty-handed to winter in London.

In the gloom of Bloomsbury he began a huge canvas illustrating the page's song from " Pippa Passes." For some time he worked at it feverishly, and finished two of the twenty-three figures. Then his interest slackened. The picture lay about in his studio for some time, its very size reproaching and depressing him. In the end he cut it up, two fragments surviving in separate frames.

For three years after this he gave up all attempt at rivalling Holman-Hunt's indefatigable output of exhibition paintings, and began working in water-colour and pen and ink. The following, taken from the list compiled by H. C. Marillier, are his only important works between *Ecce Ancilla Domini* and *Found*.

1850. *To Caper Nimbly in a Lady's Chamber to the Lascivious Pleasing of a Lute.* (Pen and ink, 8¼ in. x 6¾ in.) (Early drawing for Borgia group.)

A Parable of Love. (Pen and ink, 7½ in. x 6⅝ in.) (A lady painting her own portrait, her lover guiding her hand.)

Rossovestita. (Water-colour, 9⅝ in. x 7¼ in.) (Probably fragment of *Hist ! said Kate the Queen.*)

1851. *Borgia.* (Water-colour, 9½ in. x 10 in.)

Beatrice at a Marriage Feast Denying her Salutation to Dante. (Water-colour, 13¾ in. x 16¾ in.)

How They Met Themselves. (Pen and ink. Lost.)

Hist ! said Kate the Queen (Oil, 22½ in. x 12 in.) (A small reproduction of his original composition for his abandoned 1850 painting.)

1852. *Giotto Painting Dante's Portrait* (Water-colour, 14½ in. x 18½ in.)

Guardami ben, ben son, ben son Beatrice (the meeting of Dante and Beatrice in Paradise). (Water-colour, 14½ in. x 18½ in.)

Hesterna Rosa. (Pen and ink, 7½ in. x 9½ in.)

Dante Drawing the Angel (Water-colour, 11½ in. x 24 in.)

DR

During this time Hunt was covering as many square feet of canvas as Rossetti was inches of paper, but it is by no means an insignificant period in his life.

In the first place, he was teaching himself to paint in water-colours, and it is on his work as a water-colourist, I am convinced, that eventually his claim to distinction as a painter will stand. He never had very much respect for the materials in which he worked, none of the crafts-man's loving submission to the limitations of medium. It is often difficult to tell at first sight whether some of his work is in oil or water-colour, or even pastel or needle-work. Paint, for him, was just so much stuff in which he had to work out the effects he wanted. He is happiest as a water-colourist because it was in this medium that the effects he wanted could be most comfortably produced. The period of his great water-colours, moreover, coincides with his purest and most graceful artistic output. It was a real misfortune that the purchasing public always regarded water-colours as being in some way less worth their money than oils. Of course, they lack the physical solidity of canvas and varnish. It is well known, too, that they are far less expensive in time and materials. Ruskin alone saw the superiority and fitness of Rossetti's water-colours ; he was not happy using the full brush ; his incapacity in drawing became offensive the moment he dealt with large spaces ; the inevitable shine on an oil surface detracts from the subtlety and depth of his colouring ; the ease with which parts could be retouched and remodelled encouraged all his worst faults of pre-liminary carelessness and indecision. Only one thing lured him away from his true *métier*, the prices he could get for inferior oil paintings from less fastidious patrons than Ruskin. It is a lasting testimony to the stupidity and bias of William Bell Scott that he welcomed this decline as " emancipation " from the old-maidenly fussiness of Ruskin.

His first attempt, or at any rate the first that anyone thought worth keeping, was the *Laboratory*, a small illus-tration to a poem by Browning done some time in 1849,

when he was at work on *Ecce Ancilla Domini*.   It is interesting to compare this with the *Dante Drawing the Angel*
mentioned above.   The first is merely a coloured drawing,
done over pen and ink;   in the second the design has
become woven into the texture of the painting.   And
what a texture, built up in delicate stipple work, like the
plumage of a butterfly's wing !   It is hard to believe that
they are both the work of the same hand, with only four
years between them.

As his technique advanced he found himself groping
with new preferences in the intellectual ideas that, for
him, made up so much of the value of his work.   The
two pictures by which he was at present known to
the public were both devotional, full of ecclesiastical
symbolism and sadly Romish.   The old cry of " No
Popery " was still a powerful execration, grown all the
more bitter with the prosperity of the Anglo-Catholic
movement.   His Italian name was against him.   The
tide had not yet turned ; his aureoled doves and Madonna
lilies were ten years too early for wide popularity.   Always
sensitive to the condition of the market, Rossetti now
found his commercial instincts pressing him in the
direction to which his æsthetic feelings had always tended.

His separation from his family encouraged this change.
Though always bound to them by the warmest affection,
he saw less and less of them during the succeeding years.
His father, old and irritable, tended to ask tiresome
questions about the progress of his painting, and to
rebuke his idleness ; Maria, as has been mentioned above,
was at work as a governess ; the dame school in Mornington Crescent was not a success, and early in 1853 Christina
and his mother moved to Frome, hoping that it might
flourish a little better under the shadow of Aunt Charlotte
and the Thynnes. Gabriel no longer saw the world against
the background of the Rossetti ladies.   Rich Southern
promptings began to break through the simple ideals
of faith and purity and to seek expression.   He became
conscious of a new Romanticism pervading and colouring
his work.

The temper of this Romanticism is discernible throughout all his work, but most particularly in the work of the
next ten years, before it became overlaid with sexuality
and occultism. To a great extent it had always been
there, from the days of his little sketches at the Art School.
Millais and Hunt had done their best to crush it out of
him, but as soon as their influence slackened it welled
up again irresistibly. It was chiefly the result of a special
outlook on life and the preoccupation with a special
system of symbols.

Among the Victorians, and, for that matter, among
most modern people too, there were two main attitudes
towards the rest of the universe. There was the breezy,
common-sense attitude to life, typified by Millais as " one
damned thing after another," and there was the solemn
perception of process, typified by Holman-Hunt, an
attitude which saw the earth as part of a vast astronomical
system, and man's life on the earth as a brief phase of its
decay, and any individual life as infinitesimally small and
unimportant except as an inseparable part of the whole—
a system that appeared comforting or terrifying as the
observer was a Tennyson or a Stevenson. Most intelligent
men accepted this attitude when they took the trouble to
think about it, and based the normal activities of their
life upon the first assumption.

The romantic outlook sees life as a series of glowing
and unrelated systems, in which the component parts are
explicable and true only in terms of themselves ; in which
the stars are just as big and as near as they look, and
" rien n'est vrai que le pittoresque."

It is this insistence on the picturesque that divides,
though rather uncertainly, the mystical from the romantic
habit of mind.

It is a great mistake to suppose that Rossetti at this
period ever consciously " dressed up " his pictures to
make them attractive. It was simply that the æsthetic
excitements at the back of his mind naturally translated
themselves into forms of the Middle Ages and the Italian
renaissance. He was not merely interested in these ages,

as Scott was, as a period of history in which thrilling things happened and fine clothes were worn. It just so happened that the forms of these periods were the language in which he most easily recorded his emotions.

In an odd way, too, he began to identify himself with the Dante of the *Vita Nuova*. His intense absorption in this story throughout his life, culminating in the *Beata Beatrix*, determines the symbolism for some of his most beautiful work.

In this way he evolved for himself a unique vocabulary for artistic expressions which analysis renders less articulate.

The number of discarded designs between 1850 and 1853 show how quickly Rossetti was developing; it is in his poems that the change first shows complete expression, though these have been much rewritten. *Jenny*, written while he was painting *The Girlhood of The Virgin*, shows a sentimental interest in prostitution that is typical of his age and of no other. " It is a sermon," he said many years later, " and on a great world, to most men unknown, though few consider themselves ignorant of it."

" A great world, to most men unknown." How much of the art of the last century is implicit in that phrase. Rossetti, in middle life, plunged fairly heavily into that world, but he was never able to look upon it with the same eyes as upon the other trafficking of civilisation. Perhaps it was because it was, in his day, almost the only profession practised mainly by women. Woman, in the abstract, was always an absorbing mystery to him. Professor Abercrombie has suggested that an interest in incest is characteristic of romance; one may add that an interest in prostitution is characteristic of sentimentality.

If one turns from *Jenny* to *The Staff and Scrip* and *Sister Helen* of 1851 and 1852, one finds himself in a different world, remote, thrilling, without date or place, the world he was painfully learning to paint.

6

Besides all this, he fell in love.

Elizabeth Siddal, as is well known, was first discovered by Walter Deverell. This handsome and ill-fated young man, who looked so much like Phiz's drawings of Steerforth, had for some time been a close friend of the Pre-Raphaelites, and on the defection of Collinson he was elected to the Brotherhood. It is hard at this distance to form any judgment of the promise of so brief a career. He was obviously an attractive companion ; he is reported to have been an excellent amateur actor. Many found something to admire in his painting. At any rate, one day early in 1850 he was with his mother in a bonnet-shop in Cranborne Alley, a side-street near Leicester Square which has since been demolished, when, peering over the blind of a glass door at the back of the shop, his attention was riveted by one of the girls in the workroom.

That evening he burst into Holman-Hunt's studio full of his discovery.

" You fellows can't tell what a stupendously beautiful creature I have found. By Jove ! She's like a queen, magnificently tall, with a lovely figure, a stately neck, and a face of the most delicate and finished modelling ; the flow of surface from the temples over the cheek is exactly like the carving of a Phidean goddess. Wait a minute ! I haven't done. She has grey eyes, and her hair is like dazzling copper, and shimmers with lustre as she waves it down. . . . I got my mother to persuade the miraculous creature to sit for me for my Viola in *Twelfth Night*. . . . She's really a wonder ; for while her friends, of course, are quite humble, she behaves like a real lady by clear common sense, and without any affectation, knowing perfectly, too, how to keep people at a respectful distance."

It is fairly easy to check this description. Hunt painted her as *Sylvia* ; Millais nearly killed her by painting her in a bath as *Ophelia* ; Rossetti never ceased painting and drawing her in every conceivable disguise for ten years ; she even painted herself in the looking-glass though with a slightly comic result. She was, without doubt, astonishingly beautiful.

She was also talented. It is impossible to understand quite what her character was. She undoubtedly kept people at a respectful distance, and even preserved this elusiveness and intangibility with her constant companions and near relatives. No doubt it was the habit of self-protection which one so often finds in refined people who have grown up in unrefined surroundings. Her parentage was quite simple ; the father a Sheffield cutler or watch-maker—accounts differ—who may or may not have been dead at the time when she met Rossetti. At any rate, he never appeared ; nor did her younger brother, who was slightly dotty. William Rossetti met her elder brother and reported him as a " sensible, well-conducted young man." She seems to have been attached to her sister, whom the Pre-Raphaelites called " the Roman " on account of her nose. Everyone was very anxious to emphasise her natural air of good breeding. Swinburne wrote of her :

" To one at least who knew her better than most of her husband's friends, the memory of all her marvel-lous charms of mind and person—her matchless grace, loveliness, courage, endurance, wit, humour, heroism, and sweetness—is too dear and sacred to be profaned by any attempt at expression." William Rossetti records that she made no " faults in her speech " ; Ruskin would hardly have tolerated it if she had. She was apparently witty, though her few surviving letters give little proof of this, and she used her wit to turn aside the attempts at intimacy she feared. She was never known to confide in anyone, to offer sympathy or accept it. She resented any mention of the love between her and Rossetti, even by their closest friends. There can be no question that she loved him deeply, though how soon this came about it is impossible to say. They were probably engaged by 1851.

From the moment Gabriel met her he began to engross more and more of her time, first as a model but soon as a pupil. It is impossible to study her drawings in the Tate Gallery without being deeply moved by a pathos quite distinct from the mere knowledge of her pathetic little life. They have so little real artistic merit, and so much of what one's governess called " feeling " ; so tentative, so imitative, and flickering with the live intensity of the souls that sighed about the Blessed Damozel.

She wrote poetry, too, of unrelieved melancholy, redolent of coming tragedy.

> . . . And, mother, wash my pale, pale hands,
>   And then bind up my feet ;
>   My body may no longer rest
>   Out of its winding-sheet.

> . And, mother dear, when the sun has set,
>   And the pale church grass waves,
>   Then carry me through the dim twilight
>   And hide me among the graves.

And again :

> . . . I felt the spell that held my breath,
>   Bending me down to a living death—
>   As if hope lay buried when he had come
>   Who knew my sorrows all and some.

The following poem is so poignantly autobiographical that it deserves to be quoted in full :

WORN OUT

> Thy strong arms are around me, love,
>   My head is on thy breast ;
> Though words of comfort come from thee,
>   My soul is not at rest.

> For I am but a startled thing,
>   Nor can I ever be
> Ought save a bird whose broken wing
>   Must fly away from thee.

I cannot give to thee the love
  I gave so long ago—
The love that turned and struck me down
  Amid the blinding snow.

I can but give a sinking heart
  And weary eyes of pain,
A faded mouth that cannot smile
  And may not laugh again.

Yet keep thine arms around me, love,
  Until I drop to sleep :
Then leave me—saying no good-bye,
  Lest I might fall and weep.

How curiously this contrasts with some verses written
about the same time by Gabriel, and with her absurd
nickname :

EPISTLE TO FORD MADOX BROWN

    . . . And if from these cads
    You've superfluous brads,
    To my crib you must lug 'em
    (Dear Lizzy's a " Guggum "),
    Whose limited head
    You shall find, and a bed,
    Or for tea we will ring,
    If to get it you'll bring
    A bob or a tizzy
    (What a " Guggum " is Lizzy !).
    If you come, though, don't hollor
    At my evident squalor,
    . . . Nor as to my picture
    Throw out any conjecture.
    So now, if you come
    To where *ego sum*,
    You know the condition
    (Dear Lizzy's a pigeon),
    And now don't be witty
    Upon D. G. Rossetti.

What a contrast ! The one exuberant, slangy, expan-
sive, buoyant, widely educated and of some reputation,

conscious of untried strength and unexplored potentiali-
ties, the other wan, and prim, already crushed by the
difficulties of life, her strength failing daily, practically
uneducated and entirely unknown, with only her fading
beauty bearing the taint of underlying decay in its very
height.   In 1853 she first showed signs of consumption,
and from then onwards, until her terrible death, Rossetti
was never free from growing anxiety about their future.

It is impossible to estimate the full effect of this
tragedy. Like the young lover in the *Heptameron*,
Rossetti, in the full vigour of his youth and in the exulta-
tion of first love, found himself suddenly brought up
sharply by the icy breath of corruption and mortality in
the being most dear to him. He had for a long time been
in love with love and, when he at last found it, it withered
at his approach.   How much of the turmoil and darkness
of his later years we may attribute to this malignant and
perverse experience ! If he had met Janey Morris in
1850 . . . but it is idle to speculate.

7

Millais and Holman-Hunt meanwhile sent their
pictures to the 1851 Academy, and, rather to their surprise, they were not rejected. They were hung, however,
in far less favourable positions than those of the year
before, and the critics adopted a tone of triumphant
contempt.

"We cannot censure at present, as amply or as strongly
as we desire to do, that absurd disorder of the mind or
the eyes which continues to rage with unabated absurdity
among a class of juvenile artists who style themselves
P.R.B., which, being interpreted, means Pre-Raphaelite
Brethren," and so on ; "an absolute contempt for
perspective . . . aversion to beauty in every shape . . .
seeking out every excess of deformity," wrote *The Times*
and then more pointedly : " The council of the Academy,
acting in a spirit of tolerance and indulgence to young
artists, have now allowed these extravagances to disgrace
their walls for the last three years. . . . The public may

fairly require that such offensive jests should not continue
to be exposed. . . . That morbid infatuation which
sacrifices truth, beauty, and genuine feeling to mere
eccentricity deserves no quarter at the hands of the
public."

Only one paper, the *Spectator*, where William had
some influence, defended them. They were cut by their
acquaintances and insulted in the streets by total strangers.
Holman-Hunt's father was the laughing-stock of his
City companions. A pamphlet was issued by a clergy-
man of the Church of England beginning, "Woe, woe,
woe, to the exceedingly young men of stubborn instincts
calling themselves Pre-Raphaelites." Collinson sent in
his formal resignation to the Brotherhood, sold his easel
and lay figure, and went off to Stonyhurst with the
intention of becoming a priest.[1]

Drawings which had been commissioned by a publisher
were returned to Holman-Hunt with the curt intimation
that other arrangements had been made. He found
himself deprived of the small portrait commissions on
which his livelihood depended.

At this moment of real despair came "thunder out of
a dark sky"—two letters to *The Times* by Ruskin.

Now Ruskin at this time was a very important person
indeed in the art world, not only with the general cultured
public, but—what was far more important—with the
buyers.

> I paints and paints,
> Hears no complaints,
> And sells before I'm dry,
> Till savage Ruskin
> Sticks his tusk in,[2]
> And then no one will buy.

[1] The Church was by this time a little suspicious of its æsthetic converts,
and set him to work cleaning boots. This was not what he had learned
to expect of the tranquillity of monastic life ; he decided that, after all,
his true vocation lay in art.

[2] *Punch*. An allusion, no doubt, to the boar's head chosen for a crest
by Ruskin's father.

Modern Painters had been published in 1843, when he was only twenty-four, and at this astonishingly early age had established his place as an art critic of unexampled sensibility. Moreover, he was a young man of considerable wealth, and could prove his sincerity in the way most likely to impress the Victorian public—by buying for himself the works he commended. In 1848 he married, had a house in Park Street for the season, moved among exalted people, fastidiously choosing a friend here and there, but for the most part holding aloof from the society which would have liked to lionise him. To the end of his life he never allowed his mind to become stultified, never forced it into channels for which it was not suited. Starting with a romantic and intensely penetrating love of nature, he allowed his perceptions to widen, from Alpine scenery to Turner, from Turner to thirteenth-century Gothic, to Giotto, to Tintoretto, until, gradually assimilating all art into an aspect of nature, he passed on inevitably to sociology and politics—a development where very few were ready to follow him. At the beginning of the 'fifties when he was just developing from Florence to Venice there was no one whose approbation was more coveted.

It would have saved the Pre-Raphaelites much discomfort had he noticed them the year before, but, if he saw their work at all, he had not bothered about it. It was through the agency of Coventry Patmore that he was at last enlisted on their side. When roused, there was no hesitation in his verdict.

" As studies both of drapery and of every minor detail, there has been nothing in art so earnest or so complete as these pictures since the days of Albert Dürer. This I assert generally and fearlessly."

His only criticisms are the " commonness of feature " in the models chosen.

" I am perfectly ready to admit that Mr. Hunt's *Sylvia* is not a person whom Proteus or anyone else would have been likely to fall in love with at first sight, and that one cannot feel very sincere delight that Mr. Millais's

Wives of the Sons of Noah should have escaped the Deluge. . . . Nor is it perhaps less to be regretted that while in Shakespeare's play there are nominally ' Two Gentlemen,' in Mr. Hunt's picture there should be only one, at least the kneeling figure on the right has by no means the look of a gentleman."

But these are his only complaints. He continues :

" . . . And so I wish them *all*, heartily, good speed, believing, in sincerity, that if they temper the courage and energy which they have shown in the adoption of their system with patience and discretion in framing it, and if they do not suffer themselves to be driven by harsh and careless criticism into rejection of the ordinary means of obtaining influence over the minds of others, they may, as they gain experience, lay in our England the foundations of a school of art nobler than the world has seen for three hundred years."

This was intoxicating reading for the two buffeted young men, and between them they concocted a letter of thanks. The result was that the Ruskins drove round to see them, and, as the address was that of Millais's studio, bore him off there and then for a week's visit to Denmark Hill.

Their fortunes were practically assured. In spite of a fiery crop of anonymous protests, *Valentine and Sylvia* was awarded the prize at the Liverpool exhibition, and sold for £200. Millais won the same prize in 1853 with *The Huguenot*, and Hunt's *Strayed Sheep* won the prize at Birmingham. But the Pre-Raphaelite Brotherhood had come to an end.

The last meeting was held in April 1853 at Millais's studio. Woolner, in Australia, had despaired of gold-washing, and, returning to Melbourne, was attempting to get some commissions for portrait busts of local worthies. He had made pretty free use of his artistic connections in the Mother Country, and the good colonists, who were so often taken in by spurious reputations, were anxious to see some proof of his membership of the Brotherhood. Accordingly, the remaining members met to draw each other's portraits. These they sent out to Woolner, who hung them round his studio, and no doubt his prestige profited by them.

By the winter of 1853 Hunt had finished his best-known picture, *The Light of the World*, and the singularly beautiful *Awakened Conscience*. Rather suddenly he decided to leave England for the Near East.

Millais, engaged to be married to Ruskin's wife, was considered certain for election as an A.R.A. at the coming election. He and Rossetti went to the station to see Hunt off. As a parting present, Rossetti gave him a daguerreotype of *The Girlhood of the Virgin* inscribed with a quotation from Taylor's *Philip van Artevelde* :

> There's that betwixt us been, which men remember
> Till they forget themselves, till all's forgot,
> Till the deep sleep falls on them in that bed
> From which no morrow's mischief knocks them up.

Not to be outdone, Millais hurried to the station buffet and returned, just as the train was starting, with a large bag of sandwiches and buns.

" So now the whole round table is dissolved," quoted Rossetti sadly, as the train steamed out of the station.

But the year 1854 was opening for him genial with promise.

CHAPTER III

THE ÆSTHETES

Ruskin—The Working Men's College—William Morris and the Pembroke set—Edward Burne-Jones—Rossetti " would have all men painters "— *Arthur's Tomb, The Marriage of St. George,* the Llandaff Triptych— Rossetti as a business man—The Morris firm—Rossetti as a husband— Death of Elizabeth Siddal.

I

IT is a testimony to both the strength and the weakness of Holman-Hunt's influence that when Rossetti next set about a big painting he chose an essentially Pre-Raphaelite composition and failed to finish it.

Mr. MacCracken, a Belfast packing agent, was one of the picture collectors of the time who followed Ruskin's judgments with unfaltering fidelity. He was not particularly rich, and had rather a tiresome habit of trying to pay for his purchases in kind, a sort of schoolboy " swopping " for which Rossetti had very little use. At this stage of his career, however, he was distinctly useful. In 1853 he bought *Ecce Ancilla Domini,* after the name had been changed to *The Annunciation,* to remove, as far as was possible, the taint of Popery, and in the same year he commissioned a large genre painting, to be called *Found.* The subject, which is in the regular succession of the *Awakened Conscience* and Spencer Stanhope's *Thoughts of the Past,* is thus eloquently described by Mr. F. G. Stephens :

" The time was soon after the chilly, silvery dawn had dispersed the gloom which concealed the victim, and there was light enough to reveal her form to the young countryman, who, driving townwards to market, no sooner saw the still, fair face set in pale golden hair than he recognised the once pure maiden, formerly his betrothed, who, years before, had left his village and was lost in London. Leaping from the cart, he seized the girl's hands and held her firmly, while, shrinking to the ground, she struggled and turned her face away in vain."

This seems a very nice description.

The treatment was to be wholly Pre-Raphaelite. Miss Fanny Cornforth—the heroine of Mr. Max Beerbohm's " *Pleased to meet Mr. Ruskin, I'm sure,*" who plays a large part in Rossetti's story—sat as model for the principal figure. Rossetti had picked her up in the street, attracted to her by a shower of nutshells. The wall, after endless search by Gabriel, Christina, and all their friends, was found at Finchley and " done from nature." So was the calf and the farm cart.

But Rossetti had outgrown this didactic theme and ingenuous treatment long before it was finished. It took him a year to get properly started, and then it was only with the utmost effort that he could banish the romantic images that danced in his imagination.

In September of the next year Madox Brown notes in his diary :

" On Saturday Rossetti came, in the middle of the most broiling sun. I knew he must have come to get something. He wanted costumes to paint a water-colour of the Passover, this instead of setting to work on the picture for which he has been commissioned by MacCrack since twelve months. However, whatever he does is sure to be beautiful. But the rage for strangeness disfigures his ideas."

" *October 6th.*—Called on Dante Rossetti. Saw Miss Siddal, looking thinner and more deathlike and more beautiful and more ragged than ever ; a real artist, a woman without parallel for many a year. Gabriel, as usual, diffuse and inconsequent in his work. Drawing wonderful and lovely Guggums one after another, each one a fresh charm, each one stamped with immortality, and his picture never advancing."

Year after year the canvas stood in his studio. Mr.

MacCracken never got it, nor did the two or three other patrons who from time to time advanced him large sums for its completion. He worked at it off and on until late in his life. Eventually Burne-Jones washed in the sky and it was packed off to the U.S.A.

A more profitable investment of MacCracken's was the exquisite water-colour of *Dante Drawing the Angel* which has been referred to already. This he sent to Ruskin, who was naturally enough enraptured by it.

"MacCracken sent my drawing to Ruskin, who the other day wrote me an incredible letter about it, remaining mine respectfully (!!) and wanting to call. I of course stroked him down in my answer, and yesterday he called. His manner was more agreeable than I had expected. ... He seems in a mood to make my fortune."

In this way began a relationship of vital importance in Rossetti's life.

2

It is impossible to resist extensive quotation from the letters which passed between Rossetti and Ruskin during these years of friendship. Nothing reveals more delightfully the characters of these absurdly incongruous people at an important time in the development of both of them.

One thing that must be borne in mind throughout is that Rossetti was only a part of Ruskin's multifarious activities. During the years in which Rossetti's every activity was being overlooked and directed by Ruskin, the latter was suffering continually from ill health, and, in the intervals between almost complete prostration was working feverishly on the last volumes of *Modern Painters* and *The Stones of Venice* ; he was issuing yearly more and more authoritative *Academy Notes* to a widening public, who admired and bought whatever he commended; he was lecturing all over the country upon art and nature ; he was wrestling with the Herculean and ill-requited labour of cataloguing and arranging the many thousands of drawings left in unimaginable confusion at Turner's

Er

death ; he was teaching at the Working Men's College in Great Ormond Street ; and all the time suffering acutely from the public humiliation of the annulment of his marriage.

It is doubtful how much Rossetti ever really cared for his patron. In a conversation with Hall Caine later in his life, and in many of his letters to his family and to William Allingham, he spoke of him as if with affection ; he can hardly have helped being very proud, at any rate at first, of the enthusiasm of this very precious and influential man, but one is left with the feeling that he was never quite at ease in the rarefied atmosphere of Denmark Hill, where fruit in its season appeared on the precise day of its perfect maturity, and screens were put up on Sundays in front of the Turners. He was at heart essentially ramshackle in the ordering of his life ; he liked things to be untidy, and was far happier borrowing ten pounds in a slangy way from Madox Brown than in gracefully acknowledging the unfailing generosity of Ruskin. Besides this, for all his appreciation of the value of Ruskin's reputation he had the contempt that artists always feel for the critic ; the sort of contempt that hurt Ruskin so bitterly in his action with Whistler years later. He was never convinced by the Athanasian certainty of judgment that never resulted in creative art.

" I do not choose," Ruskin wrote at the end of their friendship, " to have any more talk to you until you can recognise my superiorities as I can yours. And this recognition, observe, is not a matter of will or courtesy. You simply do not see certain characters in me.

" There are many things in which I always have acknowledged, and shall acknowledge, your superiority to me. . . . There are other things in which I just as simply know that *I* am superior to you. I don't mean writing. You write, as you paint, better than I."

It was just such superiorities as Ruskin claimed that Rossetti, by his peculiar obliquity of vision, was unable to perceive or appreciate. He was always ready to praise artistic achievement of the most trifling merit with exaggerated respect; but that and physical beauty in woman were the only things he thought worthy of reverence.

The pathetic thing was that Ruskin was craving for friendship. He wanted sympathy, even if to be understood he had to explain himself.

" I think it well," he wrote in 1855, " to tell you something about myself. . . . You constantly hear a great many people saying I am very bad, and perhaps you have been yourself disposed lately to think me very good. I am neither the one nor the other. I am very self-indulgent, very proud, very obstinate, and *very* resentful; on the other side, I am very upright— nearly as just as I suppose it is possible for a man to be in this world—exceedingly fond of making people happy, and devotedly reverent to all true mental or moral power. I never betrayed a trust, never wilfully did an unkind thing—and never, in little or large matters, depreciated another that I might raise myself. I believe I once had affections as warm as most people; but partly from evil chance, and partly from foolish misplacing of them, they have got tumbled down and broken to pieces. . . . So that I have no friendship and no loves. . . .

" Though I have no friendships and no loves, I cannot read the epitaph of the Spartans at Thermopylæ with a steady voice to the end; and there is an old glove in one of my drawers that has lain there these eighteen years which is worth something to me yet."

He said later that only two women, one of whom—the only one he cared for—he never saw, and one man, Edward Burne-Jones, ever understood him. Rossetti hardly tried. That first " He seems in a mood to make my fortune " lay always at the back of all his friendship with Ruskin. I do not see any reason to laugh at the older and more generous man; if he was partly a prig, Rossetti was partly a cad, and it is extraordinary how little there is that is priggish in any of his dealings with Rossetti.

In one of his last letters, written after Rossetti's

marriage, he expresses some of the disappointment that had accumulated in the last seven years.

" . . . What I *do* feel *generally* about you is that, without intending it, you are in little things habitually selfish—thinking only of what you like to do and don't like ; not of what would be kind. Where your affections are strongly touched I suppose this would not be so—but it is not *possible* you should care much for me, seeing me so seldom. I wish Lizzie and you liked me enough to—say—put on a dressing-gown and run in for a minute, rather than not see me ; or paint on a picture in an unsightly state, rather than not amuse me when I was ill. But you can't *make* yourselves like me, and you would like me less if you tried. As long as I live in the way I do here you can't, of course, know me rightly. . . .

" Love to Lizzie.

" I am afraid this note reads sulky—it is not that ; I am generally depressed. Perhaps you both like me better than I suppose you do. I mean, only, I did not misinterpret or take ill anything *yesterday* ; but I have no power in general of believing much in people's caring for me. I've a little more faith in Lizzie than in you—because, though she don't see me, her bride's kiss was so full and queenly kind."

It was this failure in personal affection that finally caused the breach between the two men—this and Rossetti's failure to follow him when he began to develop from Pre-Raphaelitism to political economy[1] ; but, while the friendship lasted, it was of enormous advantage to Rossetti.

First, financially, Ruskin was willing to support Rossetti, buying all that he painted, in certain limits, at its market value. He explained his attitude towards this patronage with a sweetness and delicacy which Rossetti, who was the least squeamish of men in haggling over his wares, can hardly have appreciated.

" It seems to me that, amongst all the painters I know,

[1] " Who could read it, or anything about such bosh ? " was Rossetti's comment on *Unto this Last*.

you on the whole have the greatest genius, and you appear to me also to be—as far as I can make out—a very good sort of person. I see that you are unhappy, and that you can't bring out your genius as you should. It seems to me, then, the proper and *necessary* thing, if I can, to make you more happy, and that I should be more really useful in enabling you to paint properly and keep your room in order than in any other way.

" If it were necessary for me to deny myself, or to make any mighty exertion to do this, of course it might to you be a subject of gratitude, or a question if you should accept it or not. But as I don't happen to have any other objects in life, and as I have a comfortable room and all I want in it (and more), it seems to me just as natural I should try to be of use to you as that I should offer you a cup of tea if I saw you were thirsty, and there was plenty in the tea-pot, and I had got all I wanted.

" . . . I forgot to say also that I really do *covet* your drawings as much as I covet Turner's ; only it is use-less self-indulgence to buy Turner's, and useful self-indulgence to buy yours."

How much of their lives would not many young men give to have such a letter addressed to them ?

Secondly, without hampering his imagination, Ruskin took Rossetti seriously in hand in the formation of his technique.

" *October* 1855.—Please oblige me in two matters or you will make me ill again. Take all the pure green out of the flesh in the *Nativity* I send, and try to get it a little less like worsted-work by Wednesday, when I will send for it. I want the Archdeacon of Salop, who is coming for some practical talk over religious art for the multitude, to see it."

" 1857. . . . Just remember as a general principle, never put raw green in *light* flesh. No great colourist ever did, or ever wisely will. This drawing by candlelight is all over black spots in the high lights. The thought is very beautiful—the colour and male heads by no means up to your mark."

" 1859. . . . You shall have the picture again immediately. I have never scrubbed it—more, by token it has
never once been out of the frame since I had it. It has
the most curious look of having been rubbed—but it is
impossible unless it was taken out of the frame by you.
But this is not the only case of failure of colour from
your careless way of using colours. My pet lady in blue
is all gone to nothing, the green having evaporated or
sunk into the dress—I send her back for you to look at—
and I think the scarlet has faded on the shoe. You must
really alter your way of working and mind what you are
about."

And so on, even to such practical details as this :

" *July* 1855. . . . Meantime, as soon as you get this,
pack up your drawing, finished or not, in the following
manner :

" 1. Sheet of *smoothest* possible drawing-paper laid
over the face, and folded sharply at the edges over to the
back, to keep drawing from possibility of friction.

" 2. Two sheets of pasteboard, same size as drawing,
one on face, the other behind.

" 3. Sheet of not too coarse brown paper, entirely and
firmly enclosing drawing and pasteboards.

" 4. Wooden board, a quarter of an inch thick, exact
size of drawing, to be applied to the parcel, drawing to
have its face to board.

" 5. Thickest possible brown paper firmly enclosing
board, parcel, and all, lightly corded, sealed, and addressed
to me :

Calverley Hotel,
Tunbridge Wells,
Paid, per fast train.

Take it to London Bridge Station yourself, and be sure
to say it is to go by fast train."

Besides all this, Ruskin, who always tended amiably
to romantic affections for young girls, was entirely
captivated by " Guggum," and whatever pain and

difficulty Rossetti did not suffer in his wretched engagement and marriage was saved him by Ruskin's tenderness
and generosity.

The following are two extracts from Madox Brown's
diary :

"*March* 10*th*, 1855.—I had a letter from Rossetti,
Thursday, saying that Ruskin had bought all Miss
Siddal's [" Guggum's "] drawings, and said they beat
Rossetti's own. This is like Ruskin, the incarnation
of exaggeration."

"*April* 13*th*, 1855.—This evening a letter from Gabriel
saying Ruskin . . . had made two propositions to Miss
Siddal . . . one to buy all she does one by one, the other
to give her £150 a year for all she does, and if he sold
them for more, the difference to be hers ; if not, to keep
them. . . . D.G.R. in glee."

But " Guggum's " health made it impossible for her to
do any drawing, and the arrangement had to be put on
another footing. The £150 a year was still to be hers.

" Utterly irrespective of Rossetti's feelings or my
own," he writes, " I should simply do what I do, if I
could, as I should try to save a beautiful tree from being
cut down, or a bit of a Gothic cathedral whose strength
was failing."

And in another letter, a few days later :

" It is very possible you may feel as if it involved a
sort of pledge on your part to do a certain quantity of
work, and that, if you could not do as much as you thought
you should, you might get unhappy.

" . . . If you will put yourself in my place, and ask
yourself what you would like any other person to do who
was in yours, I believe you will answer rightly and save
both me and yourself much discomfort. For I think you
will then see that the best way of obliging me will be to
get well as fast as possible, not drawing one stroke more
than you like."

From then onwards the cornucopia of his benevolence
rained kindness on her.

She was driven to Denmark Hill, where old Ruskin,

the sherry dealer, said that she might have been born a countess, and Mrs. Ruskin, who prided herself upon her medical knowledge, was closeted with her a long time hearing her symptoms and advising change of air. " I forgot to say to you," he wrote to Rossetti, " when I saw you, that, if you think there is anything in which I can be of any use to Miss Siddal, you have only to tell me. I mean, she might be able and like, as the weather comes finer, to come out here sometimes and take a walk in the garden, and feel the quiet fresh air, and look at a missal or two, and she shall have the run of the house, and if you think she would like an Albert Dürer or a photograph for her own room, merely tell me and I will get it for her."

He sent her down, sure in his own mind that she was a dying woman, to see Dr. Acland at Oxford ; he called her " Ida," after Tennyson's Princess ; he sent her to the South of France ; he gave her ivory dust with which to make a jelly.

3

And, while all this was going on, Rossetti still lived betweenwhiles his rough gypsy life, undisturbed. This was the slangy, quarrelsome, haphazard world where he was at ease, the central figure of which was his redoubtable old friend, Ford Madox Brown.

August 16th, 1855, the time of his closest relationship to Ruskin, is a typical day in his life at this time. This is the entry in Madox Brown's diary :

" Emma [Brown's wife] went into town with Miss Siddal before Rossetti was come in from his room at the Queen's Head, so that when he did come his rage knew no bounds at being done out of the society of ' Guggum,' and vented itself in abuse of Emma, who ' was always trying to persuade Miss Sid that he was plaguing her,' etc. etc., whereas, of course, Miss Sid liked it as much as he did, etc. I did not know whether to laugh most or to be angry, so did both ; laughed at him and damned him, and at length thought it best to tell him where he could find them. . . . This appeased him, and presently off he started. I took a shower bath, not having had one since Miss Sid came, she having my room. After this, much pleased to be at peace once again, I set to work at the portion of ship's-netting that covers the piece added to the side of the panel. Went and cut a cabbage in the garden, placed it, and worked well from about half-past eleven till half-past four, when back came Betty with a note from Rossetti to say I must be at Chatham Place by five, as they were all going to the play. This just as I was getting in cue for work. In much dudgeon I dined and dressed and off to Hampstead, getting to Blackfriars in time to find a note saying I was to follow them, to Astleys of all places in the world. . . . Walked over as the crowd came out, but they were gone. So in a cheerful temper I off to Blackfriars, and there found Gabriel gone and Miss Siddal in bed."

Another entry :

" *December* 31*st*, 1855.—Gabriel was such a swell as I never saw before, but looking really splendid, everything about him in perfect taste except his shoes ; it will be some time before he goes to that length. Otherwise his brown suit was most in the fashion ; he looked handsome and a gentleman, talking of buying a ' ticker,' but not of paying me back my fifteen pounds, alas ! "

What a journey from Denmark Hill !

Ruskin did not like Gabriel's Bohemian friends, and through their eyes one gets a very different picture of him. He was spoken of as the Great Prohibited. Brown certainly had every reason to resent the studied neglect to which he had been treated.

Another Bohemian day :

" . . . Stopped up talking to Gabriel till three, then talked in bed with him till five. After breakfast concocted a letter to the Marchioness of Waterford declining to give her lessons *à domicile* by my advice. . . . While I was smoking a pipe in shirt-sleeves, ' enter to us ' Ruskin. I smoke ; he talks divers nonsense about art hurriedly in shrill, flippant tones. I answer him civilly, then resume my coat and prepare to leave. Suddenly upon this he says, ' Mr. Brown, will you tell me why you chose such a very ugly subject for your last picture ? ' I, dumbfounded at such a beginning from a stranger, look in his face expectant of some *qualification*, and ask ' What picture ? ' To which he, looking defyingly, answers, ' Your picture at the British Exhibition. What made you take such a very ugly subject ? It was a pity, for there was some nice painting in it.' I . . . being satisfied that he intended impertinence, replied contemptuously, ' Because it lay out of a back window,' and, turning on my heel, took my hat and wished Gabriel good-bye ! Ruskin . . . would not look at me as I left the room. So much for my first interview."

And another :

" Painted at William Rossetti from eight till twelve. Gabriel came in. William wishing to go early, Gabriel proposed that he should wait for five minutes and they would go together, when, William being got to sleep on the sofa, Gabriel commenced telling me how he intended to get married at once to ' Guggum ' and off to Algeria, and so poor William's five minutes lasted till half-past two a.m. . . . I went to a meeting of the sub-committee about the testimonial of Ruskin's, he having noticed my absence from the previous one with regret. Ruskin was playful and childish, and the tea-table overcharged with cakes and sweets as for a juvenile party. Then about an hour later cake and wine was again produced, of which Ruskin again partook largely, reaching out with his thin paw and swiftly absorbing three or four large lumps of cake in succession. At home he looks young and rompish. At the meeting at Hunt's he looked old and ungainly, but his power and eloquence as a speaker were homeric. But I said at the time that but for his speaking he was in appearance like a cross between a fiend and a tallow chandler. . . . At night to the Working Men's College with Gabriel, and then a public meeting to hear Professor Maurice spouting and Ruskin jawing. Ruskin was as eloquent as ever, and is wildly popular with the men. He flattered Rossetti in his presence hugely, and spoke of Munroe in conjunction with Baron Marochetti as the two noble sculptors whom all the aristocracy patronised—and never a word about Woolner, whose bust he had just before gone into ecstasies about and invited to dinner. This at a moment when Woolner's pupils of the college were all present.

"Rossetti says Ruskin is a sneak, and loves him, Rossetti, because he is one too, and Hunt he half likes because he is half a sneak, but he hates Woolner because he is manly and straightforward and me because I am ditto. He adored Millais because Millais was the prince of sneaks, but Millais was too much so, for he sneaked away his wife, and so he is obliged to hate him for too much of his favourite quality."

This is an odd and rather unintelligent explanation of the man who had described himself as "nearly as just as it is possible for a man to be in this world." Presumably Rossetti invented it to soothe Brown as they walked home from the meeting; he could hardly convince him that Ruskin sincerely despised his painting—at least, not if he wanted to soothe him. It is quite extraordinary how often Ruskin was right. He was always so positive, so catholic in the scope of his judgments, eschewing all the half blame and oblique approval of modern criticism, so easily carried away into extravagant ecstasies by the very depth of his appreciation of beauty, and yet it is only in a few cases that he ever went really wrong. He may have been over-excited by Mulready and Miss Siddal; he undoubtedly was; but he knew that Madox Brown (except in *Work* and a few sunny sketches) was a thoroughly second-rate painter, however jolly a fellow he may have been, and that Woolner, for all his uprightness, was an insignificant sculptor. He was tremendously conscious of his position as Censor of the Arts, and nothing would make him betray his trust; his manner was often provokingly supercilious and a little spiteful, but that is a different matter. Madox Brown was possessed by an overpowering belief in the clanship of the arts. He, and to a great extent Rossetti, saw the world divided into two classes, those who painted pictures and those who did not. Those who did not had one plain duty, to support those who did. Inside the circle relative merit was of secondary importance.

" It is for this reason," writes Ford Madox Hueffer,[1] " that these painters and these poets, distinguished by singular merits and by demerits as singular, made upon the English-speaking world a mark such as perhaps no body of men has made upon intellectual Anglo-Saxondom since the days of Shakespeare. . . . Anglo-Saxon writers, as a rule, sit in the British Islands each upon his little hill, surrounded each by his satellites, moodily jealous of the fame of each of his rivals. . . . But it was the union of these men in matters of art that gave them driving force against a world which very much did not want them. They pushed their way amongst buyers, they pushed their way into exhibitions, and it was an absolutely certain thing that as soon as one of them had got a foothold he never rested until he had helped in as many of his friends as the walls would hold. . . . For any one of them to leave the other of them out of his praises was to commit the unpardonable sin."

Ruskin was just one of the buying public, a little less wealthy and a little more difficult to please than Millar, or Rae, or Leathart, or Plint. Whatever was purely predatory in Rossetti's attitude to him may be attributed to this cardinal doctrine of the Madox Brown set.

4

Ruskin's scheme of life was essentially didactic. Though pure benevolence dictated a great many of his actions, there was usually at the back of his mind the ulterior intention of linking up all these isolated acts

---

[1] *Ancient Lights* (Chapman & Hall). A most delightful account of the artistic life of this period.

of grace into a great artistic and moral reformation, with himself at the head.

"I am rolling projects over and over in my head," he wrote to Lady Trevelyan in 1854. "I want to give short lectures to about two hundred at once, in turn, of the sign painters, and shop decorators, and writing masters, and upholsterers, and masons, and bricklayers, and glass blowers, and pottery people, and young artists and young men in general, and schoolmasters and young ladies in general, and school mistresses ; and I want to teach illumination to the sign painters, and the younger ladies ; and to have prayer-books all written again (only the Liturgy altered first, as I told you) ; and I want to explode printing and gunpowder, the two great curses of the age . . . and to make copies of all the fine thirteenth-century manuscripts and to lend them out, all for nothing of course ; and to have a room where anyone can go in all day and always see *nothing* in it but what is *good*, with a little printed explanatory catalogue saying *why* it is good . . . and I want to have a little academy of my own in all the manufacturing towns, and to get the young artists—Pre-Raphaelite always—to help me ; and I want to have an Academy exhibition, an opposite shop . . . in nice little rooms decorated in a grotesque manner . . . and no elbowing. I mean to write a great work on politics—founded on the thirteenth century."

The scheme widened and widened with the years, and Rossetti's genius and "Guggum's" ivory dust were a very minute part of it.

It was in this width of outlook that Ruskin claimed to be Rossetti's superior, and Rossetti, of course, just did not understand it. Only in one direction could Ruskin enlist his help, and that a very practical one.

The Working Men's College in Great Ormond Street—were the Rossettis never to get clear of the soot and fog of Bloomsbury ?—has already been mentioned several times. It played a considerable part in the artistic life of the 'fifties. F. D. Maurice, "a puzzle-headed man," founded it to provide evening classes in

literature, history, economics, and art, the lecturers
for the most part giving their services. This sort of
gratuitous "uplift" has been run to death nowadays,
and one is inclined to regard it with undue distrust.
There was nothing at all of the kind in existence then,
but even at the time it came in for a good deal of hostile
criticism, particularly in the Art School. The idiotic
William Bell Scott has plenty to say about it in his *Autobiographical Notes*. He found Ruskin's class engaged
upon detailed pen-and-ink drawings of leaves and
lichenous twigs. At his school in South Kensington they
began in the ordinary way, with spheres and pyramids,
and gradually worked up to "The Dying Gladiator."
It disturbed his professional prejudices, and he even
went so far as to be rather rude to Ruskin about it at
a house-party, bringing up as his final argument the
challenge that by his method Ruskin had never produced
a single artist of any merit.

The answer, of course, is that it was not Ruskin's hope
or intention to produce artists, or even professional
designers. For that he always advised the Academy
Schools. His object was moral ; he believed in the power
of natural beauty with the fervour which we now devote
to artificial sunlight ; he wanted to introduce into the
cramped little minds of the workmen, warped and
debauched by the industrial system, some little delicacy
of feeling, some sense of pleasure other than gin or
cruelty. Hence the leaves and the lichen, and hence
too, perhaps, his "wild popularity."

Rossetti, I think, really hoped to produce artists.
At any rate, he wanted his men to have a good time with
the paint-box.

"You should see my class for the model ! " he wrote,
"none of your *freehand drawing books* used ! The
British mind is brought to bear on the British *mug* [1]
at once, with results that would astonish you."

He gave them the use of free colour at once, and one
evening, finding Ruskin's class more cautiously at work

[1] One of Rossetti's slang words ; it means face.

on studies in Prussian blue, he confiscated the entire store, which, oddly enough, Ruskin does not seem to have minded.

It was through this school that he came into contact with William Morris and Edward Burne-Jones.

5

Morris had gone up to Oxford in 1853, at the age of nineteen, intending, like so many of the more prominent members of the Pre-Raphaelite-Æsthetic movement, to take Holy Orders. Like many wise people before and after him, he found the life there pitiably disappointing. In spite of the railway, it was still very much like the Oxford of Gibbon's time; the President of Magdalen had been elected before the French Revolution, and was not receptive of new ideas; the head of his own college, Exeter, never put in an appearance at all; the dons, idler than those of to-day and more widely ignorant, were no less tedious; hunting and whoring were the only interests of the undergraduates who were not bores; no one seemed to remember having heard the names of Newman or Pusey.

Oxford culture, as Morris hoped to find it, is a growth of very recent years, and can only be found in those red wastes of Gothic about the Woodstock and the Banbury Roads. They were all fields in Morris's time. To the end of his days " Don " and " Oxford " were two of the most bitter words in a vocabulary glowing with oaths.

The first and almost the only friend he made at Exeter was Edward Burne-Jones, like himself of Welsh descent (he was plain " Jones " at this time, but in later life he followed Hunt's example and hyphenated his name with a baptismal name). He, too, was reading for the Church. They were both bored and distressed by the University. They used to go for " angry walks " together every after-noon, and read the history of the Eastern Church aloud to each other in the evenings.

Gradually these two formed a little circle about them,

mostly of Pembroke men whom Jones knew at Birmingham. There was Faulkner, a mathematician and scientist of incisive intellect ; he did something to balance the strong theological bias of the set ; he had been ploughed in Divinity for including Isaiah among the twelve apostles. Dixon and Fulford were both reading for the Church, and both became parsons, undisturbed by the change of Morris and Jones. Dixon, afterwards a canon, was a poet of some ability ; Rossetti at one time expressed great admiration for his work. Cormell Price, Welsh too, was Morris's closest friend. He addressed him in his letters as " Dearest Crom," and signed himself " Your most loving, Topsy." Price later became headmaster of Westward Ho College in the days of Stalky & Co.

Fulford had come up from King Edward's School, Birmingham, two years before the others, leaving behind him a great reputation of genius, so that at first he took the place of leader in the set, until he was gradually over-shadowed by Morris, who developed astonishingly in the next three years. The development was all towards art and away from theology. Instead of Milman's *Latin Christianity* or the *Acta Sanctorum*, the reading of the group became *Modern Painters* and *The Lady of Shalott*.

Jones had been famous at Birmingham for drawing " devils " ; at Oxford he used to go out to Bagley Woods to draw foliage while Morris poured over the illuminated manuscripts in the Bodleian. Together they visited neighbouring churches and took rubbings from the brasses. Morris was the first of them to see anything wrong with Tennyson. The group took to reading Shakespeare in each other's rooms, drawing lots for the parts. " Topsy " suddenly discovered he could write poetry, line after line, almost without effort. When he was twenty-one he came into the then comfortable income of £900 a year.

It was in 1854, in Ruskin's " Edinburgh Lecture," that they first came upon the name of Rossetti. Morris was thinking at this time of devoting his fortune to the foundation of a monastery from which, in celibacy and communal life, the Birmingham group should engage in a " Crusade and Holy Warfare against the Age," but by the end of 1855 he was thoroughly secularised by the study of Chaucer and Browning, and the crusade had lost its conventual character. It was to be a war against the ugliness of industrial life—much the same war as Ruskin was already waging with his æsthetic clinics. It was in 1855, the year of Sebastopol, and *Maud* that Morris finally renounced his aims to priesthood and decided to take up architecture.

He now for the first time came across an example of Rossetti's work—a woodcut illustration to William Allingham's *Day and Night Songs* of which Rossetti was singularly ashamed. Morris was enraptured by it, and instantly set about drawing and engraving himself. He and the rest of his set, who now called themselves the Brotherhood, were busily producing a magazine, to be called *The Oxford and Cambridge Magazine*, Fulford taking the lead again, and " Topsy " guaranteeing the expenses. This magazine, so remote in its inception, was generally looked upon as the successor of *The Germ.* Unlike its predecessor, it appeared regularly for a year, but at a heavy loss. Ruskin expressed his sympathy with the production, and hinted at the possibility of his contributing. Rossetti gave them—everyone, in his own words, wrote " for love or spooniness "—*Staff and Scrip, The Burden of Nineveh,* and a new version of *The Blessed Damozel.*

Jones was the first of the group to meet their idol in the flesh. It was just after Christmas, 1855–6, when the magazine was first being published.

" I knew no one," he writes, " who had ever seen a painter or had been in a studio, and of all the men who lived on earth the one that I wanted to see was Rossetti. I had no dream of ever knowing him, but I wanted to look at him, and as I had heard that he taught at the Working Men's College . . . I went to the college one day to find out how it would be possible that I should set eyes upon him. I was told that there was to be a monthly

FR

meeting that very evening, in a room in Great Titchfield Street, and that, by paying threepence, anyone could get admittance, including tea . . . so without fail I was there, and sat at a table and had thick bread and butter, but knowing no one.   But good fellowship was the rule there, that was clear ; and a man sitting opposite to me spoke at once to me, introducing himself by the name of Furnivall, and I gave my name and college and my reason for coming.   He reached across the table to a kindly-looking man, whom he introduced to me as Vernon Lushington, to whom I repeated my reason for coming, and begged him to tell me when Rossetti entered the room.   It seemed that it was doubtful if he would appear at all ; that he was constant in his work of teaching draw-ing at the college, but had no great taste for the nights of address and speeches ; and, as I must have looked downcast at this, Lushington, with a kindness never to be forgotten by me, invited me to go to his rooms in Doctor's Commons a few nights afterwards. . . . On the night appointed, about ten o'clock, I went to Lushing-ton's rooms, where was a company of men some of whom have been friends ever since . . . and by and by Rossetti came, and I was taken up to him and had my first fearful talk with him.   Browning's *Men and Women* had just been published a few days before, and someone speaking disrespectfully of that book was rent to pieces at once for his pains and was dumb for the rest of the evening, so that I saw my hero could be a tyrant and I thought it sat finely upon him.   Also, another unwary man professed an interest in metaphysics ; he also was dealt with firmly ; so that our host was compelled to ask if Rossetti would have all men painters, and if there should be no other occupation for mankind.   Rossetti said stoutly that it was so.   But before I left that night Rossetti bade me come to his studio next day.   It was at the top of the last house by Blackfriars Bridge, at the north-west corner of the bridge long ago pulled down to make way for the Embankment ; and I found him painting at a water-colour of a monk copying a mouse in an illumination.

The picture was called *Fra Pace*. . . . He received me very courteously and asked much about Morris, one or two of whose poems he knew already. . . . He seemed much interested in him. . . . I stayed long watching him at work, not knowing till many a day afterwards that this was a thing he greatly hated, and when for shame I could stay no longer, I went away, having carefully concealed from him the desire I had to be a painter."

But at this stage of Rossetti's life there was no question of concealing such a desire from him ; as is shown in the quotation above, he regarded it as every man's plain duty. Not only had Jones got to become a painter, but " Topsy " too. It must have been rather agreeable for Rossetti, after having been so many people's so rebellious pupil in turn, to find himself looked upon as a master by these reverent young men. " Topsy," working for Street, the architect, at Oxford, used to come up for week-ends ; he met most of the more prominent Pre-Raphaelites, and was intoxicated by them. Rossetti kept at him all the time to make him a painter.

" I have seen Rossetti twice . . . spent almost the whole day with him last time—last Monday, that was. Hunt came in . . . a beautiful man. Rossetti says I ought to paint; now, as he is a very great man and speaks with authority and not as the scribes, I *must* try. . . . I can't enter into politics or social subjects with any interest, for on the whole I see things are in a muddle, and I have no power or vocation to set them right in ever so little a degree. My work is the embodiment of dreams in one form or another."

How those last two sentences smack of Gabriel.

For some time he attempted a feverish compromise, spending all day at the office and all the evening at a drawing school, but it was clearly impossible to keep this up for long, and in the end Gabriel won. At the end of 1856 he definitely gave up architecture. Brown was, as always, rather suspicious of these new friends. Trying to make conversation, Burne-Jones asked him whether he was not very old to begin painting.

" Oh, no ! There was a man I knew who began older," was the gruff reply; and then, some seconds later, " By the bye he cut his throat the other day."

In February 1857 " Topsy " and Jones were living together in Red Lion Square, with Rossetti as a daily visitor. He had a genuinely high opinion of their merits.

" Two young men," he wrote in 1857 to Bell Scott, " projectors of *The Oxford and Cambridge Magazine,* have recently come to town from Oxford and are now intimate friends of mine. Their names are Morris and Jones. They have turned artists instead of taking up any other career to which the University generally leads, and both are men of real genius. Jones's designs are models of finish and imaginative detail, unequalled by anything unless, perhaps, Albert Dürer's first works "— it is extraordinary how Dürer is always cropping up as the one standard of finish in Pre-Raphaelite criticism— " and Morris, though without practice as yet, has no less power, I fancy. He has written some really wonderful poetry too." But he had no real use for poetry just then any more than for architecture. Painting was the only thing. " If any man has poetry in him," he used to say, " he should paint, for it has all been said and written, and they have scarcely begun to paint it."

For two years Morris studied under Rossetti with servile deference, by far the two least profitable years in his life. Beyond a broad sense of decoration he had no gift for painting at all ; he grew moody and discontented, while Rossetti exulted in his mastery. When Jones commented on the lack of originality in his work, he said, " I've got beyond that ; I want to imitate Gabriel as much as I can." It was by no means a healthy connection for " Topsy," despite the robust mythology that has grown up about it.

They were living, Jones and " Topsy," at 17 Red Lion Square, in the same house where Deverell and Rossetti had once shared a studio. When the second wave of the æsthetic movement broke with such a decrease of strength and with so much foam of affectation and decadence, biographers found it expedient to emphasise, in rather a tiresome way, the tremendous heartiness of its pioneers. Anecdote after anecdote of brutish horseplay is invoked to show the gulf that separated Red Lion Square from Reading Gaol. It is recorded with the utmost relish how " Topsy " threw a small plum-pudding at the housemaid ; how he flew into fits of ungovernable rage, and would throw the furniture about the room, tear at his infrangible hair and beard, and champ up spoons and forks with his teeth ; how he roared downstairs, "Mary, those six eggs were bad. I've eaten them, but don't let it happen again"; how in 1859 they all joined the Artists' Rifle Corps, and paraded weekly in grey and silver uniforms ; how they tied Morris's hair into knots while he was sitting for a drawing ; how he kept an owl in the house—cruelly, one cannot help thinking—and how he would himself imitate an eagle, " climbing on to a chair and, after a sullen pause, coming down with a heavy flop."

It is typical of this whole friendship that the chief fruit of it should be the disastrous frescoes in the Union Debating Hall at Oxford. It is an ugly enough building, designed by Woodward, the arch-fiend of Oxford archi-tecture, and is now used as the principal library. It is a narrow, steep erection, with apsidal ends. A gallery runs round it, lined with shelves, and above the shelves a belt of wall, divided into ten bays, each pierced by two circular windows, and covered by an open timber roof. It was this belt of wall that fired the imagination of Rossetti and Woodward. Rossetti offered to give his services in painting it, and to find friends who would do the same, in return for the bare expenses of living and working. It was a matter which should have been put before a meeting of the society, but the building committee, who had a vague discretionary authority to see to things during the long vacation, did not wish to appear un-gracious, and were bullied by Woodward and Dr. Acland into precipitous acceptance. Arthur Hughes, Spencer Stanhope, Val Prinsep, and Hungerford Pollen were to do one each; so, under supervision, were Morris and Burne-Jones. Gabriel would do two, or even three. Before the others were barely beginning upon their sketches, Morris was down in Oxford painting away with fury. It was this that really cured him of being a painter.

No one in England at this time knew much about the very special technique necessary for mural decoration; no one knew less than these gay young Pre-Raphaelites. The surface as left by the builders was rough, damp brick whitewashed over, and upon this irregular and treacherous surface they began working in water-colours with small brushes. The result need not be imagined; it may be seen to-day at Oxford in the colourless and indecipherable remains.

The irregularity of the commission was questioned in debate next term and condoned. The painters lived very comfortably in the High Street, and were idolised by the brighter undergraduates; they dined at high table, drank with Algernon Swinburne of Balliol, grew rather discriminating about the hospitality they accepted, got bored with kind Dr. Acland, and piled up their expenses. Of Rossetti's three frescoes, one was nearly finished; the others got no further than rough sketches. Morris had great fun with a blacksmith and a suit of chain mail. The paintings crumbled and faded before they were finished; the artists packed up and went away; a Mr. Rivière was commissioned to finish them off; and there they are.

" Sweet, bright, and pure as a cloud in the sunrise," wrote Coventry Patmore, " so brilliant as to make the walls look like the margin of an illuminated manuscript."

Everyone seems to have agreed that Rossetti's, so far as it went, was outstandingly the best of the frescoes. There is a water-colour copy of it by Treffry Dunn from which it is impossible to get more than the vaguest impression of its real value. The composition looks muddled, but so would much of his best work at this period if clumsily copied. The woodcut illustrations from his drawings—how they all smarted under the Dalziels!—

all give an impression of impoverishment. The unity of his designs is so much dependent on texture.

While they were at Oxford, " Topsy " got engaged to be married, a very salutary change of interest for him. He and Rossetti were at the theatre one night when their attention was taken by the exotic beauty of a lady sitting not far away from them. She was the elder of the two Misses Burden, daughters of an Oxford resident. Rossetti had an insolent and surprisingly successful way of forcing his acquaintance upon women who attracted him—one of his *affaires* started by his suddenly pouncing upon a young girl, up from the country in a London restaurant, and pulling down her hair " to see how it looked." With a less violent overture on this occasion, he persuaded her to sit to him, and from then onwards her dark beauty, growing less and less human as the years went by, dominated his painting, usurping Elizabeth Siddal's white and gold. With a last and decisive subservience to Rossetti's taste, " Topsy " married her.

6

Meanwhile, Rossetti's relations with " Guggum " were of practically unrelieved pain and anxiety. In 1854 he wrote :

" It seems hard to me when I look at her sometimes, working or too ill to work, and think how many, without one tithe of her genius or greatness of spirit, have granted them abundant health and opportunity to labour through the little they can do or will do, while perhaps her soul is never to bloom nor her bright hair to fade, but, after hardly escaping from degradation and corruption, all she might have been must sink out again unprofitably in that dark house where she was born. How truly she may say, ' No man careth for my soul.' "

Ruskin urged them to marry, and to put " an end to the peculiar sadness and want of you hardly know what " that there was in both of them. But what with one thing and another—her continued ill health, Rossetti's continual improvidence, despite his growing income, and his natural repugnance to the restraints and responsibilities of marriage—the engagement went on desolately, and still, heaven knows why, shrouded in a sort of secrecy. A letter written to Madox Brown in 1857 deserves to be quoted in full for the curious light it throws upon their relationship.

" 14 Chatham Place,
" *February* 26*th*, 1857.

"MY DEAR BROWN,—Last night a misunderstanding occurred between Lizzie and me about what passed, when you were there, concerning the scheme of a college.

" She seems under the impression that you came there in great surprise at hearing I had not consulted her on the matter, and with the wish to speak to her yourself. Though I should be grateful to you for anything done in friendship to her, I cannot but imagine that, as my friend, you would have preferred first asking me what has passed between us before speaking to her ; especially as you could have been under no impression that I was acting in this without reference to her as well as myself ; seeing that on the night when Morris, Jones, and I came to you, and were discussing the scheme, I expressly said that I should be married by the time it came into operation, and require space accordingly in the building.

" When you first spoke on Tuesday evening of two married couples as beginning the scheme, I thought you meant Lizzie and me for the second, and, finding that you did not, I refrained from saying anything, simply because Lizzie has sometimes lately shown so much displeasure on my mentioning our engagement (which I have hoped was attributable to illness) that I could not tell how far her mother was aware of it, or how Lizzie would take my mentioning it before her.

" I *had* spoken of the scheme to her some days ago, but she seemed to take little interest in it, and I did not say much. . . . However, my wishes as to this scheme would entirely depend on hers, supposing that it would really affect her happiness ; in which case I should cease to care for it or think of it. As it is, she seemed last night quite embittered and estranged from me on this account, whether for the moment or permanently I cannot tell, and it has made me most unhappy ever since, more so than anything else could make me. I am going there to-day now, and shall probably be there in the evening. After to-day she talks of going to stay for a week at her sister's.

" Yours ever sincerely,
" D. G. ROSSETTI."

She had come back to England in the winter of 1856 from her protracted convalescence in the South, apparently a little better. But, soon after the letter just quoted, Rossetti was writing :

" She does not better in health, never eating anything to speak of, and I am most wretched about her. What to do, I know not. . . . I cannot feel any anger at her, only constant pain in her sufferings. Kind and patient she has been with me many and many times, more than I have deserved."

She was continually disappearing to health resorts, hotly pursued by Rossetti.

In April 1860 she was at Hastings, desperately ill again.

" I have been, almost without respite, since I saw you, in the most agonising anxiety about poor dear Lizzie's health," he writes to Madox Brown ; " indeed, it has been that kind of pain that we can never remember at its full, as she has seemed ready to die daily, and more than once a day. It has needed all my strength to nurse her through this dreadful attack. . . . It makes me feel as if I had been dug out of a vault, so many times lately has it seemed to me that she could never lift her head again.

. . . Lizzie, I find, prefers being alone with me, and, indeed, it would be too painful for anyone to witness. I assure you it has been almost too much for me . . . it hardly seems as if I shall ever work again."

A month after the writing of this letter they were married. The letter he addressed to Brown immediately after the wedding does little to reveal what his thoughts must have been as they set off.

" DEAR BROWN," he wrote,—" All hail from Lizzie and myself, just back from church. I am sorry I cannot give you any good news of her health, but we must hope for the best. We go to Folkestone this afternoon if possible, with a view to spending a week or so in Paris, and, if we stay long enough there, I hope Ned and Georgie will join us.

" Yours affectionately,
" D. G. ROSSETTI.

" If you are still with Top, as Ned told me you were, best love to the Topsies. The Towers of Topsy must darken the air by this."

On his honeymoon he painted again, with listless premonition of coming tragedy, a subject which had early fascinated him, *How They Met Themselves*, an illustration of the *Döppelgänger* legend. There is no one quite like F. G. Stephens for describing pictures.

" Two lovers," he writes, " are walking in a twilight world when they are suddenly confronted by their own apparitions, portending death ; she, sinking to the earth, stretches out her hands as if appealing for mercy, while he, bolder but overawed, lays his hand upon his sword. . . . The poet-painter had already made the colours of his pictures harmonise with their pathos ; this he did . . . in the presageful gloom of *How They Met Themselves*, all haggard and woebegone, in the darkness of the shadow-haunted wood, and in the colours of the lovers' dresses."

7

In the nine years between Rossetti's acquaintance with
Ruskin and the death of Elizabeth Siddal, his position as
a painter was raised and established. He was never,
until after his death, widely famous, but during these
years he took a prominent, and in many cases pre-eminent,
position in the esteem of the inner circle of rather literary
connoisseurs and the outer circle of rather illiterate
collectors who formed the artistic society of his time.

As in the case of the Morris set, it was through Ruskin
that most people first heard of him, and it was at Ruskin's
valuation that he was accepted, and thus an initial misconception of Ruskin's, much to Rossetti's advantage
became perpetuated. He got the reputation of having
been the originator of the Pre-Raphaelite Brotherhood.
We have already discussed at some length how far this
claim is tenable. Ruskin undoubtedly believed in it.
On June 15th, 1854, he wrote from Geneva :
"I know that, so far from being envious of them [Hunt
and Millais], you are thoroughly happy in their success ;
but yet you feel that there is as much in you as in them.
. . . I think that you, Hunt, and Millais would, every one
of you, have made the discovery " [the possibilities of Pre-
Raphaelite treatment of genre subjects] " without assistance or suggestion from the other. One might make it
quicker or slower than another, and I suppose that
actually you were the first who did it."

And thus in 1857 the *Athenæum*, reviewing the Pre-
Raphaelite Exhibition, refers to " Mr. Millais, the chief
of the sect ; Mr. H. Hunt, the apostle of the order ; and
Mr. D. Rossetti, the original founder of the three-lettered
race, who's generally spoken of by them in a low voice "
—can one imagine Millais ever lowering his voice ?—
" as he is supposed, from the fertility of his allegorical
sketches, to be capable of doing anything, though he does
not and will not exhibit in public."

This exhibition was an important step in Rossetti's
advance. It was held more or less privately in Russell

Place, Fitzroy Square, under the presidency of Madox Brown. The exhibitors did not give the collection any particular name, but people soon began to speak of it as " The Pre-Raphaelite Exhibition," and the name has stuck. Brown, Hunt, Millais, and Miss Siddal all sent pictures, also Collins, Hayes, Martineau, and several others. Rossetti's contributions were *Dante's Dream of the Death of Beatrice*, *Dante Drawing the Angel*, *Mary Nazarene*, *Mary Magdalene*, *The Blue Closet*, *Hesterna Rosa*, and photographs of his Tennyson designs. It is a fair selection of his work up to this time.

Dante's Dream was a more sombre sketch for the well-known painting which he finished in the last year of his life.

Mary Magdalene, usually known as *Mary at the Door of Simon Peter's House*, and *Hesterna Rosa* are pen-and-ink drawings of very great beauty. Three years separate them in date (Marillier has *Mary Magdalene* catalogued a year late).[1]

The Tennyson designs are rather unfortunate. The drawing was slipshod, and Dalziel, forced by the exigencies of the graver into some sort of definitiveness, has made them intolerably hard and ugly—for example, in the hair of the nine princesses in the *Palace of Art*, which Rossetti had left in a blur of pencil, and the background of the *Lady of Shalott*.[2]

No doubt all his work was not easily accessible for exhibition. If one were now asked to select eight of his drawings to represent him at that period, they would certainly include *Mary Magdalene* and *Dante Drawing the Angel*, but I, at any rate, would substitute *The Marriage*

[1] It must be remembered, in cases of this sort, that it is often impossible to assign an exact day to some of Rossetti's works. Until they were actually out of his hands they were always in a state of flux. He worked on them off and on, adding and taking out bits, often with unfortunate results, until they were sold.

[2] The whole commission caused endless worry, particularly to Moxon, the publisher. Rossetti was never up to time with drawings or proofs. Moxon kept writing, but Rossetti was not good at answering letters; he kept calling, but Rossetti was never up. Rossetti said it nearly killed him; Moxon actually did die.

of St. George—if it was finished in time for the exhibition,
a point I have been unable to verify—for *Mary Nazarene,*
and no exhibition either of this period or of the whole of
Rossetti's work would be wholly satisfactory that did not
include *Arthur's Tomb.*

This singularly beautiful little water-colour—it measures
only 14½ in. by 9½ in.—seems to me typical of all that was
most virile in Rossetti's imagination and most sensitive in
his technique.   Again to resort to F. G. Stephens, it is
" a brilliant study of sunlight in an apple orchard, where,
under the first laden trees (here introduced significantly),
lies the altar tomb of King Arthur, with his effigies all
in armour lying upon it, while the Queen, habited as
a nun of Glastonbury, and her quondam lover, clad in
helmet and mail, have met and hold discourse about
their former lives and sins."

But I am not sure that for once Mr. Stephens has not
let us down ; there is much more in the drawing than he
seems to have realised.

The scene, as recorded in Malory, takes place in the
convent cloister, in the presence of all the ladies and
gentlemen.

" And then was queene Guenever ware of Sir Launcelot
as he walked in the cloyster ; and when she saw him she
souned three times, that all the ladies and gentlewomen
had worke enough for to hold the queene up.   So when
shee might speake, shee called ladies and gentlewomen
unto her, and said, ' Ye mervaile, faire ladies, why I
make this cheere.   Truly,' said shee, ' it is for the sight of
yonder knight which yonder standeth ; wherefore I pray
you all to call him unto me.'   And when Sir Launcelot
was brought unto her, then shee said, ' Through this
knight and me all these warres were wrought, and the
death of the most noble knights of the world, for through
our love that we have loved together is my most noble
lord slaine.   Therefore wit thou well Sir Launcelot, I
am set in such a plight to get my soules health ; and
yet I trust, through Gods grace, that after my death for
to have the sight of the blessed face of Jesu Christ, and

at the dreadful day of dome to sit on his right side. For as sinful creatures as ever I was are saints in heaven.

" ' Therefore, Sir Launcelot, I require thee and beseech thee heartily, for all the love that ever was betweene us two, that thou never look mee more in the visage. . . . For well as I have loved thee, Sir Launcelot, now mine heart will not once serve mee to see thee ; for through mee and thee is the flower of kings and knights destroyed. Therefore, Sir Launcelot, goe thou unto thy realme, and there take thee a wife, and live with her in joy and blisse. And I beseech you heartely praye for me unto our Lord God, that I may amende me mine living.' ' Now sweet madame,' said Sir Launcelot, ' would yee that I should now returne againe unto my country and there wed a ladye ? Nay, madame, wit ye well never while I live ; for I shall never be so false to you, but the same destiny that yee have taken unto you, I will take me unto, for to please God and speciall to pray for you. . . . For I take record of God in you have I had mine earthly joy. And if I had found you so disposed now, I had cast mee for to have you into mine owne realme and country. . . . Wherefore, madame, I pray you kisse me once and never more.' ' Nay,' said the queene, ' that shall I never doe, but abstaine you from such things.' And so they departed. But there was never so hard a hearted man but hee would have wept to see the sorrow that they made ; for there was a lamentation as though they had been stungen with spears."

This affecting and decorous incident has been endowed by Rossetti with a guilt all his own. The lovers meet alone and at Arthur's tomb, and the dead king's effigy— or effigies, if Stephens insists upon a use which the *O.E.D.* condemns as " humorously pedantic "—dominates the composition. Austere and ungainly, it draws a line of obtrusive mortality across the picture. On one side is Launcelot, all the sentimental despondence of Malory aflame with masculinity, crouching and peering under the beetle-back of his shield like some obscene and predatory insect ; the head of Arthur butts him away

with almost comic vigour.   Beside the tomb, and practically
a part of it, kneels Guinever, stripped of the sententious
dignity of the abbess-queen, her stiff gesture of repugnance allying her with the archaic sculpture at her back,
the last defence of threatened chastity, Galatea repetrified.

It is in many ways a painful picture.   Three horizontals
constrict the composition until it aches with suppressed
resilience.   Remove the apple-tree and the whole composition would fly up uncontrollably through the frame ;
the thick, stiff little trunk straps it down and tortures it
unendurably.   To look at it for a long time is like looking
at a traction engine ;   only a continual exercise of reason
and calculation of stress can quell the instinctive terror
that it must inevitably burst almost at once.   And how
well Rossetti felt this.   A lesser artist, certainly any other
Pre-Raphaelite, would have twisted that apple-tree or
gnarled it and made a beautiful decoration of it ;   all
Rossetti wanted was a clamp.

Arthur's Tomb is important as the only complete expression in Rossetti's art of this stress of constricted energy
which is so characteristic of his life.   The drawings of
this period show, for the most part, a delicate enchantment and splendour of colour that are very lovable.
Everyone has his own favourites ;   my own is *The
Marriage of St. George.*

Here again the composition is cramped, but there is
no outward pressure ;   the design is built about the
diagonal and nestles within its limits, and the edges are
padded fairly comfortably.   It is more like needlework
than any of his paintings, being built of little stitchlike
strokes of pure colour. [1]

[1] A very suggestive description of it is found in one of the letters of
James Smetham, a remarkable but forgotten character, torn between
Methodism, mysticism, and painting : " One of the grandest things, like a
golden, dim dream.   Love ' credulous all gold,' gold armour, a sense of
secret enclosure in ' palace chambers far apart ' ;   but quaint chambers in
quaint palaces, where angels creep in through sliding panel doors, and
stand behind rows of flowers, drumming on golden bells, with wings crimson
and green.   There was also a queer remnant of a dragon's head which
he had brought up in a box."

The first important commission that shows the growing recognition of Rossetti's powers was for the painting
of a triptych for the Cathedral of Llandaff, in Wales,
which was being restored by John Seddon. It was first
offered to him in 1855, much to the annoyance of Madox
Brown, who would have been very grateful for the work.
His explanation of the choice was entered in his diary
on Good Friday : " It is to toady to Ruskin."

Oddly enough, it did not attract Rossetti much, but
he, too, needed the money, and, after some bargaining,
he agreed to do it for £400. The subject chosen was
" The Seed of David," one side-panel representing David
as the Shepherd, the other David the King, with, in the
centre, a Nativity, with the Adoration of a Shepherd and
a King. He made some water-colour sketches straight
away, but it was not until 1860 that he really got to work
upon it, and then it was four years before it was finished.
He never enjoyed the work, and was ashamed of it afterwards. *David the Shepherd* certainly is very limp and
undistinguished, but the opposing panel, *David the King*,
is full of rich decorative quality, and contains one of
the few examples in Rossetti's work of really successful
foliage. The truth was that Rossetti could not by then
take any real interest in a composition in which male
figures predominated. *David the King* is a face emerging
from a gorgeous study of feathers and brocade ; *David
the Shepherd* is a man and nothing more, and hence its
failure. The central panel is good, sound church decoration, with little to be said about it either way.

Mention has already been made of his pen-and-ink
drawings. Two important additions to this series are the
Hamlet and Ophelia of 1853 and the *Cassandra* of 1861.
Though neither of these compares with the *Mary at
Simon Peter's Door*, there is a depth and completeness
about them that characterise all his work in this medium.
They are particularly interesting as enabling one to judge
his drawing and composition apart from his colour. The
making of a pen-and-ink picture is practically a lost art
in England to-day. Mr. James Guthrie is probably the

only living artist who makes drawings in pen and ink which are not intended for photographic reproduction, or do not derive their technique from drawings so intended. For the rest, the drawing has merely become the raw material of the zinc process block. This is not a particularly deplorable development, but, from Beardsley onward through Phil May to almost every black-and-white designer and illustrator living, there has been a new attitude to pen drawing based on the initial conception of a white page to be decorated with black lines, and the fewer lines, so long as they are significant and rightly disposed, the better. The idea of making " a picture," with all its depths and variety of tone, has simply disappeared. Anything that will not " translate " into a line block is felt to be false to its medium.

Rossetti really made " pictures " with his pen in a way that, even in his day, very few people troubled to do. He did not leave white spaces in his work any more than he would leave bare patches of canvas in his paintings. One is so used to the technique of modern second-rate illustration that one simply does not realise at first how thoroughly stylised it is.

Mary Magdalene was later turned into an oil painting and it was for a long time Rossetti's intention to paint *Cassandra*. With its crowded and palpitating drama it would have made a magnificent picture. One can imagine how, under Rossetti's brush, the gold and bronze would have glowed with the fires of Troy. The reason that it was never done is typical of Rossetti's later years. No one would commission it. His patrons had grown to beware of paying large sums in advance for large compositions ; besides, Rossetti wanted such very large sums. The collectors all wanted something that would represent in their galleries what they regarded as typical of Rossetti. That meant, in William Rossetti's words, " female heads with floral adjuncts." These Rossetti could turn out without much effort. He wanted a large price, but there was every probability of getting the picture some time. For

GR

a large composition such as the *Cassandra* he wanted
fabulous sums, and the chances were that he would never
get it finished. The monotonous series of women's
heads that begins with *Bocca Baciata* and extends throughout the rest of his life was not so much due to a failure of
Rossetti's imaginative energy as to his grasping desire
for money. Had he been orderly in his manner of life,
or less self-indulgent, he could have afforded to risk a bad
price, or even no price at all; he would have preferred
to exercise some restraint on his comfort so that he might
be free to paint as he wanted to. Instead, as will be seen
later, he attempted to torture his frivolous subjects into
expressing all the ideas which he repressed. That is
what I mean when I say that he lacked the *moral* stability
of a great artist.

This degradation of his own attitude towards his art
begins where his dependence on Ruskin ends.

"Yesterday," he writes to Madox Brown in January
1861, "I sold for £25 a coloured sketch which had taken
me about half an hour—*that* paid."

While he was painting for Ruskin, or for any of
Ruskin's friends,[1] as the letters already quoted show, he
was working under discipline. In 1858 he was brought
into touch with a Leeds stockbroker, Mr. T. E. Plint,
the first of a long series of wealthy and undiscriminating
purchasers. Something has already been said of the
laudable humility with which these men approached the
arts. Plint was ready to pay much higher prices[2] than
Rossetti had yet received for any of his work, and, what
was still more important, would pay in advance. Rossetti
fastened upon him eagerly, and spoke of him with pitying
contempt.

[1] "I extend my notions of my deservings to such a conceited extent as
to plead not only for myself but for my *friends*. That is to say, Miss
Heaton and other people, when they put themselves into my hands and
say, 'What pictures shall I buy?' ought, I think, not to be treated as
strangers, but as, in a sort, my clients and protégés."—Ruskin to Rossetti,
1855.

[2] It is sad to note that when his collection came to be sold in 1865, it
only fetched a very small fraction of what he had paid for it.

"Just now I have only been saved from further 'avuncularism,'"[1] he writes in 1859, "by a visit of old Plint, who has bought two pen-and-ink drawings of *Hamlet* and *Guenevere*—one for 40 guineas, the other for 30 . . . O wondrous Plint! Did you see that glorious stroke of business—the joining together of a head and a landscape into one great work here? Plint bites already, and will buy, I suspect."

By September 1860 his commercial preoccupation was growing all-absorbing. The following letter, also to Brown, is typical of his change of tone:

"1st, Gambart offers 50 guineas for the head and won't give more, but says . . . I should paint him another for better wages, as I understood him. I then wrote to old Marshall, who no doubt is away, as I have had no answer yet. So I believe in another day or so I shall have arrived at the due pitch of starvation to accept Gambart's terms.

"This being thus, I don't see how I can possibly paint Gillam's water-colour just now without downright ruination. Nevertheless, I *must* do so, unless a plan will do about which I wanted your advice. It is this. I have nearly finished *Cassandra*, pen-and-ink; at least, with hard work might get it done within a day or two after the end of this month, which is Gillam's quarter day for my work. Now one of his commissions is for a £50 pen-and-ink (*Hamlet*). Do you think I might propose a substitution of *Cassandra*, for this is ready for delivery (I remember he seemed taken with it), and defer beginning the Dante series till next term? I really do not like infringing Gillam's compact, nor, strictly speaking, ought I to sell this drawing for £50. Or mightn't I ask him an additional £10? . . . It would enable me to devote a little clear time to poor, dear Plint."

What a change from the man to whom, six years ago, Ruskin was writing, "It seems to me just as natural I should try to be of use to you as that I should offer you a cup of tea if you were thirsty, and there was plenty in the tea-pot, and I had got all I wanted."

But " poor, dear Plint " got his revenge by dying quite suddenly in 1861. The details of his transactions with Rossetti have never, to my knowledge, been made public, but there were certainly large sums involved, which he had advanced for work which had never been finished, or, in some cases, begun. At the winding up of the estate it was necessary that these sums should be returned to the trustees unless the pictures were immediately forthcoming. It was a great blow to Rossetti, and accounts for the tremendous output of his married years.

To sum up this rather disconnected account of Rossetti's work, he had, between *Found* and February 1862, painted twelve pictures in oils. Four of these were on panels for furniture, one for William Morris at 17 Red Lion Square and two later for the Red House at Upton, " The Towers of Topsy," and one for himself. One was a *St. Catherine*, commissioned by Ruskin ; another was *Bocca Baciata*. This study of Mrs. Schott —Fanny Cornforth—was the first of the series already alluded to, which includes, in the period under discussion, four more oil paintings, all done during his married life from various models (one of them—*Burd-Alane*— is of doubtful authenticity). The other two are the Llandaff Triptych and an unimportant little design called *Love's Greeting*.

Forty-three water-colours are catalogued by Marillier ; it is probable that there were more. Of these, seven are Dantesque in subject, either from the *Vita Nuova* or the story of Paolo and Francesca da Rimini ; seven are Arthurian or mediæval, of which the beautiful *Sir Galahad at the Shrine* of 1859 should be noted, besides the *Arthur's Tomb* already mentioned. Two of them— *Before the Battle* of 1858 and *The Angel of the Grail* of 1857 —are closely connected with the exquisite series of little paintings that made this period the richest of Rossetti's life. The three most perfect of these are *The Tune of*

Seven Towers, The Blue Closet, and *The Marriage of St. George.* The rest, for the most part, are subjects taken from incidents in the Italian Renaissance, richly conceived and executed. A particularly happy departure from the usual choice of subject is the *Dr. Johnson at the Mitre,* begun on his honeymoon, and finished soon after his return to England.

There are also the three superb pen-and-ink drawings of *Hamlet, Mary Magdalene,* and *Cassandra,* some designs for stained glass, and innumerable " Guggums." " A drawer full. . . . God knows how many, but not bad work, I should say, for the six years he had known her ; it is like a monomania with him. Many of them matchless in beauty, however, and one day will be worth large sums " (Madox Brown's diary).

Ruskin, too, wrote in 1860 : " I looked over all the book of sketches at Chatham Place yesterday. I think Ida should be very happy to see how much more beautifully, perfectly, and tenderly you draw when you are drawing *her* than when you draw anybody else. She cures you of all your worst faults, when you only look at her."

Besides these, of course, there was the pathetic fresco at Oxford.

Rossetti's reputation, by this time, was extremely high in an extremely small circle. The name Pre-Raphaelitism had become generally current after the dissolution of the Brotherhood, and Rossetti's name was generally spoken of as the foremost of the movement, but, as his work was not accessible to anyone outside his own circle or Ruskin's, the praise and blame that the movement excited were by outside critics mostly attached to the other painters. There was by 1862 no trace at all, that I can discern, of his early apprenticeship. The Pre-Raphaelite movement, as conceived by Hunt and systematised and explained by Ruskin, still went on. Millais had practically dropped out ; what with the requirements of the London season and the imperative call of " fishin' and shootin'," he had barely time to get

his Academy pictures done, without bothering about his
early scruples. After all, you can see Nature and all
that from the back of a horse just as well as cramped over
an easel, and in far better company, what's more. But
Hunt was still unswervingly faithful, and a new group of
disciples followed at his heels. Ruskin's lectures had
made the aims of the movement intelligible, and people
took sides according as they liked the aims or not. There
is a very amusing pamphlet, issued privately and widely
circulated in 1860, by one who did not like them. It
is called *Pre-Raphaelitism Tested by the Principles of
Christianity*, by W. Cave Thomas. He takes up the
issues with creditable vigour at their vital point. There
is now no nonsense about " puerile drawing " and " wilful
disregard of perspective "; he admits that the Pre-
Raphaelites have attained to unrivalled truth to nature.
His point is that it is flat blasphemy to be truthful to
nature. It is a breach of the second commandment,
which forbids representation of anything that *is* in heaven
or earth, as distinct from their ideal intended by the
Creator. Pre-Raphaelitism, said Mr. Thomas, was a
glorification of the imperfections introduced into Eden
by the fall of Adam. It is a good point ; at any rate,
it shows a marked clearing of thought after the irrelevant
criticism of 1851, and moves the discussion on to ground
that is quite significant when one considers the solemn
sense of divine authority with which Holman-Hunt
pursued his career.

Rossetti had quite diverged from this movement, but
linked up with it, to some extent by Madox Brown, there
was another school, also termed Pre-Raphaelite, of which
Burne-Jones was to be the central figure. It is best,
perhaps, to call this second school the Æsthetic Movement, keeping it in one's mind very distinct from the
decadents who succeeded to much of its inheritance.
We have already seen the beginnings of this school in
the Morris set at Oxford and at Red Lion Square. It
now rallied about the new firm of Morris, Marshall,
Faulkner & Co., and though he had little affinity with the

real aims behind it, Rossetti's personal connection with the founders brought him into close touch with it.

"The Shop," as they called it, had very little about it of the educational crusade which Ruskin had propounded to Lady Trevelyan; it had still less of the modern spirit of arts and crafts, in which the vicar's daughter—plucky little thing—teaches basket-making to the Mothers' Union. However superficially unbusinesslike it may have been in some of its dealings, it was essentially a business concern; they may have wanted to raise the standard of domestic decoration throughout the country and revive the dignity of hand labour, and they succeeded in this indirectly, but their immediate aim was to produce beautiful and expensive things for people who appreciated them and could get them nowhere else.

It was not entirely new for people to have beautiful things made for them, but it was unbelievably rare. Holman-Hunt had had some furniture made to his own designs, and so, of course, had "Topsy" and Ned Jones when they began furnishing Red Lion Square—notably a settle of such massive proportions that when it was moved to Upton the canopied top was railed off and used as a minstrels' gallery. But carpentry was almost the only trade in which the tradition of hand workmanship survived at all. Glass, china, wallpapers, stuffs, silver plate, could only be procured in debased machine-made patterns. When "Topsy" came to equip his house at Upton, he found that it was not only impossible to buy anything tolerable ready made, but that it was almost impossible to get things made to order. The original idea—attributed to Marshall, a gifted sanitary and civil engineer of Rossetti's acquaintance—was for a co-operative society of artists, who should employ their own workmen, provide each other with designs for whatever they wanted, and receive payment in kind. This scheme was soon expanded into the firm of Morris, Marshall, Falkner & Co.

At the head, for several reasons, stood the uncouth figure of "Topsy." For one thing, he and his mother between them provided by far the largest share of the capital ; the other main reason was that he had nothing else to do. The other members of the firm were engaged in pursuing careers and earning their livings in various specialised ways ; " Topsy," having abandoned painting, was able to diffuse his great talents, in a way that the others could not afford to do, over the whole business of decoration, disclosing a genius for this broad and varied art quite as great as any of the other members, Rossetti excepted, showed in their specialised forms of it.

Falkner was " Topsy's " old Pembroke friend, who abandoned a mathematical fellowship at University College, Oxford, to manage the business side of the firm.

Phillip Wells, the architect of the " Towers of Topsy," was an important member. The other three were painters—Arthur Hughes, Madox Brown, and Rossetti. All seven subscribed towards the initial outlay, and were to be paid either in kind or out of the profits of the firm. It was mainly with the hope of its proving a profitable investment that Madox Brown joined in. Associating with his juniors in a subordinate position was not much in his line. Rossetti, as I have said, came in because of his friendship with the other members, and because Morris could not yet undertake anything without his *imprimatur.*

The prospectus, in which Rossetti is said to have had a hand, states their aims with laudable moderation and directness.

" The growth of Decorative Art in this country," it ran, " . . . has now reached a point at which it seems desirable that Artists of reputation should devote their time to it. . . . These Artists, having for many years been deeply attached to the study of the Decorative Arts of all times and countries, have felt more than most people the want of some one place where they could either obtain or get produced work of a genuine and beautiful character. They have therefore now established themselves as a firm for the production, by themselves and under their supervision, of :

" I. Mural Decoration, either in Pictures or in Pattern Work, or merely in the arrangement of colours, as applied to dwelling-houses, churches, or public buildings.

" II. Carving generally, as applied to architecture.

" III. Stained glass, especially with reference to its harmony with Mural Decoration.

" IV. Metal Work in all its branches, including jewellery.

" V. Furniture, either depending for its beauty on its own design or the application of materials hitherto over-looked, or on its conjunction with Figure and Pattern Painting. Under this head is included Embroidery of all kinds, Stamped Leather, and ornamental work in other such materials, besides every article necessary for domestic use.

" It is only requisite to state further that work of all the above classes will be estimated for, and executed in a businesslike manner ; and it is believed that good decoration, involving rather the luxury of taste than the luxury of costliness, will be found to be much less expensive than is generally supposed."

This last statement, though possibly true in the comparative form in which it is stated, gives a false impression. The products of " The Shop " were always quite beyond the reach of any except the wealthy.

A really luminous history of the Morris firm has yet to be written. In the present study we are only concerned with it as far as it affects Rossetti, and that is very little.

He did not, as we shall see in the next chapter, make use of " The Shop's " services when he came to furnish his house in Cheyne Walk. The only designs which he is known to have done for them are for stained glass, and possibly some tiles. Of these, one is an agreeable but unremarkable series illustrating the story of St. George and the Dragon. It consists of six rectangular drawings, none of which was executed. The others are two pointed windows of Adam and Eve for St. Martin's Church, Scarborough, one of Morris's first important commissions. He has made no attempt to adapt his designs to the shape of the windows—as some designers delight to do, exulting in intricate traceries—but has made his drawings in two rectangles, filling up the interstices with diapers. This is typical of his whole conception of the relation between artist and craftsman, but he has, rather surprisingly, taken full advantage of the vigour of line which the leading of a window facilitates. The way in which he has brought the leaves across the bodies, in bold, geometrical masses, is a departure from his usual conception of pattern. The head of the *Adam*, too, is particularly interesting.

In 1857 an Exhibition of English Paintings was held in New York, to which most of the Pre-Raphaelites sent contributions. On both sides of the Atlantic attempts were made to persuade Rossetti to do the same, but he declined. Captain Ruxton, the organiser, said that great interest was felt in his work in America, but this interest, if it existed to any appreciable extent, must have been limited to a very few. Rossetti corresponded with Professor Norton of Massachusetts, and sold him a picture—*Before the Battle*.

Except for the members of "The Shop," few of Rossetti's friends were artists, and he had a large and growing literary connection. Swinburne was a devoted friend, Patmore and Browning close acquaintances, and even Tennyson—in William Rossetti's phrase—was "not without a perceptible liking and regard for him." This connection was considerably strengthened by the publication in 1861 of Rossetti's translations from the *Early Italian Poets*, the work of a much earlier period, substantially emended. Ruskin advanced £100 towards the expenses of their publication—his last service to Rossetti, I think. The work was well received, and sold steadily. By 1869 the edition was nearly exhausted, and, after Ruskin's £100 had been repaid, Rossetti earned £9 from their sale.

The edition contains an intimation of the forthcoming publication of a book of original poems, but this was postponed in tragic circumstances.

8

The two years of Rossetti's married life were a time
of concentrated industry. The marriage meant little;
it had been so long delayed that it had lost its significance.
It was no longer the consummation of his early love, but
simply another stage in an inevitable and painful relationship. Perhaps he still loved his wife; his every mention
of her is redolent of devotion; but it was love of a
different quality from the exultant pride of ten years
before. You cannot spend weeks on end ministering
at a sick-bed and regard your patient as a " stunner."
At the very blossoming of his genius and reputation
he was marrying a dying woman, consecrating the past
and preserving inviolate a remembered and hardly to be
repeated happiness; there was nothing to look forward to.

Ten years is a long time, particularly if they are spent
as Rossetti had spent the time of his engagement; it
would be absurd to suppose that he brought to his
marriage the same fresh idealism and untarnished chastity
in which he had fallen in love. Throughout his life
Rossetti was impelled by a highly passionate nature,
easily roused and insistent of satisfaction.

There is nothing to be gained by raking up and
chronicling the details of his various amours except in
so far as they determined any changes in his art. They
were, for the most part, so far as one can gather, swift
and unscrupulous; characterised by insolence of inception, energy of enjoyment, and vagueness of termination;
he relished the adventure of promiscuity and of grotesque
encounter.

In 1857 he had an obscure quarrel with Holman-
Hunt which caused a permanent severance of their
friendship. William Rossetti, in his admirably candid
biography,[1] refers to it thus:

[1] " Several truths were stated in a mild tone, not because I wished to
force them upon public attention, but because they had previously been
stated by others in an acrid tone." William Rossetti, preface to *Ruskin :
Rossetti : Pre-Raphaelitism.*

" I understand perfectly well what it is that Mr. Hunt
terms ' the offence,' but will not dwell upon any details ;
only remarking that, if my reader chooses to ask the old
question, 'Who was the woman ?' he will not be far
wrong, though his query may chance to remain for ever
unanswered. . . . It behoves me to add that Mr. Hunt
was wholly blameless in the matter ; not so my brother,
who was properly, though I will not say very deeply,
censurable."

Besides this, he had got, if the phrase may be allowed,
into a rut of habitual irregularity ; in the ordering of the
actual routine of his life he was wholly and blindly selfish.
He did what he wanted to, when he wanted to, because
he wanted to. He ate with a sporadic and incalculable
appetite ; worked in alternating bouts of feverish application and profound indolence, generally preferring the
night for any sort of activity, artistic or social. His
boisterous good humour was by no means unfailing. He
luxuriated in a chaotic untidiness of clothes and posses-
sions. He was lacking, in fact, in every domestic virtue
except affection, and with that he was endowed to an
overpowering degree. He was an odd mate for the
lovely wraith he bore back to Chatham Place. But she
was used to him and his manner of life, and, by upbringing, did not expect the calling and card-leaving of the
Victorian bride. She was herself supremely incapable
of managing servants or looking after house. It suited
her very well to sit for a painting until half-past nine and
then to dine " on tick." If by some miracle she could
have regained her health, and matched his vitality with
some of her own, the marriage might have been, in its
way, serenely successful. As it was, she was simply
physically over-powered, faltered, and flickered out in
the darkness and alone.

On their return from their honeymoon, they lived at
Chatham Place, except when, for part of the time, they
had a small house in Hampstead as well, to be near the
Browns and for the good of " Guggum's " health.
They saw practically no one except the Browns and the

Morrises, except very occasionally the other Rossettis
—Christina and " Guggum " did not get on over-well.
Swinburne was their most constant companion ; he
adored them both, as was his way, extravagantly. They
saw a certain amount of Patmore and of the Brownings.
The only new friend they made—Alexander Gilchrist,
the author of *The Life of Etty*—died almost at once.

In spite of his industry, Rossetti began to grow fat ;
" awfully fat and torpid," he wrote to Brown in 1861.
" Guggum " grew thinner and feverishly restless. The
phthisis which had been undermining her health for
years was now aggravated by incessant attacks of acute
neuralgia. In April 1861 she gave birth to a still-born
child. From then onwards she gave way to melancholy,
which often took the form of resentment and jealousy
against her husband. In the succeeding winter she was
authorised by her doctor to take frequent doses of
laudanum. On February 11th, 1862, she died of an
overdose.

Rossetti, his wife, and Swinburne dined together at
the Sablonière Hotel in Leicester Square. Rossetti saw
her home, advised her to go to bed—for she was complaining of torpor—and went out to the Working Men's
College. Returning at eleven, he was unable to wake her ;
a laudanum bottle was empty at her side. At half-past
seven next morning she died, without having recovered
consciousness. Four doctors were present at her death,
after every attempt to rouse her had been made in vain.
At some time a little before five, Rossetti arrived at
Madox Brown's house at Finchley wild with anxiety.

A coroner's jury brought in a verdict of " Accidental
Death." It is significant of Rossetti's reputation with
the general public, and of the journalistic methods of the
time, that the account of the inquest, in the only paper
that reported it, was headed by the severe announcement :

" DEATH OF A LADY FROM AN OVERDOSE OF LAUDANUM."

The few people who could have told the full story of

that last evening are now in their graves, and nothing beyond the orthodox account found in the official biographies has ever been authoritatively recorded. Perhaps there is no more to recount.

There are, however, two stories that were widely circulated at the time and widely believed, which throw some light upon the emotional storm through which Rossetti passed in the next few days, and the permanent effects it appears to have had on his development.

The first is that on the night of his wife's death, Rossetti was not at the Working Men's College, but in the company of another woman with whom he was carrying on an intrigue. He returned to find his wife unconscious, and was left with the insatiable suspicion that she had known of his betrayal and taken her own life in consequence.

The second and more convincing version is that Rossetti was, as was stated at the inquest, innocently engaged at the Working Men's College, but that his wife was now in a condition when she construed his every absence as infidelity; she took her own life, leaving beside her bed a letter for Rossetti reproaching him with his cruelty towards her.

Six days elapsed before the funeral, during which Rossetti was subject to paroxysms of uncontrollable grief. On the second or third day, gazing, as he had been doing continually, at his wife's face, serenely beautiful, so that William had been moved to quote :

> *Ed avra in sè umiltà sè verace*
> *Che parea che dicesse, Io sono in pace,*

Rossetti became convinced that she was not really dead ; she was in a trance, the result of the laudanum. Breaking through all remonstrances, he summoned the doctor again ; surely she could not be dead ? The doctor could only assure him that she was.

" The Roman " came up for the funeral, which took place on February 17th in Highgate Cemetery, in the grave in which Professor Rossetti was already buried, and where later Mrs. Rossetti and Christina followed him.

While the coffin was still open at Chatham Place, Rossetti, leaving his friends in the outer room, went in alone to where it lay.

" The poems he had written, so far as they were poems of love, were chiefly inspired by and addressed to her. At her request he had copied them into a little book presented to him for the purpose. . . . He spoke to his dead wife as if she heard, saying, as he held the book, that the words it contained were written to her and for her, and she must take them with her, for they could not remain when she had gone. Then he put the volume into the coffin between her cheek and her beautiful hair, and it was . . . buried with her in Highgate Cemetery."[1]

Brown disapproved of the whole business.

---

[1] Hall Caine : *Recollections of D. G. Rossetti.*

CHAPTER IV

THE GOOD YEARS, 1862–1867

Tudor House—Rossetti's income—His collection of bric-à-brac and animals—Charles Augustus Howell—*The Beloved*—Rossetti's compositions.

I

IN the days immediately following his wife's death, Rossetti lived with his family and with the Madox Browns, almost prostrate with sense of loss and sense of guilt. It was very slowly that he emerged from the shadows and began to rearrange the scattered particles of his daily life, but when he did so it was with characteristic strength. Spiritually as well as physically he had great recuperative powers. He moved into temporary chambers in Lincoln's Inn, began working again, and looked about him for a new home. It is not true to say that he ever fully recovered from the shock of his wife's death or the strain of the ten years preceding it, but he managed to thrust them into the background of his life, where they remained always present with varying obtrusiveness, colouring and permeating all that he did, but never obscuring his immediate objects. He was outwardly a free man, once more unencumbered by human obligations, with a widening reputation and prosperity; the loss which had fallen upon him with such cataclasmic suddenness was one which he must long have schooled himself to expect; years of dragging misery had elapsed in one night of horror. Only the guilt remained. He started on a new life, bravely enough, but with a part of his soul dead and festering within him.

Many years before he had been attracted by Tudor

House, No. 16 Cheyne Walk.   Here he now settled in
October 1862, and here he remained with brief excursions
into the country until the last months of his life.   It was
a house singularly suited to the ripening of his personality,
large, intricate, picturesque, and rather decayed.   Outside, where Chelsea Embankment now runs, the side of
the road sloped down to the river with muddy slats and
cobbles and patches of dirty grass, broken by jetties and
wharfs and encumbered with all the agreeable long-shore
litter of boats and ropes and rigging.   A short distance
away were Cremorne Gardens, one of those centres of
the polka and fireworks and disreputable company where
gaiety was localised in the Victorian era.

Behind the house lay nearly an acre of dank, unkempt
garden, under it a warren of cellars which at some remote
time had probably led down to the river.   The house
itself is not particularly old.   It took its name[1] from the
legend that it had been used by Henry VIII as a nursery
for Elizabeth and Mary.   If there was any truth in this
it must have referred to some earlier building, of which
no doubt the cellars were a part, upon the same site.
Nothing in the existing structure is earlier than the time
of Queen Anne.   It stands back a little way from the
road behind a flagged courtyard.   Bay windows had been
built out from the plain brick front.   Describing the
house as it appeared at a later date, Sir Hall Caine writes:

" The interior was at once like and unlike the exterior.
The hall had a puzzling look of equal nobility and
shabbiness.   The floor was paved with beautiful white
marble which, however, was partly covered with a strip
of worn cocoa-nut matting ; the ceiling was in one of its
sections gracefully groined, and in each of its walls, which
were lofty, there was an arched recess containing a piece
of sculpture . . . three doors led out of the hall, one at
each side, and one in front, and two corridors opened
into it, but there was no sign of a staircase, nor had it any
light except such as was borrowed from the fanlight that

---

[1] It is now called Queen's House, presumably for the same reason.

HR

looked into the porch. . . . The changes which the building must have undergone since the period of its erection had so filled it with nooks and corners as to bewilder the most ingenious observer to account for its peculiarities. . . . The studio was a large room, probably measuring thirty feet by twenty, and structurally as puzzling as the other parts of the house. A series of columns and arches on one side suggested that the room had almost certainly been at some period the site of an important staircase with a wide well."

This studio, attractive enough as a room in which to sit about and talk—and it was greatly used for this in the first years of Rossetti's tenancy—was never wholly satisfactory as a workroom. From time to time suggestions were made and plans drawn out for its substantial alteration, and even for the erection of an entirely new room in the garden, but in the end Rossetti contented himself with enlarging the main window.

The best room in the house, and next to the studio the most important, was the drawing-room which ran across the front of the house looking on to the river. This was used also as a dining-room when Rossetti gave a party.

The rent was only £110 a year,[1] but the house was far too large for Rossetti to keep up by himself even if, at this sociable period in his life, he had had any desire to do so. The first inmates were William Rossetti, Algernon Swinburne, and George Meredith. These each had separate sitting-rooms where they could entertain their friends and they only met in the evenings for dinner ; at least this was the arrangement, but it soon resolved itself into Rossetti and Swinburne sharing the house. There is considerable confusion in the reports of Meredith's tenancy. He himself in later life denied that he ever lived there at all, but there is a letter extant addressed by him to William Bell Scott in 1862 and written on the

---

[1] When Rossetti renewed the lease ten years later he was deprived of his garden and the rent was doubled.

note-paper of the house. One story is that he was so
revolted by Rossetti's table manners that he walked out
of the house after breakfast on his first morning ; another
is that he could not afford even the modest rent charged
by Rossetti and, attempting to economise by starving
himself, was offended by the genial chaff which has been
mentioned before as a characteristic of Pre-Raphaelite
intercourse. Anyway, the arrangement was certainly
not a success and did not last, at the most, for more than
a few weeks. William Rossetti was up to the end a
constant visitor, but the necessity of looking after his
mother and sisters soon ended his tenancy. He was
steadily making a reputable literary career for himself
and he was very much in awe of his brother.   •

Swinburne stayed on for five years and wrote *Atalanta
in Calydon* and most of *Poems and Ballads* there, but in
the end it became convenient for him too to set up on his
own. Ruskin suggested that he too should become a
tenant of the house, but this incredibly incompatible
combination never came about.

Another inmate of the house who plays an incon-
spicuous but not entirely negligible part in Rossetti's
life was H. Treffry Dunn, a Cornishman, whom Rossetti
engaged in 1863 to succeed a Mr. Knewstub as his
professional assistant. The proper share taken by such
assistants in their masters' work is always a difficult and
rather awkward question. Mr. Dunn's services were
certainly not confined to the mixing of colours and
priming of canvases. Any investigation into the full
extent of his participation must reflect considerably
upon the value of many works in public and private collections. It is sufficient to say that after Rossetti's death
several heads that had been abandoned by the master as
unsatisfactory were resuscitated by the executors and
brought up to the sale-room standard of completion by
Mr. Dunn, and that it is impossible to be quite satisfied
that in every case he confined himself to the purely
mechanical work which, presumably, was usually rele-
gated to him by Rossetti.

2

A number of records have been left by Rossetti's friends and acquaintances of the life that he lived during the first five years at Cheyne Walk. All agree in describing him as fitfully melancholy, but often cheerful and even high spirited. He slept until late, painted industriously, and in the evenings was sociable and hospitable. His personal appearance may be judged from an excellent photograph taken in 1862 by Downey of Newcastle. He is wearing a black Inverness cape buttoned at the throat and hanging open in front. Its heavy folds and the attitude he has adopted, one elbow akimbo, the other hand resting heavily upon a massive and ornamental piece of photographer's furniture, emphasise his physical solidity. His head was compared by his friends to Chaucer's and to Shakespeare's, but there is also something about it of a despondent Napoleon. His forehead, as in his youth, is dominantly rotund, and his eyes, hidden beneath its prominent bar, deepset in shade and melancholy. His mouth is almost hidden by his moustache and beard, which are dark and well trimmed. He preserved practically the same appearance throughout his life, though towards the end he grew a little thinner in body and face, and after 1872 he did not shave his cheeks, so that his white face was set in a continuous fringe of dark hair from temple to temple.

Now for the first time in his life he found himself in receipt of a large income. He kept no accounts, but mentions in a letter to William that in 1865 he made £2,050, in 1867 £3,000, and in 1876 £3,725. He appears to have regarded this sum as his average, but it is doubtful whether he ever made so much again. In spite of his exceptional avidity and acumen in making money, he exhibited complete indifference in spending it. As late as 1867 he had no banking account, but kept his money, often very considerable sums, loose in a drawer, from which he would disburse handfuls of sovereigns whenever they were required for household purposes or to women or impecunious friends. He never made any attempt to cut a figure in smart society, though there were many hostesses who would have eagerly taken him up and honoured him. He always dressed with slovenly sombreness. He never kept a carriage or horses. He never gambled or frequented expensive restaurants. But his money oozed from him as quickly as it came. No doubt he was robbed and imposed upon in all directions, but probably he was quite aware of the fact. He liked to surround himself with odd and disreputable people so long as they amused him, and he did not mind paying for his amusement. Besides loans to casual borrowers who seldom went away disappointed as long as they had an intriguing story to tell, there were regular allowances being paid to Lizzie Siddal's family, to one at least of his models, and of course wages to Treffry Dunn and his servants. But his chief expense was his engrossing enthusiasm for collecting. This appears to have come upon him as soon as he settled at Cheyne Walk, and to have lasted with unabated zeal until about 1868, when it practically ceased. He collected almost anything that attracted his attention, particularly china, furniture, and animals.

Of the last he had at one time and another a Pomeranian puppy called Punch, an Irish wolfhound called Wolf, two brown owls called Jenny and Bobby, some rabbits, dormice, hedgehogs, white mice, squirrels, a mole, a chameleon, some salamanders, a deer, a wallaby, some kangaroos, two wombats, a Canadian marmot, a woodchuck, an armadillo, a racoon, a Brahmin Bull, a jackass, and numerous birds including peacocks, Chinese horned owls, talking grey parrots, a raven, and a grass parakeet. These lived a life of conflict and depredation in and about the house and gardens and those of his neighbours. The armadillo disappeared for several weeks, and suddenly appeared through the floor of a basement kitchen some distance away, to the great alarm of the cook, " who opined that if it was not the devil, there was no knowing what it was " ; the deer stamped out all the tail feathers of the peacock, who in turn made so much noise that a clause was in future introduced into all the leases on the Cadogan Estate forbidding them to be kept in the neighbourhood. The racoon was particularly ferocious and destructive.

It does not appear that Rossetti lavished any personal affection upon his various pets, except perhaps upon the first of the wombats ; he met their frequent deaths and disappearances with fortitude ; some indeed died or disappeared almost the moment they were acquired, and some, such as the Brahmin Bull, which Rossetti bought for twenty pounds at Cremorne Gardens because it had eyes that reminded him of Janey Morris, proved quite unmanageable. But he liked to have them about the place, and he particularly delighted in visits to Jamrack's shop, where in an acrid atmosphere, beasts, from all countries chattered and rattled against their bars.

His china collection was one of the first of its kind in England. Every night he and his friends used to dine off priceless old plates which his ramshackle servants broke in the pantry, but his chief delight was blue and white Nankin. The fashion was still very new ; a Mr. Huth had a large collection, and so had the Italian Ambassador, the Marquis d'Azeglio ; Whistler was a keen rival and so was Charles Augustus Howell, who will figure again in this story, but the " trade " in general had not become aware of the craze, and prices were proportionally low. Pieces of exquisite design and colour could be picked up for a few shillings. The trade too, both for china and all the antiques which Rossetti loved, was practically unorganised. There was no army of buyers, sent out by the dealers to scour the small shops for possible bargains. It was Rossetti's utmost delight to drive round in a cab, loading it with china and brass and carved oak picked out from the litter of second-hand furniture shops and pawnbrokers. The only rivalry was with other collectors. When one of this elect little circle had made a particular " find," invitations were sent out and a dinner-party would be given. Then the new pot would be uncovered and its owner would be triumphant until the next discovery. In this genial way Rossetti amassed an enormous collection, both of valuable china and general bric-à-brac, which filled Tudor House from cellar to garret.

Old oak was then very little in demand, and Rossetti bought up large quantities of old carving which he had made into curious composite chimney-pieces of his own design. He collected musical instruments, though solely for their design and as properties for his pictures ; he never showed any interest in music, and in later life was inclined to regard it as an invention of his enemies devised expressly for his own discomfort.

He collected old stuffs and curtains. He and Whistler anticipated by many years the Japanese craze which engrossed collectors in the early 'nineties.[1] The drawing-room in Cheyne Walk was full of Japanese work, embroidery, prints, screens.[2]

It is greatly to be hoped that, before he is wholly forgotten, someone who knew him will write a life of Charles Augustus Howell. His fame, so brilliant and fascinating in his lifetime, is already very dim ; he belongs to that race of adventurers whose evanescent genius is purely social and who, unless by some freak of chance they become Prime Ministers, or, in a better day, the favourites of kings, are forgotten almost as soon as the actors and actresses of the stage. A connoisseur of art, a forger, a liar, the least loyal and most enchanting of friends, Howell passes through the history of his period, now as a political conspirator, now as a picture dealer, now as a gentleman of fashion, knowing everyone, going everywhere, always discredited, always triumphant. He was the son of an English father and a Portuguese lady of rank who claimed descent from Boabdil il Chico. He

[1] Rossetti and Whistler were the first collectors in London , actually the fashion was begun in Paris by Tissot, the painter.

[2] It is odd that, unlike Whistler, his work seems to have been entirely unaffected by this hobby. I can discern no Japanese or even Oriental tendencies in his painting.

is described as resembling Velasquez's Philip IV. His early youth was spent in the by-ways of cosmopolitan society, where he claimed to have lived romantically by diving for guineas in a sunken galleon. Rossetti came across him in 1856 and instantly took him to his heart. He was the "Munchausen of the Pre-Raphaelite Circle." Whoever was at the moment prominent, whether murderer or minister, Howell claimed close acquaintance with him. He had an illimitable fund of scandal about everyone. For some years he even lived with Ruskin on terms of warmest intimacy and acted for him as almoner to his charities. In 1858 he became involved in the Orsini plot to murder Napoleon III, and left the country. On his return in 1864 Rossetti warmly welcomed him back to his circle.

With a ready *flair* for what was to be the next fashion, Howell began to collect Nankin china. He had infinite leisure for searching old shops, a very keen discernment of worth, and superb assurance in making a bargain. He never assembled a large collection, because he was under the continual necessity of reselling his purchases. He did this however for a handsome profit, and many of the best pieces in the collections of the time had passed through his hands.

There is an amusing story of him recorded by Treffry Dunn.[1]

" On one occasion, Howell's rambles took him to some out-of-the-way and unfrequented part of Hammersmith, which at that time abounded in small furniture-dealer's shops. In one of these old furniture shops, Howell, with hawk-like eye, espied the corner of a blue dish peeping out from a pile of miscellaneous odds and ends in the window. It was not so much the shape of this visible portion of crockery, but the colour, that attracted him ; it was the blue, the sweet, rich blue only to be found in the choicest Nankin. He entered the shop, and began prying about, asking the price of first this thing and then

[1] *Recollections of D. G. Rossetti and his Circle,* by Treffry Dunn (Elkin Mathews).

"ABSURD, AFFECTED, ILL-DRAWN, INSIPID,
CROTCHETY, PUERILE"—The *Athenæum*
(*Ecce Ancilla Domini*, 1850)

Tate Gallery   *Compare diagram on page* 144

FANNY CORNFORTH
MRS. SCHOTT
(*Woman with a fan*, 1870)

"ONE OF THE GRANDEST THINGS LIKE A
GOLDEN, DIM DREAM"—*James Smetham*
(*The Marriage of St. George*, 1857)

Tate Gallery

Compare diagram on page 144

ELIZABETH SIDDAL
(*Beata Beatrix*, 1863)

DANTE GABRIEL ROSSETTI
1862
Photograph by Downey of Newcastle

ALEXA WILDING
(*Monna Vanna*, 1866)

Compare diagram on page 145

THE APOTHEOSIS OF THE STUNNER
(*The Beloved*, 1866)

Tate Gallery

JANE MORRIS
(*Proserpine*, 1874)

that in the window until at length, as though by an accident, the whole of the dish that had lain almost hidden was exposed to view. It was a veritable piece of Imperial ware, and a fine specimen, too ! His afternoon's work was done ; he had secured a prize which would fill Dante Gabriel's soul with envy when he saw it. A cab was called, and away he drove home, chuckling with delight to himself over his acquisition.

" That evening was spent in arranging the menu of a choice little dinner, which was to be given in order to display his treasure, and in selecting the names of those of his friends who should be chosen to see the dish. Invitations were written and duly sent. Dear Gabriel's name, of course, was first on the list ; then that of Whistler—as he was one of the triumvirate of Chinese worshippers ; then came the Ionides Brothers, Leonard R. Valpy, George Howard, George Price Boyce, Burne-Jones, Morris, old George Cruikshank, John William Inchbold, and several others who were habitués of the house.

" As it had got about that Howell had something to show that would knock them all into fits, there were no absentees. The table was set, and the guests had all arrived, brought thither not only by the prospect of spending a pleasant evening, but also by curiosity to see what Howell had to exhibit. When the substantial party of the feast came to a full end, Howell felt his guests were in a sufficiently appreciative state of mind, and so the dish, for the advent of which each one of the party had been on the tip-toe of expectation, was at length produced, Howell himself bringing it in, carefully wiping it with a silk handkerchief. There was a concentrated ' Oh ! ' from all assembled at the table, which, having been partially cleared, had space enough to allow the dish to be placed in its centre, that all could view and admire it. And it bore the closest inspection, for it was certainly as good a piece of Nankin as could be found in the best of a lucky day's hunt. Rossetti waxed enthusiastic over it ; he turned it round, and examined it from every point of view, and not a flaw could he find, nor the ghost of a crack, or a suspicion of an inequality of colour in it. Everyone congratulated Howell on his being the possessor of such a beautiful specimen of ' Blue.' After it had been admired and breathed upon, coveted and delighted in, fondled and gushed over, hustled and almost fought for—in short, after having created as much squabbling and controversy as, once upon a time, the partition of Poland did among the Powers, the dish was tenderly removed by its owner, and carefully deposited in its shrine on a cabinet in an adjoining room. Whilst the ladies of the party were upstairs wrapping themselves up for their journey, and the men were downstairs occupied with their hats and overcoats, Rossetti was hanging about the hall in a thoughtful kind of way. He had on the Inverness cape which he generally wore at night, and I saw him go into the room where the dish was deposited, to have, as I thought, a last look at the treasure, but—shall I tell it ?—he hastily dislodged that dish by stealth, concealed it beneath the cape of his cloak, and carefully wrapped its ample folds around it, that none could perceive what he carried under his arm. Having so done, he took leave of Howell and his wife in the most charming innocent manner possible.

" On our arrival at his door, having dismissed the cabman, he let himself in, and pulling out the dish from under his cape had a good look at it by the gaslight in the hall, chuckling the while with glee, for in his mind's eye he saw the long face Howell would pull on discovering his loss.   He cautioned me not to let him know anything which would give him a clue as to the disappearance of the dish, or its place of concealment.   Then, finding his way to the back hall, he proceeded to carefully hide it in the recesses of the massive oak wardrobe that stood there, and, the more effectually to conceal it, swathed it round and round with model's dresses and other artistic draperies for the custody of which the wardrobe was employed. Having done all this to his satisfaction, Rossetti took his candle and went to bed.

" Next morning, when he made his appearance at the breakfast-table, we had our usual chat respecting the day's work, and whatever else required to be discussed.   In the course of our conversation, Rossetti said, suddenly :

" ' Dunn, I shall give a return party to that of Howell's last night.   This is Tuesday : I'll ask him for Friday, and tell him he must come as I have picked up a piece of " Blue " that I think will rival his.'

" Accordingly, he wrote him a note to that effect, and also dispatched invitations to most of those who were present at Howell's party, and to a good many more, making altogether enough to fill the dining-table, which was able to accommodate at least twenty.

" On the afternoon of the day of the dinner, Howell called in a cab, bringing his factotum with him, a useful fellow by whom he was generally accompanied in his expeditions.   He left his man waiting in the cab, and on gaining admission to the house, and hearing that Rossetti was in the studio, he went in and found us both there.   After an inordinately long confabulation over everything that could be talked about, but without a word concerning the dish, Howell, by and by, went from the room upon some pretext or other and left Rossetti busily painting away.   As I afterwards learnt, Howell guessed pretty shrewdly who had his dish, and where it was to be found.   Instinct took him to the old wardrobe ; softly opening its massive doors, he peeped in, then, searching about with his hands, felt his precious dish underneath the pile of draperies that Rossetti had heaped over it.   To remove these and disentangle his property was the work of a few seconds ; recovering his prize, he softly stole away along the back hall, round to the front door, which he opened, and went out to his man who was waiting his instructions.   To him he handed the dish through the window, receiving in return another of the same size and shape.   Howell went back, and after putting this dish into the wardrobe in the place of the other, re-entered the studio, and with the accompaniment of Irish cold and the indispensable cigarette, resumed the conversation for another hour or so. When he could find nothing more to talk about, he took his leave in order to dress for the dinner. Rossetti was strangely unsuspicious of Howell's movements; I suppose he thought the hiding-place he had fixed upon was so secure that it never occurred to him to go and see what Howell had been up to and whether the dish was still there.

"At the appointed hour, our guests came flocking in until the whole of them had arrived. When they were assembled in the dining-room and had taken their seats round the table they formed a goodly company. The dinner was well served, a professional cook having been engaged to prepare it, and a distinct success; the wine was excellent and the conversation sparkling. At last Howell managed to divert the talk to the subject of Blue china, and the dish of his that had excited so much admiration on the night of his party, whereupon Rossetti declared that he had something just as fine. Howell challenged him to produce it, so off went Rossetti to the wardrobe most confidently; he fished out the dish and brought it away swathed in drapery, just as he supposed he had left it. In a few minutes he returned to the dining-room with the package, and began to carefully remove the wrappings. As the dish became uncovered, a curious, puzzled expression came over his face, and when it was entirely exposed to view, he stood still in blank astonishment. For a few moments he was silent; then his pent-up feelings burst out in a wild cry.

" ' Confound it ! See what the spirits have done ! '

" Everyone rose to look at the dish. A dish it was, certainly, but what a dish ! Instead of the beautiful piece of Nankin that was expected, there was only an old Delft thing, cracked, chipped, and discoloured through the numerous bakings it had undergone. The whole party, with the exception of Howell, who looked as grave as a judge, burst into a roar of laughter. Rossetti soon recovered himself and laughed as heartily as any of his guests at Howell's ingenious revenge."

It has seemed worth quoting at some length, because

it is so redolent of the peculiar flavour of the Rossetti circle; the robust practical joking, the real æsthetic enthusiasms, and with it all the stealth that seems inseparable from everything about them, even their humour.

This circle was now at its widest and most cheerful. Except for Madox Brown, none of his early friends belonged to it. He had quarrelled with Hunt and drifted apart from Millais; in 1864 he quarrelled with Woolner, who had come back from Australia intolerably censorious. Burne-Jones and Morris were still close friends and so, when he was in England, was Browning. George Augustus Sala, the "young lion of the *Daily Telegraph*," Frederick Sandys, Whistler, and Bell Scott made up his parties with nondescript rascals of all classes, who appeared and disappeared as quickly and attracted as much notice as his animals. His connection with Fanny Schott went on, but there was no company into which she could be introduced without offence.

In 1865 Rossetti joined the Garrick Club and a little later the Arundel. Here he came into contact with most of the critics and writers of the time, but he made few friends among them, nor did he as a rule get on well with other painters. He had little patience with their vanities and rivalries; he had his own set, who amused him and whom he could dominate, and he was fairly contented with it.

He was not at this time a heavy drinker. He liked wine, and at his dinner-parties would drink a good deal of it, but was never seen to be affected by what he drank.

In 1863 he went to Belgium on a short visit, and in 1864 to Paris, but he was never at ease travelling, and after that never left England; he disliked the country. His life had become indissolubly bound to the ramshackle house in Cheyne Walk, and to all appearance was as solid and as comfortable.

3

During these years Rossetti took a keen interest in occultism. It was natural that he should do so. He had been brought up, as we have seen, subject to the distracting influences of his mother's and sisters' Anglo-Catholic piety, his father's speculative mysticism, and the crude Liberal atheism of many of their circle. Of his present friends William Bell Scott and his brother William were frankly, and in the former's case, rather aggressively, agnostic; by Ruskin he had been brought into close touch with an infectious species of Christianity, both mellow and precious; by Patmore with Catholicism; by Browning, rasping Protestantism; by Swinburne, paganism. Now, with the death of his wife, he was confronted in an intensely personal form with the problem of survival. If there were any assurance of immortality or means of communication he was avid to find them, to whisper into the past some word to the frail creature that had fluttered out of his life, of the emotion he had felt as he laid his poems beside her body.

Spiritualism at this time had scarcely emerged from the stage in which it attracted notice as a more exciting sort of drawing-room conjuring. The mediums, some genuine, some purely fraudulent, had their fees to earn and their audiences to satisfy, mostly composed of uncritical women. Occasional sceptics would strike a sudden light, reveal the wires behind the tambourine, and another reputation would be gone. Scientific investigation on regular critical lines was unknown. Genuine mediums would add a spice to their entertainments by using the same tricks as the charlatans.

Rossetti must have been taken in as often as the other spiritualists of the time. His friends, particularly Bell Scott, despised him for his credulity. Howell, always to the front where anything new was to be exploited, expressed his enthusiasm, gave *chic* little parties for whatever medium was most fashionable that season, and played frequent practical jokes on Rossetti, even to the spiriting away for a few hours of his entire collection of blue china; he always had a wink for the unbelievers to assure them that he was one of them.

From 1865 to 1870 Rossetti attended séances regularly,

and met Mrs. Fawcett and Mrs. Gupry; at his home he attempted with Whistler to get some results from table turning and the planchette, but each doubted the other's honesty and no good results seem to have been obtained.

On one occasion[1] he gave a large party for Mr. Bergheim, the mesmerist. Morris was present, the Master of Lindsay, Leyland, the picture buyer, Sala, and of course Howell.

A large marquee had been erected in the garden, filled with couches and rugs, and flowers in Oriental profusion. The conversation was almost exclusively about the occult. The Master of Lindsay described how he had been present at a séance when Daniel Home had floated into the air over his spectators' heads and, dimly discernible in the darkness, had flown about the room tapping on the ceiling, and how he had even floated out of the window and come in again by another.

Howell had himself experienced all the manifestations that the others had witnessed. He and Richard Burton had gone into trances and visited fabulous spheres.

Sala, more prosaic but none the less blood curdling, described a visit to Constance Kent at the criminal lunatic asylum at Broadmoor. He had seen the infamous Edward Oxford who had shot at Queen Victoria and Richard Dadd who had murdered his father on Blackheath Common.

At length Bergheim arrived with two young women. The display was essentially an entertainment.

" Hearing that they were on their way to the tent, he mesmerised them before they appeared, so that they both entered in a clairvoyant state. Rossetti's surprise at this was great. Not long after, Bergheim asked him to act in an improvised little drama that he had thought of. Rossetti was to be a sailor, and act with the medium selected as though he were going to join his ship, which was about to sail on a long-service cruise. So, taking

---

[1] I am unable to give a date for this incident, which is recorded at some length by Treffry Dunn. I imagine that it was somewhere about 1868–70.

his cue, he told her a prettily-concocted tale of his being ordered away that night on Her Majesty's service, which the girl listened to with greatest emotion. Another of the party then came forward, and represented himself as a naval officer sent by the captain to take him aboard ; the anchor having been weighed, the captain was anxious to set sail. When this was told her, and she found her sailor must leave her, she got into a terribly excited state, and threatened to stab the man who would separate them. At last, however, she allowed Rossetti to be taken away, and as soon as he had disappeared through the tent awning and could no more be seen, she fell to the ground in a fit of hysterical weeping.

" Another of the party, a somewhat heavy man, was then asked to lie down on the ground, which he did. The mesmerist directed the medium's attention to him, scolding her as if she were a careless nursemaid in charge of a small child, and telling her that there was a carriage and a pair of runaway horses galloping down a supposed lane, and that unless she could rescue the child in time it would inevitably be run over and killed. In a terrible fright, she ran to the suppositious child, picked him up, and carried him away to a safe place with all the ease that a grown-up young woman would a child of three or four years of age."

After 1870, with the general derangement of Rossetti's life, these activities came to an end. Moreover his attitude towards them suffered a deep change.

Many years later, when Sir Hall Caine first came to London, something in his magnetic eye and prophetic manner suggested to his friends that he was destined to become the great medium of the age. Efforts were made to induce him to be tested for psychic powers. In no way averse, Sir Hall mentioned these proposals to Rossetti. To his great surprise the information was received with the utmost agitation. A word of discouragement would have been enough, but Rossetti threw his whole soul and voice into passionate entreaty.

" For God's sake, Caine, have nothing to do with them.

The spirits are real—I know that better than any man, but they are not good spirits. They are devils, devils from Hell."

What occult experience Rossetti had undergone during those intervening years of degradation and delusion, one can never know. If there was any such incident, real or imagined, the secret of it died with him. But one can only surmise that something of unusual gravity must have occurred to change his interest into horror.

4

For some time after his wife's death, Rossetti was incapable of any prolonged concentration. He drew a crayon portrait of his mother and painted a small oil picture of a gypsy girl, called *Girl at a Lattice*, which shows a marked falling off from the technical facility of the Llandaff Triptych. He also executed a replica of the *Paolo and Francesca* diptych for Leathart.

His first important painting is the *Joan of Arc*. For some reason this picture has come in for an enormous amount of admiration, and in later years he found a ready market for replicas of it. William Rossetti counted it as one of his brother's highest achievements, and he himself, writing to Mr. Valpy, said of it that " neither in expression, colour, nor design had he ever done a better thing." This estimate, however, may be taken more lightly when it is remembered that Mr. Valpy was a possible purchaser, and that in Rossetti's letters to clients almost identically the same phrase occurs quite frequently about other pictures.

It is difficult to see what attraction people found in it, exhibiting, as it does, in a marked degree, all the faults of his later work. It consists of a face and hands set uncomfortably into a muddled assemblage of hair, brocade, and bric-à-brac. From the earliest time he had shown a childish inclination to paint into his pictures all manner of extraneous objects that attracted his attention, without reference to their relevance to the subject

IR

or value in the composition. As long as his mediæval predilection persisted, the result was naïve and harmonious. If you can stand that sort of picture at all, you will not take exception to the furniture of the cell in *Fra Pace* or the dragons head in the *Marriage of St. George*, but the details of *Joan of Arc*, the unco-ordinated medley of church furniture, unhistorical costume, and trivial ornament from coral necklace to lily, are lamentably typical of that " stage property " school of design which the Pre-Raphaelite Brotherhood had intended to overthrow. The hard line of the chin and forehead, accentuated by the hard line of the sword blade combine with the shapeless mass of the hair and shoulder to complete a thoroughly ugly and unworthy piece of work.

The truth, as has been suggested before, is that Rossetti was unrestrained, as no other artist of importance had been before, by any adequate æsthetic system either devised by himself or imposed upon him by convention. He was guided entirely by his own momentary preferences for a face or piece of patterned stuff, and by those of his clients, but there was in him, errant and erring, a streak of the purest genius, and it is typical that his next work should be a painting of consummate delicacy and beauty, unsurpassed in his own age and comparable with the greatest creations of the past.

This is the *Beata Beatrix*, which hangs in the Tate Gallery, where it was bequeathed by Lady Mount Temple. It bears the date 1863, the year in which most of it was painted, but it was a long time before he finally allowed it to leave his hands. It is, perhaps, the most purely spiritual and devotional work of European Art since the fall of the Byzantine Empire. This statement is offered as a considered judgment and not as an ecstatic outburst. Anyone who, confronted with its sublime and pervasive sanctity, can speak of it coldly in terms of saturation, and planes and plastic values (as many people, hatless and dishevelled, may be heard declaiming daily in the Tate Gallery) has constricted his artistic perceptions to an antlike narrowness. There are manifestations of the human spirit that transcend the materials in which they are discernible; this picture is one of them, and it cannot be dealt with by the workaday machinery of technical valuation, however high-sounding the phrase and however little understood.

The symbolism of the picture is explained by Rossetti in the following terms :

" The picture illustrates the *Vita Nuova* embodying symbolically the death of Beatrice as treated in that work. The picture is not intended at all to represent death, but to render it under the semblance of a trance, in which Beatrice, seated at a balcony overlooking the city, is suddenly rapt from earth to heaven.

" You will remember how Dante dwells on the desolation of the city in connection with the incident of her death, and for this reason I have introduced it as my background, and made the figures of Dante and Love passing through the street, and gazing ominously at one another, conscious of the event ; while the bird, a messenger of death, drops the poppy between the hands of Beatrice. She, through her shut lids, is conscious of a new world, as expressed in the last words of the *Vita Nuova*—that blessed Beatrice who now gazes continually on His countenance—*Qui est per omnia saecula benedictus.*"

The colour scheme is a sombre harmony of gold and green and purple, a crimson dove bears the grey death poppy in his beak. On the frame, designed by Rossetti himself, are inscribed the first words of the quotation which Dante uttered when Beatrice's death " despoiled the city of all dignity." *Quomodo sedet sola civitas!* " How doth the city sit solitary that was so full of people ; how is she become a widow that was great among the nations."

Into the dimly aureoled head of Beatrice, Rossetti has painted all that was most tender and most devout in his memory of his wife. No model sat for him. From his most intimate memories and the innumerable sketches that had strewn the studio at Chatham Place, he built up painfully and reverently the disembodied vision of his

early love. It was a worthy memorial, the swan-song
of his own delicacy and depth of feeling.

As a work of art it may well serve as a test case in the
objective and plastic theory of painting to which almost
all our modern critics are committed. This theory,
varied a little from journal to journal according to the
personal predilections of the writer, has been devised
very lately in comparison with the antiquity of graphic
and plastic art, owing to the necessity of interpreting to
the public and the art editors and advertising managers
who have usurped the places of Leathart and Leyland as
patrons of the Arts, the intentions and achievements of
the schools of painting since Cezanne. It provides, in
the hands of the ablest exponents, a lucid and illuminat-
ing justification of apparently new aspects of form in
terms of the academic tradition of Latin Europe. Post-
impressionism is shown as the fulfilment of this tradition.
But this has only been possible by the cutting down of the
pure artistic impulse and perception to the narrowest
conceivable limits. Everything that comes within the
limits is now more coherently and intelligently arranged
than ever before, but here and there isolated and obviously
not insignificant cases occur of artists who cannot be
brought into these limits. The difficulty which Mr.
Roger Fry showed in coping with Jerome Bosch in his
book on *Flemish Art* is an example of this. *Beata Beatrix*
is another. You can if you are so disposed dismiss with
a clear conscience half at least of Rossetti's work as
artistically negligible ; you can go further and denounce
his whole reputation as a fraud, but as long as *Beata
Beatrix* hangs in the Tate Gallery there is a problem to be
faced. You can say that this picture simply does not
rouse any emotion in you and therefore is not a work of
art ; you are then in the position of the old-fashioned
Academicians who cannot imagine what all these people
see in Matisse ; there is no contact for argument. Or
you can say that it does arouse very definite and deep
emotion, but that, as it is not a picture which can be
explained by the same standards as Poussin or Picasso,

this emotion is not æsthetic but some other kind of emotion altogether improper to a picture. Now if this emotion were the sort that is roused by pure illustration, you are well armoured to resist it. But this is not the case. The heart does not go out in human sympathy in the way that it does to the unlucky family of Martineau's *Last Day in the Old Home*. It is not romantically aroused by Lizzie Siddal's beauty or pathetically reminded of her death or stirred by some remembered quotation from Dante, though no doubt all these considerations are present to a certain extent. Is this illicit emotion so different from that aroused by, say, the *Mona Lisa* or the mosaics at Daphne? Is there conceivably something we have missed in our austere stringing together of individual geniuses on the gut of our generalisations?

It is more than a little shocking to find Rossetti in 1869 submitting even this sacred memorial to the profitable process of replication. Perhaps it is significant that the reserve which he had till then earnestly observed with regard to it should first be broken through in the year when he rifled the grave in Highgate Cemetery to recover his buried poems. The first replica was a crayon drawing for Mr. William Graham, for whom three years later he and Dunn made another version in oils, adding for the sake of distinction some white doves and a predella. Other copies followed for various patrons in oil, crayon, and water-colour, with the " questionable profusion " that characterised this branch of his activity.

To 1863 also belongs a negligible little oil painting called *Helen of Troy*, which Swinburne described as " Helen with her Parian face and mouth of ardent blossom, framed in broad gold of widespread locks "; a water-colour drawing from one of the St. George stained glass designs, and *Belcolore*, *Brimfull*, and *A Lady in Yellow*, three trivial but quite pretty little studies of female beauty.

From 1864 onward Rossetti became more or less settled in his choice of subject and manner. Large three-quarter length female figures, usually in historical or pseudo-historical costume, and surrounded by a medley of bric-à-brac, and bearing sonorous titles, found a ready and rich market and well suited Rossetti's personal inclinations. They are of two main types, a dichotomy typical of Rossetti's outlook, fair and voluptuous or dark and pensive according to whether Fanny Schott or Janey Morris was uppermost in his thoughts. Janey Morris predominates after 1868. It is wrong to suppose that he employed no other models, and he greatly resented the imputation, which was frequently repeated in his own time ; but the fact remains that all the voluptuous figures do bear a most confusing resemblance to Mrs. Schott, and all the pensive ones— even those that are designedly portraits of quite other people—to Mrs. Morris.

The bric-à-brac, though the same objects of virtue often recur again and again, would fill an antique shop. There can be no explanation of their irrepressible re-appearances except that he liked the things and enjoyed painting them. There is a shell-like wheel of seed pearls which may be discovered either in prominent or remote parts of his pictures with such consistency that it almost amounts to a signature ; there is also a crystal heart and a coral necklace that can usually be discerned somewhere about the composition. Enterprising schoolmasters have been known to employ some of the reproductions of this period as tests of observation, requiring their pupils to write down the objects which appeared more than once.[1]

Fazio's Mistress was the first of this type, a richly executed study of Fanny Schott which was shortly followed by *A Lady in White Dress Combing her Hair* (the title obviously is not Rossetti's) and later by *Lady Lilith*. This large study of " Body's beauty " took some time to complete. It is in intention the embodiment of carnal loveliness. Mr. F. G. Stephens describes it with strain-ing fluency.

" She appears in the ardent languor of triumphant

[1] After prolonged scrutiny, one boy wrote down " Woman " and left it at that.

luxury and beauty . . . the abundance of her pale gold hair falls about her Venus-like throat, bust, and shoulders, and with voluptuous self-applause . . . she contemplates her features in the mirror. . . . The haughty luxurious-ness of the beautiful modern witch's face . . . does not belie . . . the fires of voluptuous physique . . . she has languor without satiety. . . . Thus occupied, she is reckless how much or how little of her bosom and shoulders is displayed in a delicious harmony of colour with the warm white of her dress, heedless of the grace of her attitude and the superb abundance of her form."

Rossetti's own description is in *The House of Life*, Sonnet No. 77.

Of Adam's first wife, Lilith, it is told
(The witch he loved before the gift of Eve)
That, ere the snake's, her sweet tongue could deceive,
And her enchanted hair was the first gold.
And still she sits, young while the earth is old,
And, subtly of herself contemplative,
Draws men to watch the bright web she can weave,

Till heart and body and life are in its hold.
The rose and poppy are her flowers ; for where
Is he not found, O Lilith, whom shed scent
And soft-shed kisses and soft sleep shall snare ?
Lo ! as that youth's eyes burned at thine, so went
Thy spell through him, and left his straight neck bent,
And round his heart one strangling golden hair.

Mrs. Schott sat as the model for this picture.[1]

A less happy achievement of the same year was *Venus Verticordia*. At least four versions exist of this picture in various mediums—all more or less lamentable. The large oil painting in which the idea originated was not finished for four years. A water-colour done for Mr. Rae can therefore claim priority, and is generally treated as the original version.

[1] Later, in 1873, when Rossetti was consumed with what usually proved to be a mischievous itch to retouch all his work, the head of Lilith was repainted from another model. But Fanny shines through it all.

It represents a half-length nude figure emerging from and surrounded by banks of flowers. The model was a young cook whom Rossetti picked up in the streets; handsome as presumably she was, there is little about her vapid little face to suggest the Goddess of Love. Her hair, like an ill fitting and inexpensive wig, is arranged like *Helen of Troy's*, falling behind one shoulder and over the other; in one hand she holds an arrow aslant the composition and in the other an apple. All about are masses of honeysuckle and roses. Upon these Rossetti spent enormous sums of money, ordering them regally from every possible source until his studio was heaped with them, and he was obliged to institute a rigid curtailment of his household expenses to pay his florists' bills.

He wrote a sonnet for it in accordance with what now became the usual custom and had it inscribed on the frame.

His warmest admirers—F. G. Stephens excepted—were obliged to admit that the picture was not a success. Ruskin was so repelled by it that he finally severed his irregular connection with his old friend.

Rossetti had had singularly little practice in painting from the nude, partly owing to his lack of early training and partly owing to his habitual neglect of whatever was not directly profitable. Among the circle of buyers with whom he dealt there was no demand for such works; the worthy old men were frankly shy of them, and Mr. Valpy even went so far as to refuse place in his collection to a figure wearing a sleeveless gown. It would never do to put such a thing where his wife and daughters might see it. Rossetti was quite happy with the textures of velvets and brocades which pleased his sense of pattern while concealing his ignorance of anatomy, and so it happened that he knew less about this essential branch of painting than the average student. The result, as has been said, is lamentable.

" I really do not think the large picture chargeable with anything like Ettyism, which I detest, but I am sure the little one has not a shadow of it," he wrote to Rae.

It does not seem to occur to him that the comparison is in this case entirely against himself.

The other productions of this most fertile year include two curiously mediæval water-colours, *How Sir Galahad, Sir Bors, and Sir Percival were fed with the San Grael, but Sir Percival's sister died by the way,* and *The Madness of Ophelia.* Either of these might from their conception have belonged to the days of Ruskin, but there is a marked coarsening of the brush work. He was already losing his facility for water-colour work.

He also executed in this medium a drawing called *Monna Pomona,* representing a seated girl holding an apple and accompanied by " floral adjuncts."

Besides these, and *Morning Music,* another water-colour reminiscent of an earlier period and often so attributed, he and the invaluable Treffry Dunn turned out no less than six replicas of former successes—two *Joans of Arc,* two versions of *How They Met Themselves,* a *Saluto di Beatrice* triptych for Lady Ashburton, and a copy of the left compartment of the same work for William Graham.

Next year, 1865, he added *The Blue Bower* to the Fanny Schott series, a very gorgeous work carried out in a rich harmony of blues and greens, blue tiles at the back, blue cornflowers, blue turquoises in the golden hair, and "the lady herself in a fur-lined robe of green, such green as that which the sea knows and of which she shares the secret with a chosen few of the world's great colourists."

Another female head painted in oils was called first *Bella e Buona* and later *Il Ramoscello.* There is little remarkable about it.

The Merciless Lady, a little water-colour of three figures drawn during this year, is another example of his fitful reversions to his earlier manner. It represents a lover between two ladies, one dark and sad, the other fair and gay ; his hand is held by the dark one, but his attention riveted to the other, who is singing to him to her own accompaniment. In this picture he has even returned to the carpentered security of the *Marriage of St. George,* fitting the figures snugly into a sort of pen.

Washing Hands is, with *Dr. Johnson at the Mitre*, Rossetti's only excursion into eighteenth-century genre. He describes it in a letter :

" The drawing represents the last stage of an unlucky love affair. The lady has gone behind the screen (in the dining-room perhaps) to wash her hands ; and the gentleman, her lover, has followed her there, and has still something to say, but she has made up her mind. We may suppose that others are present and that this is his only chance of speaking. I mean it to represent that state of a courtship when both of the parties have come to see in reality that it will never do, but when the lady, I think, is generally the first to have the strength to act on such knowledge. It is all over in my picture, and she is washing her hands of it."

In 1866 Rossetti's art reached the highest pinnacle of pure visual splendour in the two great pictures that flame and sparkle upon the walls of the Tate Gallery, *Monna Vanna* and *The Beloved*. If, as he feared he might, he had lost his sight in 1867, he would have passed into the darkness with the knowledge that in these two superb paintings he had enriched his fellow-men with the most sumptuous visions of barbaric glory that had ever burst into the grey city of his exile. All these adjectives are used deliberately and for what they are worth. It is the moment when the real Rossetti enthusiast, if such a one survives, holds his breath and strains his imagination for words of adequate luxury. We who are less single hearted can echo his phrases word for word, but with a slight and significant shifting of implication.

There is little need to describe them at length. *Monna Vanna*, which, though painted subsequently to *The Beloved*, may, as the less dazzling, be dealt with first, is on the whole more than a little absurd. It is all sleeve; face, hair, hands, " floral adjuncts," and jewels, including the inevitable wheel of pearls, are all there, and painted with the utmost elaboration, but all one can see is sleeve. These other things have to be sought out, the great swirl of gold and white, prolonged and accentuated by the folds of the dress, stands out from the picture as though at some yards distance from the rest of the body, like the partially deflated envelope of an airship designed by some tipsy maharajah. At any gust of wind it may again take flight, dandling at its bow the little china hand with its ring and wristlet. And this is not an impertinent comment; one cannot help feeling that about it, and no picture can be held to be altogether a success that gives that impression, however sumptuous and sensuous and ballasted with brilliantly painted accessories.

There is nothing so outrageously distracting about *The Beloved*. It is by far Rossetti's most successful achievement in sheer virtuosity. Except for *Dante's Dream* it is the only important composition of his later period that contains more than two figures. There are four half-length, life-size figures and two more partially concealed behind them. He has lavished upon them all his skill and all his sense of luxury. The pity is that his skill was not supreme and his sense of luxury was largely superficial.

Ford Madox Hueffer very happily describes this picture as " a sort of peacock's fan of women's heads."

" As regards its splendour of colour and the passion of its design," wrote Mr. Stephens, " *The Beloved* need not fear comparison with the greatest works of the sixteenth century in Venice."

" I mean it to be like jewels," Rossetti wrote to Rae, by whom it was commissioned. One is in no doubt about the intention. Everything that was gorgeous in Rossetti's wardrobe has gone into it, everything that was intoxicating in contemporary standards of womanly grace and loveliness. He has let himself go unrestrainedly, and one may fairly judge from this work the value of this aspect of the painter's aspirations.

The picture represents the bride of the Song of Solomon, " brought unto the King in raiment of needlework " and accompanied by " virgins that be her fellows." There is no attempt at a spiritual or symbolic interpretation

of the theme. The allegorical interpretations that head
the chapters of the authorised version of this poem are,
of course, not merely the efforts of puritan divines to
excuse the rather incongruous appearance in their canon
of an Oriental love-song of unrestrained passion, though
people ignorant of the sexual imagery of the mystics are
often inclined so to regard them. Rossetti, at any rate,
leaves them entirely alone. His picture is of a royal
wedding, pure and elaborate.

"My Beloved is mine, and I am his ; let him kiss me
with the kisses of his mouth : for thy love is better than
wine."

It is the apotheosis of " the stunner."

In contrast to the quintessential femininity of the rest
of the picture, the foreground is occupied by a negro
page, heavily bejewelled, who carries in his hands a little
gold vase of roses. In the first stages of the work this
place was taken by a negro girl, for whom a number of
studies survive. The boy was put in her place at the
repainting some years later. The deep bronze colour of
the skin and the well-felt modelling of the negro head are
perhaps the best isolated piece of painting that Rossetti
ever accomplished. Behind him stands the bride,
arrested in the act of lifting her veil and revealing an
oval face of pure Caucasian loveliness. On one side of
her stands a Jewish virgin, on the other a gypsy carrying
branches of japonica and tiger lily. Two other virgins
peep over her head as though eager to " get into the
papers." The model for the bride was a Miss Mackenzie
—the only example of Rossetti's employment of a professional model. The dresses and accessories are a
blaze of colour ; the pair of gold and scarlet aigrettes
made of Peruvian feather work which are pinned to the
bride's veil have always attracted special admiration.

There is a suggestion about their lips, which Stephens
was quick to appreciate, that the bridesmaids are singing.

" Of his skill in the high artistic sense, implying the
vanquishment of prodigious difficulties—difficulties the
greater because of his imperfect technical education—

there cannot be two just opinions as to the pre-eminence of Mr. Rae's magnificent possession. It indicates the consummation of Rossetti's poems in the highest order of modern art, and is in harmony with that great poetic inspiration which is found in every one of his more ambitious pictures. This example can only be called Venetian because of the splendid colouring which obtains in it . . . the intention of Venetian art is exalted, if that term be allowed, while its form, colouration and chiaroscuro are most subtly devised to produce a whole which is thoroughly harmonised and entirely self-sustained."

There are the claims made for *The Beloved* by its most eloquent admirer, F. G. Stephens—that it is technically irreproachable, that it is inspired by Rossetti's highest genius, and that it establishes his claim to eminence among the greatest colourists of the world.

From all these propositions one must in some measure dissent. There is a good deal that is disagreeable about the technique, the harsh discord in treatment, for example, between the gold vase in the page's hand and the gold ornament on his chest. Moreover I have never been able to satisfy myself that the perspective of this ornament is correctly realised. It does not seem to lie flat upon his chest, but to decline from it at a noticeable angle. The relative distances too between the various objects seem continually confused, and it is from this straining to focus the eyes where no focus is possible that much of the dazzling effect originates which Stephens regards as so great a merit. The high modelling of the negro's head accentuates the formlessness of the bride's, which floats nebulously among her draperies. I am not trying to suggest that this was not a work embodying enormous skill, but that only still greater skill could have carried it off successfully.

As regards the colouring, it is absurd to compare it with the work of the great colourists, unless Stephens understood by this category something quite different from what it means to modern critics. Rossetti has undoubtedly succeeded in covering the surface of his

canvas with a number of exceptionally brilliant and har-
moniously arranged pigments.   That is probably what
Stephens meant, and it is in fact a highly exacting achievement.   The green of the bride's sleeve was not a matter
of squeezing out a tube.   Anyone who has painted at all
in oil colours knows the heart-breaking way in which
apparently vivid colours on the palette become muddy
and toneless on the canvas.   If they wished to, very few
people could rival the brilliance of the scintillation that
this picture shows.   It is instructive on a student day to
glance at some of the attempts to copy it.

But this is not the aim of a great colourist in the sense
that Rubens is supreme in that category.   When one
hears this absurd claim one thinks of the portrait of the
Archduke Albert in the National Gallery ; of the depths
in the reds and blacks, of the subtlety and strength of
the plumed hat, of the economy and richness of a great
colourist.   Rossetti loved bright things like a child or a
peasant, but that sensitiveness to the modification of
colour and that profound feeling for its structure that
make a great artist were unintelligible to him.

His next important picture which was begun this year
but not delivered until 1870 was the *Sybilla Palmifera*,
which represents the second half of the Sacred and
Profane Love of which *Lady Lilith* was the first.   An
austere priestess, painted from a Miss Wilding, to whom
Rossetti now began the payment of a regular retaining
fee and who sat for many of his pictures, sits under a
stone canopy carved with cupid and skull.   She holds in
her hand a palm branch, while a burning lamp, a brazier
of incense, and two butterflies complete the composition.

Early in 1867 he painted *Joli Cœur*—a thoroughly
vulgar study of a young girl complete with coral necklace,
crystal heart, and pearl wheel, with melting eyes and
provocative mouth, typical of the beauty albums of
the day.

The Loving Cup, of which several replicas exist, was
also done in this year.   It is a well-painted and unpre-
tentious study of a girl in crimson, standing with a gold

cup against a background of embroidered linen and brass plates.

The rest of the year was spent for the most part in finishing off the works already mentioned and, as will be recorded in the next chapter, in serious anxiety about the state of his eyesight.

The Return of Tibullus to Delia is a water-colour that only deserves mention as a departure from his usual subjects.

5

A few words may be added at this point about the general tendency of Rossetti's compositions. As we have seen, his choice of subject was now practically restricted to pictures of beautiful women of various types and with various accessories and costumes ; with this change came a change in the rhythms underlying his composition. These rhythms are always purely linear ; as we have seen, he was untouched by any impulse towards the coherent arrangement of form in space which is now taught in Art Schools as the primary impulse of art.

His early pictures are for the most part a diaper pattern in two dimensions, a result following directly from the precepts of Millais and Hunt. As we have seen, the organised vitality of the baroque seemed artificial to them. They sought to diffuse the interest of the composition into every part of the canvas. The result is in Rossetti a unifying rectangularity in which, probably unconsciously, he attempts to hold the composition into its frame by repeating its lines and corners throughout the design.

In the accompanying figures an attempt is made, by contrasting the main lines of *Ecce Ancilla Domini*, *The Marriage of St. George*, *Monna Vanna* and *The Question* of 1875, to show four phases in his development of rhythmic unity in the use first of right angles, then of the diagonal, later of a single curve, and at the last of contrasting curves.

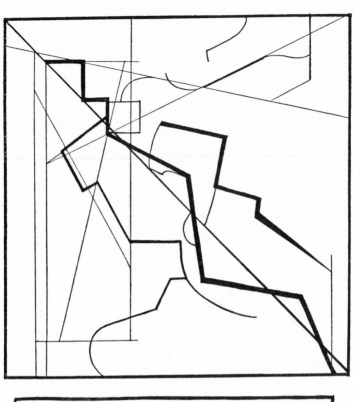

THE MARRIAGE OF ST. GEORGE (1857)
Elaborate geometric design balanced on the diagonal
Compare plate facing page 95

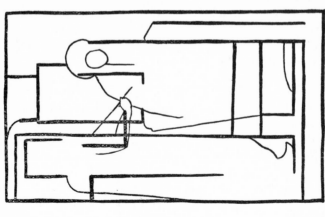

ECCE ANCILLA DOMINI (1850)
Simple rectangular design
Compare plate facing page 42

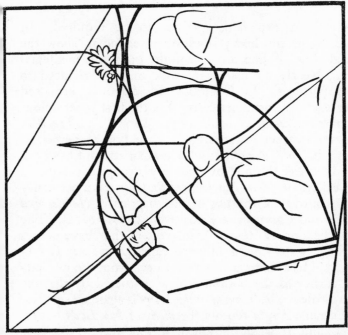

THE QUESTION (1875)

Elaborate straight lines and radiating curves

MONNA VANNA (1866)

Simple accentuated curved motive

Compare plate facing page 138

KR

Very little explanation seems to be required. In the diagrams the heavy lines are intended to show the general flow of line and the light ones the incidental detail. Nearly all his early work may be reduced to diaper patterns. In *Fra Pace* two diagonals are used rather coarsely, forming a heavy X ; the first water-colour of *Dante's Dream*, *Galahad at the Shrine*, and *The Blue Closet* tend rather towards an accentuation of perpendiculars ; in *The Tune of Seven Towers* an attempt has been made to break the line by one very strong diagonal and one weaker one ; *The Marriage of St. George* is a peculiarly happy contrast of the use of the diagonal ; *Hamlet and Ophelia* and *Cassandra* are positively chess-boards. The first indication of Rossetti's interest in the curve occurs in a little water-colour of 1859 called *My Lady Greensleeves*. Here there is a marked curve from the top left-hand corner to the bottom left, accentuated by the line of the girdle. *Dr. Johnson at the Mitre* is again all squares, but *Lucretia Borgia* repeats the *motif* of *My Lady Greensleeves*, and it is significant that this feature is more marked in the second than in the earlier version. In *Love's Greeting* the change is more marked, and from then onwards, with exception of *Cassandra* already mentioned and of *Tristram and Iseult*, continues to be a regular feature of Rossetti's work. *Lady Lilith*, *Beata Beatrix*, *Monna Vanna*, *Sybilla Palmifera*, *The Return of Tibullus to Delia*, are notably built upon single arches. Later compositions will be dealt with as they occur.

CHAPTER V

SHADOWS

Insomnia—Fear of blindness—Penkhill—Poems.

I

It was in 1867 that Rossetti's health first began to cause him real anxiety.

The year before, he had contracted a uræmic complaint which, though inconvenient and at times extremely disagreeable, was not at present a source of danger to him. It required periodical surgical treatment for its relief, and, when this could be obtained without delay, it caused very little trouble. After one of these minor operations, he was again at work at his easel within fifteen minutes. Only on one occasion, when the operation had been delayed and his constitution was already shaken, did he suffer any serious effects from it. He had, as has already been mentioned, singular recuperative powers over any physical infirmity.

His real trouble, that finally ate out his vitality and overthrew his whole robust spiritual constitution, was nervous. Throughout the jovial five years at Cheyne Walk of hospitality and industry he had never been free from the gnawing melancholy, partly perhaps the result of some prenatal or childish influence, but certainly intensified by, and centralised in, the death of his wife. However gay the punning and rhyming, the slang and the chaff, of the Pre-Raphaelite Circle, at the end of it, when Madox Brown's last burst of abuse had died down and Howell's latest adventure had been exploited to its utmost and most fantastic end, he was left alone in the great velvet-hung bedroom with his own unfathomable and incommunicable despair.

In 1867 his melancholy and restlessness began to give place to relentless insomnia. Others afflicted by this terrible disease have contrived in some measure to adapt themselves to it, to reserve their waning vitality, manage with what sleep they can get, and when not sleeping to take adequate rest. Rossetti was the last person to be able to do this. He became unable to rest and unable to work ; the days dragged by in fretful melancholy. He lost interest in his collections, and became morose with his friends. More and more his thoughts and conversation tended to the subject of suicide.

At the same time he became threatened by another and overwhelming calamity. He found trouble with his eyes, and became convinced that he was losing his sight. He stumbled about his studio attempting to work, knocking into objects whose distances he misjudged, and complaining always of a film as of curling smoke or effervescing champagne always before his eyes. He became dazzled in bright light and confused in dim. He complained that after he had turned away from an object he still retained its image, so that, looking from the face of a friend to the plain wall, he could clearly discern the silhouette of the head even to the extent of recognising a profile. This terror of blindness, aggravating, and in turn aggravated by, his insomnia, made the following years pitiful to his friends. His income was maintained chiefly by a steady output of replicas. One can only surmise how much of them was the work of Dunn and how much of the faltering master.

In the spring of 1868 he was induced by his friends to leave London for a rest and change of air, and, accompanied by William Bell Scott, he visited Penkhill Castle in Ayrshire, the home of Miss Boyd, an amateur artist, and close friend of Scott's.

Penkhill was an ancient family seat, recently renovated by the Boyds and embellished with a detestable fresco by William Bell Scott, and, though Miss Boyd was not aware of it at the time, heavily mortgaged by her brother. It was a curious house-party, consisting of these three and

an elderly lady, a relative of the Boyds, called Miss Losh.
The object of the party was to lighten the burden of
Rossetti's depression, and to some extent it was successful. Miss Losh took a singular fancy to him, intending,
Scott thought, to play him off against himself as an
influence in her niece's life. Rossetti would come down
to breakfast at noon, and Miss Losh would watch him,
mangling his food in the way that had revolted Meredith,
and making rings with his cup on the valuable tablecloths.
" He has genius," she would say to Miss Boyd, " and is
not like us." She was a woman of some means, and
entreated Rossetti to accept money from her, so that he
could be quite independent of painting until his sight was
restored. Rossetti told Scott of this offer, adding that
he would never take a penny of the old lady's money ;
it was found at her death, however, that he had profited
to a considerable though unspecified extent by her
generosity, and had apparently made no effort to
repay it.[1]

In the evenings Scott and Rossetti sat up to his
accustomed bedtime, drinking very heavily. Rossetti
had never liked spirits, and had only begun to drink
them as a means to sleep. In the cellars of his hospitable
hostess he found a whisky which appealed to his sense of
taste, and it is from this visit that his steady over-
indulgence in spirits dates. William Rossetti thinks
that this habit proved as injurious to his body as, later,
chloral proved to his mind. It was, at any rate, a habit
which he continued until almost the end of his life.

However deplorable the effects of his visit may have
been in this direction, there is no doubt that he went back
to Cheyne Walk considerably strengthened both in body
and mind. His friends at Penkhill had put a new hope
into his life. If he was to be deprived of his painting,

---

[1] Scott caused great offence by recording this incident. It seems to me
worthy of repetition as typical of Rossetti, and not particularly discreditable.
William Rossetti mentioned £100 as the probable amount. Scott obviously
thinks it was more. Rossetti's IOU was destroyed by the old lady's
executors.

let him, like blind Homer or Milton, live for his poetry.
During the last years he had written nothing except an
occasional sonnet for a picture, or a bawdy rhyme ; now
he began to assemble the scattered fragments of his work,
to re-write and revise, and, with a growing sense of
power, to compose. He began to concern himself with
the foundation of a literary reputation ; considered, and
at the last moment rejected, the project of a publication for private circulation ; contributed sonnets to the
Fortnightly Review and to a pamphlet review of the
pictures of the year. In his sleepless nights he began
reading poetry more thoroughly, collecting curious and
inspiring words.

Next year he returned to Penkhill, and it was clear
that all his interests were now centred in his poetry.
Crouched in a little cave not far from the castle, he
wrote *Troy Town* and *Eden Bower*—a new version of
The Stream's Secret. Painfully, and only with partial
success, he tried to piece together from memory the
early poems which lay buried in Highgate Cemetery.
Without them no volume of his poems would be complete. They contained much of his best and most
impassioned work. But it was no good. In a moment
of sentiment, it seemed, he had sacrificed his poetic
reputation, little knowing how much it would mean to
him seven years later. Delicately at first, and with increasing insistence as they found that the scheme was not
so violently repugnant as they had feared, his friends
began to press their point. The poems were not lost
irrecoverably. A little resolution and they might again
be in his hands. And then, playing upon his vanity,
they asked whether he had the right, for a personal
feeling, however laudable in itself, to withhold a work of
art from the world. Gradually his consent was won.

But meanwhile his health was still far from satisfactory.
The insomnia continued, with its attendant depression
and instability ; he drank heavily, and indulged in various
sleeping-draughts. Two events are recorded by Bell
Scott during this record visit to Penkhill which give

some suggestion of the turmoil of mind in which he lived.

They went out one day, Miss Boyd, Scott, and himself, to visit one of the sights of the neighbourhood, which, like many other such sights in different parts of the country, is called the Devil's Punch Bowl. It is a natural basin of black granite in the depths of a dark chasm, into which a jet of water falls from a great height. It is a place which might well tempt anyone who for two years had brooded almost unceasingly upon self-destruction. The three stood on a narrow ledge of rock looking down into the depths below them, half hidden in the mist of the falling water. Looking at his friend's face, Scott saw that Rossetti was looking down with an expression of unnatural fascination. He never at any time in his life showed interest in natural scenery. One thought only was present, " A step and I should be free." The two watched him, helpless ; he gave a deep sigh and drew back, and, putting his hand into that of his friend, walked a little way like an old man. Then the three sat down ; no word was spoken, but they all knew how near Rossetti had been to death at that moment.

The other incident took place a few days later. Scott and Rossetti were walking in a lane when they came upon a live chaffinch which, far from being afraid of them, exhibited marked signs of friendliness. Rossetti picked it up, and it nestled in his hands and caressed him with its beak. Scott was inclined to make light of the incident, but was checked by Rossetti's intense gravity as he said, " It is the soul of my wife, come to revisit me." He carried the bird back to the castle with the utmost reverence, but what became of it is not recorded. Scott also mentions, however, that at the time that Rossetti found the bird, the great bell at the castle gates was violently rung, and was still ringing when the servant arrived and found no one there, or near there. It may be worth adding that, after Rossetti left Penkhill, for some months, every evening, his voice could be heard reading aloud in his empty room. These incidents are

probably not of any great value in themselves, but they
suggest the atmosphere of occultism that surrounded
Rossetti, and may possibly be significant when considered
in conjunction with his early interest and later abhorrence
of spiritualism.

On his return to London he permitted and assisted
in the preliminary formalities necessary for the recovery
of the manuscript of his poems. Mr. Bruce, later Lord
Aberdare, the Home Secretary, signed the order for
disinterment. This took place at night, under Howell's
supervision, and while it was being done Rossetti sat
alone at the house of a friend in a fever of conflicting
emotions. A fire was lighted beside the grave and the
coffin opened. It is said that the body was not unduly
disfigured, but some of the hair came away with the book.

The morality of this violation of the tomb has been
widely debated ever since the story was disclosed to a
shocked public. Everyone has his own opinion upon
such a question ; it is, fortunately, one upon which one
is rarely called upon to decide. The burying of manuscript poems has never been a European funeral custom.
What we should or should not have done in like circumstances does not seem important : what Rossetti should
or should not have done does. The taboo of dead
bodies that is effective among all but the highest and
lowest civilisations is presumably sanitary in origin.
There is no reason why one should look upon the grave
as more sacred than the dung-heap. The point is that
Rossetti did so look upon it, and it is his reluctance to
comply, coupled with his compliance, that clearly indicates a real degradation in his character. In burying
the poems he was, according to his lights, performing a
sacramental act, and in digging them up he violated
that sacrament, and one can discern no motive for this
violation other than frank, disagreeable vanity.

When the poems had been dried and disinfected they
were handed over to Rossetti, and he began the hideous
task of piecing together his work from among the stains
and worm-holes of seven and a half years in the grave.

Already he seems to have regretted his resolution, and to have been conscious of a curse upon the work. It was certainly a beginning ominous of ill, and his predictions were terribly fulfilled.

2

The volume appeared on April 25th, 1870, and was greeted on all sides with a pæan of unanimous and unqualified praise. This was not altogether unexpected.

The *Fortnightly Review* said of it that it had the fullest flavour and fluency of impulse, and the impulse was always towards harmony and perfection. It had the inimitable note of instinct, and the instinct was always high and right. What he would do was always what a poet should do, and what he would do was always done.

But that, as one might perhaps guess from the alliteration, was by Rossetti's friend Swinburne.

The *Academy* had pages of unqualified approval and homage written with the full heart and glowing phrases of one little accustomed to the niggling patronage of literary criticism ; he was Rossetti's friend William Morris.

The *Athenæum* trumpeted the arrival of a great new poet. But, then, was not William Rossetti a most important person on the *Athenæum* staff ?

And so with all the critical journals of the country. Everywhere there appeared a host of reviewers eager to add their sonorous, and no doubt sincere, tribute to the new master ; but all of them were more or less directly associated with the man they reverenced.

A great deal has been said about Rossetti's share in this matter, and his brother has been at some pains to sum the matter up with a fine show of considered impartiality.

" The articles were written by competent men," he wrote " (some of them about the most competent in the country), who considered the critical opinions in them to be true. Rossetti was no part or parcel of the writing of them ; they were published under the ordinary conditions governing critical reviews. But it would have been all the better if Rossetti had not cared, and had not known who was writing or not writing, or who was publishing and not publishing."

But why all this fuss about it ? Of course, Rossetti " worked the oracle " (to quote the phrase to which his brother took such exception). Who in his position would not have done so ? A few months ago a reviewer on one of the foremost literary magazines of the present day applied for a certain book to review. He was informed by the editor that it could not be sent him, as the author was a member of the permanent staff of the paper and " desired to exercise the time-honoured prerogative of reviewing his own work."

Anyone knowing " the conditions governing critical reviews " will readily understand that Rossetti was only complying with the universal custom of his and almost all other ages in seeing to it that his friends had the writing of these articles. There is no question that he did take pains to see to it. One might go further, and say that it would scarcely have been seemly if the work of a poet of such high but limited reputation should have been entrusted to hack-writers possibly ignorant of his eminence. He was fortunate in being able to do on a large scale what William Bell Scott, and the others who complained about his success, had always attempted to do on a small scale.

There was, however, one bad fairy at the christening, and his " little drop of gall in the ocean of *eau sucrée* " was fraught with such calamitous consequences that he and his article are best dealt with in a separate chapter.

3

The poems do, within their limits—which are narrow —constitute a real contribution to the poetic literature of the century. So far, in this study, Rossetti has been dealt with almost solely as a painter, for it was in this way that he regarded himself, and was regarded by his friends. We have seen that in the 'fifties his attitude was that " if any man has any poetry in him he should paint," and the reason he gives for this judgment is significant of his poetic attitude : " It has all been said and written, and they have scarcely begun to paint it."[1]

Later he attached more importance to his writing, and in 1871 wrote from Kelmscott to Ford Madox Brown : " I wish one could live by writing poetry. I think I'd see painting damned if I could "; but I think that too much can be made, and has been made by some of his biographers, of phrases of this kind impetuously let drop. The writings of prominent men are full of such expressions, and usually denote only a momentary weariness of the job in hand or a passing attraction which they wish to vivify.

Between 1862 and 1868 Rossetti certainly gave little serious thought to his writing, and when he took it up again it was only *faute de mieux* while he was confronted with his possible incapacitation from painting.

The 1870 edition of Rossetti's poems is not of any particular rarity. One of the first things that strike one is its length. It really is a book. The first section, which is the size of most books of modern verse, contains twenty-four longish poems ; of these, several have already been mentioned. *The Blessed Damozel, My Sister's Sleep,* and *Jenny* had appeared in *The Germ,* and are reprinted with considerable emendations. *The Burden of Nineveh* and *Staff and Scrip* had appeared in *The Oxford and Cambridge Magazine* ; other poems had been printed from time to time in periodicals.

The House of Life in 1870 contained fifty sonnets and eleven songs, one of which—*Sea Limits*—has already been mentioned as one of the contributions to *The Germ.*

Then followed twenty-two further sonnets, many of them addressed to his pictures, and including those printed in the preceding chapters.

These poems afford, by their very heterogeneity of subject and method, an important record of Rossetti's development during the long period they cover. They

[1] Conversation with Burne-Jones ; see under 1857.

are, one and all, intensely personal and intensely sensual. They reveal a mind of deep, if rather irregular, sensibility, which reacts and resounds to every stimulus of sensual impression, visual, audible, or tactile, and which concerns itself exclusively with the relations existing between events and bodies capable of giving such impressions. They deal with human relations, and pre-eminently with amatory human relations. It is, no doubt, exactly this which Rossetti meant when he said of poetry that it had all been said and written. He was dealing with a subject of universal preoccupation from a universally recognised point of observation. Even in his treatment there is no hint of an intellectual process at work ; it is all a sonorous re-echoing of dark perceptions. It is instructive to compare these poems with *Fifine at the Fair*, at which Browning was at work at about this time —the one speculative, abstruse, tense, and vibrant with modernity ; the other rich, odorous, picturesque, with not a statement that any child may not understand, not an emotion that any man may not share. Despondency, desire, sense of loss, realisation of transience and of mortality, hope, all the common emotions ornamentally expressed—no wonder that he should think it had all been done before. But for these very reasons they are poems that have given, and always will give, genuine pleasure, and for these very reasons, too, are of interest to the biographer.

It is part of the underlying sensuality of Rossetti's poetry that it really needs to be read aloud. The actual form in which words are presented has a great influence in determining their psychological effect. With Rossetti the shape of his poems upon paper means nothing, but the vocal sound of them means everything. The peculiar resonance so much remarked upon in his own voice has to be evoked before many of his rhythms and rhymes, particularly the feminine rhymes which he employed so extensively, can be appreciated. Read these for yourself purely intellectually, without pronouncing the words, and the effect is lost ; read them aloud and loudly, allowing the voice to fall into softness at the end of the lines, and if it does not make you feel shy, Rossetti's intention is in some way realised.

A particularly notable example of this is *Troy Town*, with its refrain in each verse :

(O Troy Town !)
(Oh, Troy's down !)
(Tall Troy's on fire !)

And *Sister Helen*, where the refrain undergoes slight modulation at each repetition :

(O Mother, Mary Mother,
Three days to-day between Hell and Heaven !)

(O Mother, Mary Mother,
What sight to-night, between Hell and Heaven ?)

(O Mother, Mary Mother,
God shall not hear between Hell and Heaven !), etc.

Read aloud, these refrains achieve exactly the effect for which they were designed, exercising a hypnotic influence on the hearer, drawing him into the poem, making it hauntingly memorable, and giving it a certain liturgical solemnity. But printed upon a page, the effect is exactly the opposite. One sees the italics coming, and finds them an interruption which one overcomes by skipping. There is something slightly ludicrous in reading these repetitions silently to oneself ; a sort of shyness throws up an immediate barrier to the poet which is the more serious as the reader is the more sensitive.

Perhaps the most completely successful poem in the first section of the book is *Staff and Scrip*, of which some mention has already been made. It is a narrative poem of immense vigour, telling a story from the *Gesta Romanorum* of a pilgrim who dies fighting for a queen against a duke who has harried her lands. It represents Rossetti in his first youth and power, contrasting sadly with the egocentric melancholy of *The House of Life*.

The dramatic force of the opening stanzas has seldom been equalled :

> " Who rules these lands ? " the Pilgrim said.
>   " Stranger, Queen Blanchelys."
> " And who has thus harried them ? " he said.
>   " It was Duke Luke did this :
>   God's ban be his."
> The Pilgrim said : " Where is your house ?
>   I'll rest there, with your will."
> " You've but to climb the blackened boughs
>   And you'll see it over the hill,
>   For it burns still."

Sister Helen, which was written about the same time, is described by A. C. Benson as " probably the highest achievement of his art." Here again there is no prelude. The tragedy is in the first lines, again in the form of a question, and here all the more poignant in that the question is put into the mouth of a child :

> " Why did you melt yon waxen man,
>   Sister Helen ? "

It tells the story of the death by witchcraft of the son of the Baron Keith of Keith. The terrible story unfolds slowly and deliberately to its appointed end, with the refrain rising through and through it like the wind through a woman's sobbing. The brothers of the dying man come to intercede with the witch, then the father, finally the bride herself, but all in vain ; the wax melts. the man dies, and the lost soul sighs on its way.

> " Ah ! what white thing at the door has cross'd,
>   Sister Helen ?
> Ah ! what is this that sighs in the frost ? "
> " A soul that's lost as mine is lost,
>   Little brother ! "
>   (O Mother Mary, Mary Mother,
> Lost, lost, all lost, between Hell and Heaven !)

The Blessed Damozel is the only survival, besides the sonnets to the pictures, of the religious phase of Rossetti's art. In passing, it is of interest to those who care for the obstetrics of poetry to note a change which he made in the version since its original appearance in *The Germ.*[1]

> Her blue, grave eyes were deeper much
> Than a deep water even,

has become :

> Her eyes were deeper than the depth
> Of waters stilled at even.

It is amusing to see how " even " has remained in the same place as a totally different word.

The House of Life as it appeared in 1870 was just less than half of the sequence as it now stands. Rossetti was particularly anxious that this should be regarded as one poem, and not as a collection of separate poems. The sonnets that compose it were, as a matter of fact, written at isolated occasions throughout his life, and in a widely different succession from the order in which they were finally arranged ; the idea of forming them into a coherent and interrelated whole came much later. Many of them were written as early as 1848 ; but in their final arrangement they form an ordered expression of Rossetti's general outlook upon love from its most physical to its most spiritual aspect, and upon a universe transfused with love and seen in terms of it.

In a letter to the *Athenæum* in 1872, Rossetti stated that the three sonnets called " The Choice " (Nos. 51, 52, and 53 in the final sequence) sum up the general view taken of the relations existing between body and mind. They do not, however, make it altogether clear upon which side the balance is weighted. The first begins, " Eat thou and drink ; to-morrow thou shalt die," and expresses very eloquently the apologia of the normal

---

[1] There was also an intermediate state in which it appeared in *The Oxford and Cambridge Magazine.*

sensualist in terms closely akin to those of *The Rubáiyát of Omar Khayyám*, a poem, incidentally, whose merits Rossetti was one of the first to acclaim.

The second begins, "Watch thou and fear ; to-morrow thou shalt die," in which he reminds the sensualist of the uncertain duration of his pleasures.

> . . . in yonder sky,
> Now while we speak, the sun speeds forth ; can I
> Or thou assure him of his goal ?

The third begins, "Think thou and act ; to-morrow thou shalt die," and shows the sensualist "outstretched in the sun's warmth upon the shore." How vast is the extent of possibility still unachieved. But the revelation, one cannot help feeling, is rather depressing than stimulating.

> Miles and miles distant though the last line be,
> And though thy soul sail leagues and leagues beyond—
> Still, leagues beyond those leagues, there is more sea,

and, however much weight they may have had in convincing the Victorian public of their author's essential earnestness of purpose, there remains at the end of it a conviction that the sensualist was not in fact discouraged from his pleasures for very long.

The sonnets which he held as most typical of himself are *Still-born Love, Known in Vain, Lost Days,* and *The One Hope* (Nos. 55, 65, 86, and 101 in the final sequence).[1] They are indeed singularly beautiful, melodious, melancholy, haunting. It is very significant that he should choose these as most expressive of his deepest and most final conclusion about his life. The first deals with frustrated love :

> The hour which might have been, yet might not be,
> Which man's and woman's heart conceived and bore,
> Yet whereof life was barren.

[1] Hall Caine : *Recollection of D. G. Rossetti.*

The second and third with frustrated achievement :

> When Work and Will awake to gaze
> After their life sailed by, and held their breath,

and :

> The lost days of my life until to-day,
> What were they, would I see them on the street
> Lie as they fell ?   Would they be ears of wheat
> Sown once for food and trodden into clay ?
> Or golden coins squandered and still to pay ?
> Or drops of blood dabbling the guilty feet ?
> Or such spilt water as in dreams must cheat
> The undying throats of Hell, athirst alway ?

And the last with death :

> When vain desire at last, and vain regret,
> Go hand in hand to death, and all is vain,
> What shall assuage the unforgotten pain
> And teach the unforgetful to forget ?

Vain regret, waste, frustration—these, when all was summed up, the good taken with the bad, the gay hours with the grey, the accounts finally entered, added, and audited, were the stark conclusions of Rossetti's philosophy. *Vanitas vanitatum.* All he can bring from the abundant sources of a life of great richness and complexity is the ancient cry of outraged and bewildered humanity confronted with a world not of its own making, and governed by laws outside its comprehension or control.   And with the traditional despair is mingled the traditional hope instinctively and distantly apprehended. Still arguing from premises that it knows to be false but dares not abandon, humanity stretches out to some other system where compensation will be more equitable and consequences will follow that will be more consonant with the will to survive and the will to procreate.   The hope that Rossetti acclaims when

Lr

> Wedded souls now hand in hand
> Together tread at last the immortal strand
> With eyes whose burning memory lights love home

is one that he discerns, not from the promise of experience, but from its poverty, and it is a light of which he is only fitfully conscious.

> Ah ! who shall dare to search through what sad maze
> Thenceforth their incommunicable ways
> Follow the desultory feet of Death ?

And sometimes it is a hope that brings with it in full measure the bitterness he knows to be a part of all human experience.

> . . . After death
> God knows I know the faces I shall see,
> Each one a murdered self, with low last breath.
> " I am thyself ; what hast thou done to me ? "

But it is a hope he dare not lose.

> Ah ! when the wan soul in that golden air,
> Between the scriptured petals softly blown,
> Peers breathless for the gift of grace unknown—
> Ah ! let none other alien spell soe'er
> But only the one Hope's one name be there—
> Not less nor more, but even that word alone.

CHAPTER VI

' THE FLESHLY SCHOOL '

Robert Buchanan—Chloral—Jane Morris—" Past question not entirely sane "—Attempted suicide—Sale of his china.

I

FOR some time a literary duel had been going on between the Pre-Raphaelite Circle and Robert Buchanan. There are probably few people to whom this name has now any significance except in connection with his attack upon Rossetti, but in his time he enjoyed most sorts of success fairly fully. He was a poet, a journalist, a playwright, a prominent figure at first nights and on racecourses, a novelist, and the loyal friend of a few quite important people.

The trouble had started as far back as 1866, when Swinburne included in some article a contemptuous reference to David Gray, a young man of literary aspirations who had died in London after failing to make his name famous. Now Robert Buchanan had come to London with Gray, and, as his only friend, leapt to arms in defence of his reputation. The defence, as is customary in controversy of this kind, took the form of an attack upon Swinburne. In one article he compared him to Giton in the *Satyricon* of Petronius, and in the *Spectator* of September 15th published some verses from which these are an extract :

Up jumped, with his neck stretched out like a gander,
  Master Swinburne, and squealed, glaring out through his hair :
" All virtue is bosh ! Hallelujah for Landor !
  I disbelieve wholly in everything ! There ! "

. .   .   .

Till Tennyson, flaming as red as a gypsy,
　Struck his fist on the table and uttered a shout :
"To the door with the boy !　Call a cab !　He is typsy !"
And they carried the naughty young gentleman out.

They seem to me to be very amusing verses, and, in any case, to compare quite favourably with the comic rhymes that were circulated within the Pre-Raphaelite Circle, but, as far as Robert Buchanan was concerned, they were a declaration of war.

William Rossetti's defence of Swinburne was, of course, an attack on Buchanan.　"The advent of a great new poet," he wrote, "is sure to cause a commotion of one kind or another ;　and it would be hard were this otherwise in times like ours, when the advent of even so poor and pretentious a poetaster as Robert Buchanan stirs storms in tea-cups."

When William Rossetti's edition of Shelley was published it was no surprise to anyone in literary circles to see it described by Buchanan as " the worst edition of Shelley that has ever seen light."　But he was one man with no influence against a powerful and preposterously loyal circle of able and eminent men.　A mere interchange of incivilities could hurt him far more than it could ever hurt them.　Buchanan waited for an opportunity for a real full-dress assault, and this opportunity occurred in the publication of Gabriel's poems.　Gabriel had, of course, taken no part in the battle so far, but he was sailing under the gayest Pre-Raphaelite colours, he bore the hated name, and the chorus of praise by all the people whom Buchanan detested most, inflamed him to the utmost savagery.

The poems, as we have seen, appeared in the spring of 1870, but it was the autumn of 1871 before Buchanan's attack appeared, and when it did, in the *Contemporary Review*, it did so, oddly enough, under the name of Thomas Maitland.

The origin of this pseudonym has never been satisfactorily explained.　In those days there appeared to be something unseemly in the sight of one professional poet attacking another pseudonymously. Buchanan, the moment the fact became known, loudly avowed his authorship. According to him, it was all a mistake of the editors, and later, when everyone concerned except poor Gabriel was magnanimously accepting apologies from everyone else, his adversaries chose to believe this rather bald explanation. At the time it failed to shield Buchanan, and gave everyone a reasonable excuse for the bitterest vituperation and the bruiting about of such satisfying epithets as " coward," " craven," and " assassin."

One can really assume very little patience with Robert Buchanan's thesis. It was called *The Fleshly School of Poetry*, and was a coarse, ill-intentioned tirade upon the moral standards of the Pre-Raphaelite poets, particularly of Swinburne, Morris, and Rossetti. As the most recent publication, Rossetti's poems bore the chief brunt of the assault.

It began, as all such articles invariably do, with a general denunciation of the sexual depravity of the time. Sensuality was held up as the peculiar characteristic of even that period. " It lies," he wrote, " on the drawing-room table, shamelessly naked and dangerously fair. It is part of the pretty poem which the belle of the season reads, and it breathes away the pureness of her soul like the poisoned breath of the girl in Hawthorne's tale. It covers the shelves of the great Oxford Street librarian, lurking in the covers of three-volume novels. It is on the French booksellers' counters, authenticated by the signature of the author of *Visite des Noces*. It is here, there, and everywhere in art, literature, and life, just as surely as it is in the *Fleurs de mal*, the Marquis de Sade's *Justine*, or the *Monk of Lewis*. It appeals to all tastes, to all dispositions, to all ages. If the querulous man of letters has his *Baudelaire*, the pimpled clerk has his *Day's Doings*, and the dissipated artisan his *Day and Night*."

Well, that is all fairly plain sailing. There has

presumably always been a public for even the mildest pornography, though the " dissipated artisan " seems a little too good to be true, even in Mr. Buchanan's shameless age.

Buchanan then proceeded to analyse this universal sensuality, and he came straight to his point, tracing the origin of " these abnormal types of diseased lust and lustful disease " directly and uncompromisingly to the Rossetti set, whom he described as " a sort of demi-monde not composed, like that other in France, of simple courtesans, but of men and women of indolent habits and æsthetic tastes, artists, literary persons, novel writers, actors, men of genius, and men of talent, butterflies and gadflies of the human kind, leading the lazy existence from hand to mouth." In these resided that " fever-cloud generated first in Italy and then blown westward, sucking up on its way all that was most unwholesome from the soil of France."

" This is our double misfortune," he wrote, " to have a nuisance and to have it at second hand. We might have been more tolerant to an unclean thing if it had been in some sense a product of the soil."

He then proceeded to an examination of Rossetti's poems, showing how he and his friends had " bound themselves into a solemn league and covenant to extol fleshliness as the distant and supreme end of poetic and pictorial art ; to aver that poetic expression is greater than poetic thought, and, by inference, that the body is greater than the soul, and sound superior to sense."

Had his attack been mainly directed against Swinburne he might have made out a tolerable case, but the examples he has to quote from Rossetti fall rather flat after so much preliminary denunciation. The poem to which he takes particular exception is part of the sonnet sequence, *The House of Life*, called *Nuptial Sleep*. As this sonnet was omitted from the 1881 edition and by William Rossetti from the collected edition of his brother's poems, it may be as well to quote the offensive passage :

At length their long kiss severed, with sweet smart,
  And as the last slow, sudden drops are shed
  From sparkling eaves when all the storm has fled,
So singly flagged the pulses of each heart.
Their bosoms sundered, with the opening start
  Of married flowers to either side outspread
  From the knit stem, yet still their mouths, burnt red,
Fawned on each other where they lay apart.

In reading it one has to resist the temptation of being priggishly " modern." It is just the sort of poem, both in sentiment and sibilants, that schoolboys write in abundance, and the editors of school magazines have some doubts about accepting. As an example of Rossetti's art it is well left in obscurity. But the point is that it really did shock a large section of the educated public of its time. Buchanan, though the motive for his attack was admittedly personal and malicious, genuinely thought he was fulfilling a moral duty at the same time as gratifying his spite. In this view he was encouraged by many able and fairly broad-minded people. Tennyson, in conversation with him, described the sonnet as the " filthiest thing he had ever read "; Cardinal Manning, Lord Houghton, Lord de Tabley, to mention only a few names, sent him letters of congratulation. Browning seems to have given both sides reason to quote him as their supporter.

There were other phrases in the book, such as " munching necks with kisses "[1] and " gripping and lipping limbs," which were regarded as indecent.

Now, as has already been pointed out, there was much that was disingenuous and much that was fantastic in Buchanan's indignation. It is all nonsense to talk about " abnormal types of diseased lust and lustful disease." Buchanan was a common and prudish lowland Scot, Rossetti a Southern artist, and he had shocked Buchanan by his insistence on the physical side of love, and that was

---

[1] A fairly vivid description of what, I understand, was Rossetti's amatory practice.

Buchanan's way of expressing his horror. Cleared of its irrelevances and absurdities, the charge for which Rossetti is held answerable comes under two heads; first, that as a man he had a coarse and shallow attitude towards sex, in which he regarded the physical pleasures of union as more important than the emotions aroused; and secondly, that as an artist he had broken through the wholesome reticence of civilisation in expressing his attitude.

The second accusation is, of course, fully justified. He had in fact shocked people by mentioning in a sonnet sequence subjects which were considered proper to the smoking-room. He had never been able to simulate a patience he did not feel for the moral prejudices of his adopted country. It was largely a consciousness of this constitutional divergence from the ordinary public that had kept him so long in seclusion. Now, to gratify his vanity, he had exposed himself to the opinions he had so long despised, and he had to bear the consequences. It is no defence to say that no other age would have found anything reprehensible in his work. If he chose to disregard the standards of contemporary taste, as all great artists have had to do, he should also have held himself aloof from the protests he incurred.

The first charge is more important, as it raises the whole question of Rossetti's attitude to the relations of soul and body which has already been glanced at from time to time. It is absurd to say that he ever regarded the body as more important than the soul. There is nothing in his work that can possibly justify such an assertion. It is possible, however, that Buchanan was guided in this by the rumour of Rossetti's protracted liaison with Fanny Schott. "What Gabriel saw in her," was a frequent speculation among his closest friends, and his recurrent devotion to this apparently soulless woman may well explain the reputation which he undoubtedly bore, in certain circles, of being an unromantic sensualist.

He was, of course, what would now be described as "highly sexed," and the physical relief of his passion was necessary to his well-being, but there was little in his attitude towards women of the cynicism that usually accompanies sensuality. Woman was for him a mystery, and just as in his early life the story of Dante became for him an allegory pregnant with implications, so in later life he came to regard Woman as being in some perceptible but scarcely definable manner the mediating logos between flesh and spirit.

He was never ascetic, either in the obvious sense of the ordering of his life or in the wider sense of his attitude towards physical realities. The beauties of texture and the beauties of line were for him inseparable from the abstract beauties they reflected. He professed belief in a duality of flesh and spirit in which the throat and lips of women expressed one part and the eyes the other. This " elimination of asceticism from mysticism " is held up as the cardinal feature of Rossetti's art in a most interesting article, entitled *The Truth about Rossetti*, published by Watts-Dunton in the *Nineteenth Century* a short time after Rossetti's death.

When Rossetti came to reply to Buchanan, as he felt obliged to do, he was able to demonstrate from his work the shallowness of the criticisms. But the effects of the article were deep-rooted.

2

To all outward appearances, Rossetti in 1871 was very well able to support himself against any journalistic slanders. He appeared to those outside his own circle as a very prosperous and self-satisfied man, so accustomed to praise as to invite criticism. This must be borne in mind when considering the storm of reproach which afterwards fell upon Buchanan. He thought he was attacking a man very much stronger than himself—so much so that any stealth was justifiable that might help to equalise the odds. Actually, as only Rossetti's intimates knew, he was a very weak man indeed.

We have seen how in 1869 his reason was so

over-clouded with melancholy as to make people fear
for its stability ; how he was tortured with insomnia, and
convinced, in spite of the assurances of his doctors, that
he was on the verge of blindness. In 1870, probably at
about the time of the publication of his poems, he was
introduced by a Mr. Stillman to a remedy that promised
to relieve him of all these troubles ; this remedy was the
newly discovered narcotic, chloral. Stillman unques-
tionably did this with the very best will in the world.
Little was as yet known about the operation of the drug,
and it was widely supposed at the time to have all the
virtues of other narcotic drugs without any of their evil
consequences. This has since been shown to be false.
Rossetti from now onwards until about the end of his
life became increasingly dependent upon increasing
doses, and the collapse which happened in June 1872 is
directly attributable to the effects of this drug.

He took it in fabulous quantities. The normal
medicinal dose for an adult is, I believe, anything from
ten to twenty grains. Rossetti's daily consumption was
rarely less than a hundred. In a queer way he took a
certain pride in his prowess, and would boast of the
strain that his system survived. He believed that he
took much more, and, had the quantities that he claimed
to have drunk been the true ones, he could not conceivably have lived to tell of it. The truth was that
he was deceived by his friends as to the amount he took.
As he increased his consumption, so much the more
they diluted the solution. His medical adviser, Dr.
Hake, saw to it that the chemist by whom it was dispatched to him sent it in a far weaker strength than he
imagined, and, once in the house, his friends and his
brother, made every effort to dilute it further. Rossetti
would thus claim to have made three hundred grains
his standard dose when actually he was taking only a
third ; but even that was a prodigious amount, and
probably more than any other man has ever taken con-
sistently throughout an industrious period in his life.
To make matters worse, since he found the taste of the

drug disagreeable, he acquired the habit of gulping down large glassfuls of neat whisky after each dose. William Rossetti thinks that the failure of his brother's health was as much due to whisky as to chloral. He usually took these doses at night, and after each was rewarded with a few hours' unconsciousness. It was not the most healthy or the most refreshing sleep, but at least it was repose, complete and impenetrable, and this must be borne in mind when considering the effects of the drug upon his life as a whole.

We know from many poignant descriptions what Rossetti became after he became addicted to chloral; we have no means of knowing what he might have been without it. It is quite certain that he could not have lived for much longer as he had been living between 1867 and 1870. Insanity and probably suicide could have been the only result. It is conceivable, of course, that he might have found some other and innocuous remedy for the insomnia that was ruining his life. Mesmerism was tried upon him later, and with some success. It might have cured him in 1870, but this is far from likely. We do know that the immediate result of his regained sleep, morbid and trance-like as no doubt it was, was that he was once again able to start painting in earnest, and that never, when the whole world was jangling discordantly about his ears, was his brush unsteady or his sense of colour false. The drug, for him, was always a means to an end; it was no gate of horn through which he passed in search of new sensations or new dreams. He spoke of it openly and sensibly as one of the necessary things for his work.

" The fact is," he wrote to Madox Brown, " that any man in my case must either do as I do or cease from necessary occupation, which cannot be pursued in the day when the night is stripped of rest."

His life from the publication of his poems to the publication of *The Fleshly School* was fairly placid and uneventful. He began painting and drawing again with renewed power. From this time begins the remarkable succession of female three-quarter-length studies with Mrs. Morris as his model, which are always regarded as his most characteristic work. The first of these—*Mariana*—was the first important oil painting he had undertaken for three years. He also began work on the larger *Dante's Dream*, and brought it nearly to completion before his temporary abandonment of work in 1872.

His connection with William and Janey Morris was closer than it had been since their marriage, and when, in 1871, they moved from the Red House at Upton to Kelmscott Manor, in Oxfordshire, he became co-tenant with them there.

It is, of its kind, a house of insurpassable charm, with a sweetness and repose which Gabriel appreciated but could never fully share. He was glad to be away from people for a little and to be near Janey Morris. He spent the summer there, but the autumn found him again in London, plunged into the controversy aroused by *The Fleshly School* article.

At first he seems to have accepted the situation with more show of moderation than most of his friends. William Bell Scott describes his arrival at a dinner-party in the evening when Thomas Maitland's identity had been discovered, unable to think of anything or say anything except to repeat in a voice of thunder the hated name : " Buchanan ! Buchanan !" But William Rossetti makes it clear that here, as in so many places, Scott's memory was confused. He did, however, settle down to write a reply in pamphlet form, called *The Stealthy School of Criticism*, of which a large number of copies were printed before he suddenly decided to have the edition destroyed. It was, by all accounts, a point-to-point rejoinder of unbalanced vehemence, wisely abandoned. He contented himself with a moderate and cogent letter to the *Athenæum*, which appeared on December 16th, 1871. In this letter he goes straight to the real point at once.

" Any reader," he writes, referring to " Nuptial

Sleep," "may bring any artistic charge he pleases against
the above sonnet, but one charge it would be impossible
to maintain against the writer of the series in which it
occurs, and that is, the wish on his part to assert that the
body is greater than the soul.   For here all the passionate
and just delights of the body are declared—somewhat
figuratively, it is true, but unmistakably—to be as naught
if not ennobled by the concurrence of the soul at all
times.   Moreover, nearly one half of this series of sonnets
has nothing to do with love, but treats of quite other
life-influences.   I would defy anyone to couple with
fair quotation of sonnets 29, 30, 31, 39, 40, 43, and others
the slander that their author was not impressed, like all
other thinking men, with the responsibilities and higher
mysteries of life ; while sonnets 35, 36, and 37, entitled
'The Choice,' sum up the general view taken in a
manner only to be evaded by conscious insincerity.
Thus much for *The House of Life,* of which the sonnet,
'Nuptial Sleep' is one stanza, embodying, for its small,
constituent share, a beauty of natural universal function
only to be reprobated in art if dwelt on to the exclusion
of those other highest things of which it is the harmonious
concomitant."

This letter was the full extent of Rossetti's participation in the conflict, and he acquitted himself with dignity
and good sense.   William restrained him from issuing
a challenge to a duel.   Unfortunately, the other com-
batants did not share Rossetti's studied moderation,
which, indeed, was with him purely superficial.   Provoked by the taunts of cowardice hurled at him for his
pseudonymous disguise, Buchanan early in the next
year republished *The Fleshly School* in pamphlet form and
under his own name, with considerable additions and
expansions.   The result was a controversy of incredible
vindictiveness and purely ephemeral importance, which
lasted for many years, and so discredited Buchanan that
for a long time he was unable to publish his serious work
under his own name.   Writing of it to Sir Hall Caine
soon after Rossetti's death, he said :

"My protest was received in a way which turned irritation to wrath and wrath into violence ; and then ensued the paper war which lasted for years. If you compare what I have written of Rossetti with what his admirers have written of myself, I think you will admit that there has been some cause for *me* to complain, to shun society, to feel bitter against the world ; but happily I have a thick epidermis and the courage of an approving conscience. I was unjust, as I have said ; most unjust when I impugned the purity and misconceived the passion of writings too hurriedly read and reviewed *currente calamo* "—he had, after all, had eighteen months in which to consider them— " but I was at least honest and fearless, and wrote with no personal malignity. . . .

" I make full admission of Rossetti's claims to the purest kind of literary renown, and if I were to criticise his peoms *now* I should write very differently."

Before Rossetti's death he dedicated a novel, *God and the Man*, to him, with the inscription :

TO AN OLD ENEMY

I would have snatch'd a bay leaf from thy brow,
    Wronging the chaplet on an honoured head :
In peace and charity I bring thee *now*
    A lily flower instead.
Pure as thy purpose, blameless as thy song,
    Sweet as thy spirit, may this offering be ;
Forget the bitter blame that did thee wrong,
    And take the gift from me !

Rossetti was unwilling to believe that these verses were intended for him. Buchanan himself speaks of them as his *amende*, " a sacred thing between his spirit and mine." Well, no doubt it was agreeable to Buchanan, of whom no one has now heard except in this very connection, to elevate himself, in the rôle of honourable foe, to equality with a world-famous artist. That is all very well. The truth simply remains that, by writing a vulgar and abusive article, Buchanan involved himself in the destinies of a great man with tragic consequences that he could not possibly have foreseen. There is no place for an *amende* in such circumstances.

3

For some time disturbing rumours had been going about concerning the state of Gabriel's nerves. There had been an unpleasant scene in which he had received from Browning a copy of *Fifine at the Fair*, and, reading it, had flown into an insupportable rage at what he extravagantly considered a reference to himself in the closing lines ; almost instantly he had relented, but as quickly the black mood returned. He was convinced that Browning had intended to insult him, and from that time his severance from his distinguished old friend was absolute. The same thing had happened when " Lewis Carroll's " *Hunting of the Snark* appeared ; he discerned in the verses an elaborate satire on himself, and from thenceforward could not even bear to hear the author's name mentioned. By the beginning of June he was devoured by that distressing and not uncommon delusion that the whole world was banded together against him in a conspiracy of infinite ramifications.

There can be no question but that the *Contemporary Review* article, and still more its repetition in pamphlet form, was responsible for giving this particular twist to his constitutional melancholy and suspicion. Other articles had appeared during the early spring, echoing, to a certain extent, Buchanan's insults. There had been one in the *Edinburgh Review*, and another in the *British Quarterly*. These had been further fuel to the fire that consumed him. Malevolence stared at him in the eyes of strangers in the street ; every tiny mishap in his everyday life—a tube of paint mislaid, a plate cracked—had become in his mind the work of his enemies.

Unconsciously, too, his friends encouraged him in his suspicions. Madox Brown, like the hardened old campaigner he was, was never really at ease with the world unless, beard bristling and oaths flying, he had some tangible enemy to confront. There was nothing that gave him more zest for his work than to kick down his stairs some stranger innocent of any intended impertinence. He loved to picture himself with his back to the wall, fighting tooth and nail against hostile club committees, and county councils, and academy boards. Of course there was a conspiracy against them, and the more the merrier ! Let 'em all come !

But poor Gabriel had none of this stalwart nautical background. For twenty years he had withheld his pictures from public exhibition ; as long as he had had any social life at all he had kept himself from the open competition of general society and lived among the little circle who knew him and loved him and could forgive his follies.

Now, with his stamina shaken by chloral and alcohol, he collapsed pitifully under the unwonted strain of notoriety.

On June 2nd, 1872, William Rossetti went to call at Cheyne Walk after an absence which for various reasons had been prolonged rather beyond its usual limits. To his overwhelming distress, he found his brother " past question not entirely sane."

While William was with him, Mr. Lefevre called to complete the purchase of the *Bower Meadow*, for which the sum of £735 had been decided on. Far from employing the suavity which was habitual to him when negotiating with dealers, Gabriel received him with every manifestation of intense embarrassment and excitement, offered to cancel the contract if Mr. Lefevre did not consider the picture worth the money, and could only be convinced with the utmost difficulty that the dealer's satisfaction at his purchase was quite sincere.

He had for some time past been attended for his malady by Dr. Hake and Dr. Marshall, with whom he was on terms of intimate friendship. William now summoned to him a stranger, Dr. Maudsley, who specialised in nervous and mental disorders. Gabriel was alternately defiant and terrified, asserting that he was " no doctor, but someone foisted upon him for a sinister purpose."

While he cowered in his studio the three doctors and William held a consultation. It was clear that complete cessation from work and change of air were essential. An asylum was ominously suggested. What the effect of such a course, seemingly the consummation of all his suspicions, would have been upon Rossetti it is terrible to think. Fortunately, another plan was suggested by Dr. Hake and readily adopted. The kindly old doctor had a comfortable house at Roehampton, then an accessible but secluded rural retreat. Here, he suggested, Gabriel should come to live with William until they could arrive at some opinion about the probable permanence of his delusion.

On Friday, June 7th, Gabriel was induced to move, and with William and Madox Brown[1] drove down to Roehampton in a four-wheeled cab. It was a dismal journey. Gabriel sat listlessly in his place, complaining irritably that a bell was being rung in the roof of the cab. On their arrival, late in the evening, he abused the driver with some violence for this entirely imaginary nuisance. On arriving at the house he went to bed, but slept little.

Next day his melancholy had deepened. He seemed to have very little interest in the proposals for his change of residence. In the afternoon he and William went for a walk, and, as ill luck would have it, met a cavalcade of gypsy caravans preparing for the fair on Whit-Monday. He gazed for some time at their booths and awnings, and then, convinced that it was a demonstration organised by his enemies to humiliate him, hurried back to the house.

Later, after dinner, he expressed a desire to be read to. William took down a volume of Merivale's *Roman Empire*, and, opening it at random, began to read. He had not read many sentences before he discovered to his chagrin that he had hit upon the passage which describes the

[1] There is considerable uncertainty in the records whether or not Madox Brown was present on this occasion.

MR

devices employed by Caligula to insult and ridicule his courtiers. Gabriel peremptorily forbade him to stop, and sat nodding his head, his face alight with fascination.

Next morning Rossetti did not appear, and Dr. Hake, visiting his room before luncheon, found him sleeping peacefully. The party were cheered at the news, and began to hope that the turning-point in his illness had come, but, visiting him again at about four o'clock, Dr. Hake returned with a grave face. The sleep seemed far from healthy, and he feared an apoplectic seizure. All efforts to rouse him proved unavailing, and a local doctor was summoned. He pronounced that Gabriel had suffered an effusion of serum in the brain, and that his life was practically hopeless; even if he survived, he would be permanently insane.

In terrible distress, William hurried to London and, sending Madox Brown to Savile Row for Dr. Marshall, broke the news, of which Mrs. Rossetti had already some premonition, to his family. Christina was herself seriously ill, but Maria and Mrs. Rossetti instantly set out for Roehampton, hardly expecting that they would find Gabriel alive.

But during William's absence Dr. Hake had made the discovery of an empty laudanum bottle by the side of the bed. Rossetti's coma was explained, and the case, though still critical, was not hopeless. The Rossetti ladies never knew of this discovery. So that no hint of it should get about, William and Hake made with their own hands the black coffee which Marshall prescribed, and themselves washed out the saucepan. By means of this and the inhalation of ammonia, Rossetti was kept alive through the night, and at some time on Monday afternoon recovered consciousness. It was immediately clear, however, that his mental condition was, if anything, changed for the worse. He admitted his intention of suicide. All Friday and Saturday he had secreted the poison in case of need. On retiring to bed on Saturday evening, he had heard himself addressed by a voice in his room in terms of " gross and unbearable obloquy."

Despairing of ever freeing himself from his ubiquitous and insuperable enemies, he had taken the poison and rolled over to sleep.

4

Never was the loyalty of Rossetti's friends more severely tried than during the months succeeding this incident. Not only was he still partially insane, but he found himself paralysed in his left side, and for the rest of the summer a complete cripple.

On Thursday he returned to London, and was taken in by Madox Brown while arrangements were made for his future. Selflessly and ungrudgingly his friends rallied round the fallen master. Mr. Graham, the purchaser of so many of his pictures, put his two Scotch houses, Urrard and Stobhall, in Perthshire, at the painter's disposal. His friends were for the most part busy men, and relays were arranged in which they should look after him. He left London on June 20th accompanied by Madox Brown and Dr. Hake's undergraduate son, George. This young man, who seems to have been willing enough and satis- factory at first, became Rossetti's professional companion and secretary for some years. They went first to Urrard and later to Stobhall, where Bell Scott relieved Madox Brown. He in turn was relieved by Dr. Hake. After a time they again moved, this time to a farmhouse at Trowan, near Creiff. Here Rossetti expressed a wish to continue painting, and Treffry Dunn came down from London with his colours and brushes.

For the anxious watchers it was like the return of the dove to the ark with the first sign of dry land in his beak. Rossetti's physical recovery was astonishingly rapid, but with his returning strength there was at first no sign of a return of artistic impulse. It was as if it had dried up within him. He would never write another word of poetry, he declared, or paint another picture. With his return to normal health, too, he resumed his habit of taking chloral, and Hake, though at still greater pains to dilute his doses, did not dare to forbid them, for fear of more terrible consequences.

William Bell Scott claims the credit for having induced Rossetti to resume writing poetry.

Stimulated by the praise that had at first welcomed the publication of his poems, Rossetti had been, in the eighteen months that intervened between that and *The Fleshly School*, in the full flower of his poetic genius. *Rose Mary* and many of the most beautiful lyrics of the second volume belong to this period. During his stay at Stobhall, Scott with " infinite solicitation " coaxed him into attempting a sonnet.

" The outcome was an effort so feeble as to be all but unrecognisable as the work of the author of the sonnets of *The House of Life*, but, with more shrewdness and friendliness (on this occasion) than frankness, the critic lavished measureless praise upon it, and urged the poet to renewed exertion. One by one, at longer and shorter intervals, sonnets were written, and this exercise did more towards his recovery than any other medicine, with the result, besides, that Rossetti regained all his old dexterity and mastery of hand. The artifice had succeeded beyond every expectation formed of it. . . . Encouraged by such results, the friend went on to induce Rossetti to write a ballad, and this purpose he finally achieved by challenging the poet's ability to compose in simple, direct, and emphatic style. . . . Put upon his mettle, the outcome of this second artifice practised upon him was that he wrote *The White Ship* and afterwards *The King's Tragedy*."[1]

His painting at Trowan only took the form of some spasmodic work upon a replica of *Beata Beatrix*, but it was an enormous relief to his friends to see him again with palette and brushes in his hand. Among other considerations, there had been great anxiety as to how Rossetti was going to be able to support himself in the

[1] Hall Caine: *Recollections of D. G. Rossetti*. The story is here given without name or date, but there is no doubt, I think, that it refers to Scott and to the period of their residence at Stobhall.

laxity, almost amounting to luxury, to which he had grown accustomed in his prosperity.

His finances were in a bad way. He had never saved a penny, and even in the time of his full output and large income was often short of ready money for his immediate needs. He was now faced with the prospect of an indefinite cessation from work. William and Madox Brown took the matter in hand, paying what little money he had into Brown's account and together drawing joint cheques for his expenses. They arranged with his patrons to whom work was owing to wait for settlement until Rossetti's condition became more certain, and stored his paintings, finished and unfinished, in Scott's house, where they could be properly looked after. Obliged to raise money for his present expenses, they arranged, with his consent, for the sale of the entire collection of blue china. They obtained the fair price of £650, and so secured his immediate future. He seems to have shown singularly little regret at the loss of his collection.

If anything could have shaken his belief in the malevolence of the world towards him, it should have been the superb loyalty with which his friends devoted themselves to his interests throughout this summer. It was no small sacrifice for them to leave their homes and their work and shut themselves up for weeks on end with a man suffering from acute melancholia and delusions of conspiracy. But, unfortunately, the poison had eaten deeply into Rossetti's soul. Though cured from its more distressing manifestations, his mind was never again in his life entirely free from groundless suspicions of even his dearest friends. These will be noticed from time to time in the concluding pages of this narrative as they occur forcibly enough to deserve repetition.

Late in September he undertook the journey south, accompanied by George Hake, and on the 24th he arrived at Kelmscott, which for the next two years he made his permanent home.

CHAPTER VII

KELMSCOTT, 1872–1874

Kelmscott Manor—Incompatibility of Rossetti's manner of life and Morris's—The series of Jane Morris pictures.

I

IN the twelve years succeeding his marriage, " Topsy " Morris had become, in the words he used of himself some time later in the Thames Police Court, " an artist and literary man pretty well known throughout Europe." His literary work, which alone would have been the life's task of any ordinary man, was done in the intervals or during the actual exercise of the business of the Morris firm. One by one he rediscovered, learned, and taught the processes of ancient craftsmanship, and poured into them his own abundant vitality and invention. He composed pages of verse, any ten lines of which it would have prostrated Rossetti to produce, as he sat at the loom at Merton Abbey. If a man could not compose poetry as he was weaving tapestry, he used to maintain, he could not do it anywhere.

The Life and Death of Jason appeared in 1867, and met with wide approval, not only from the critics, but from the general public. The first part of the *Earthly Paradise* appeared in 1868. From then onwards the Icelandic sagas began to usurp the pre-eminence of Chaucer in his imagination. Early in 1869 he and Magnusson published their translation of the *Saga of Gunnlaug Worm-tongue*, and in 1871 he made his first visit to Iceland, a journey undertaken with all the devotion of pilgrimage, which had the deepest effect on his later development. From then onwards " the glorious simplicity of the terrible and tragic but beautiful land, with its well-remembered stories of brave men,"[1] was always present in his mind as the background against which everything was seen and the standard by which it was judged, and by comparison there was little in modern life that did not appear trivial and unclean.

One of the few things that stood the test was his home at Kelmscott, where he found sacramentally embodied all that he held of high account of beauty and sweetness and dignity.

It is architecturally very perfect, but it is not a particularly large house. Indeed, when one considers that Morris, Mrs. Morris, the two Morris children, Rossetti, and George Hake were regular inmates, Treffry Dunn at frequent intervals for long periods, and sometimes Theodore Watts-Dunton, and that besides them there seems to have been a regular flow of Morris's guests, one is more than a little bewildered to think how they all fitted in, and where they can possibly have slept.

There is no drive up to the house. It is approached through a little door in the stone wall, which opens into a narrow strip of paved path between clipped yews— one of them a very fine dragon, designed by Morris himself. Another little door leads into the house. There must have been a good deal of bumping of heads. The rooms, which lead from each other, are low and small, darkened with paint and patterned hangings; there are little embrasures filled with china, in which there is just room to stand alone. The garden, too, is tiny and ornamental, set out in little paths where two cannot walk abreast, bordered by low box hedges, and walled with mellow Cotswold stone and great ramparts of yew. It is the very antithesis of the gloomy wilderness in Cheyne Walk or Brown's mansion in Fitzroy Square. It is significant that Morris, who was the wealthiest of the circle, was at home in such constricted space. Perhaps it was his Welsh blood, prompting him to the native

---

[1] Mackail: *Life of Morris.* This quotation from one of Morris's letters actually refers to his second journey.

cosiness of caves and hovels. Rossetti and Madox
Brown could face gloom and discomfort, but they would
not be cramped. Like some amiable mole, "Topsy"
Morris was happiest when his tawny form was curled
up within these thick walls. They alone remained
unchanged in Utopia, born of the earth and the native
rightness of man, as it had watched through a dark age
for the Renaissance of beauty. It was thus that the
wanderers in *Nowhere* found it :

"Almost against my will my feet moved on along
the road they knew. . . . The garden between the wall
and the house was redolent of June flowers, and the
roses were rolling over one another in that delicious
superabundance of small, well-tended gardens which at
first sight takes away all thought from the beholder
save that of beauty. The blackbirds were singing
their loudest, the doves were cooing on the roof ridge,
the rooks in the high elms beyond were garrulous with
young leaves, and the swifts wheeled about the gables.
And the house itself was a fit guardian for all the beauty
of this heart of summer. . . .

"Yes, friend, this is what I came out for to see ; this
many-gabled old house, built by the simple country
folk of the long past times, regardless of all the turmoil
that was going on in cities and in Courts, is lovely still
amidst all the beauty which these latter days have created,
and I do not wonder at our friends tending it carefully
and making much of it. It seems to me as if it had
waited for these happy days, and held in it the gathered
crumbs of happiness of the confused and turbulent
past."[1]

Here, in small compass, lay everything for which his
art and his work was striving—peace, fellowship, love,
childhood, beauty, simplicity, abundance. "O me !
O me !" he cried. "How I love the earth and the
seasons and weather, and all things that deal with them,
and all that grows out of them—as this has done."[2]

---

[1] William Morris : *News from Nowhere.*   [2] Ibid.

Here he returned from Iceland, " all querulous feeling "
killed in him, and the " dear faces of wife and children
and friends dearer than ever,"[1] and here, in the autumn,
came Rossetti, drug-soaked, crazy, haunted and driven
by suspicion, a dark shadow across the sun-bathed
water-meadows, the very embodiment of " the confused
and turbulent past."

It was never in much doubt which would prove the
stronger, the hallowed peace of Kelmscott or the unquiet
soul of the artist. From the first he and his attendant,
George Hake, were an incongruous element in this household, of which harmony was the essential achievement.
He was, of course, devoted to the Morris family. He
still retained some part of the old free-hearted geniality
that had endeared him to " Topsy," and it shone out less
infrequently here than elsewhere. He loved the children
and the animals—particularly "Dizzy," the fat dog, and
an Icelandic pony, also fat—and it was romping with them
that most of his happiest hours were spent. Jane Morris
was now in the full maturity of her profound and lustrous
beauty, and her nearness about the household intoxicated
and inspired him. But his manner of life was inelastic
and in many ways depraved. Week by week the packets
of chloral arrived from his London chemist. The very
routine of his day was an affront to the order and dignity
of Morris's life. Here, from Sir William Richmond's
diary,[2] is an account of two days at Kelmscott : " A
quarter to six saw us astir ; half-past at a breakfast of fish
and eggs ; a little later, hard at work for pike and perch,
dace, chub, with paternosters and spinning ; a few
sandwiches and a bottle of claret fed us during the leisure
moments until dark ; dinner, sleepy talk about poetry
and art till nine, and then *such* sleep." " East wind
prevented really very good luck, but hard work gave us a
good basket . . . then, to wind up, we started yesterday
to scull down to Oxford, thirty-two miles, and did it in

[1] Mackail. This is part of the letter quoted above.
[2] A. M. W. Stirling : *The Richmond Papers.*

ten hours, doing the work of locks and weirs ourselves, dined at University common room, and were back at home by 12 p.m." Rossetti's day began somewhere about noon, and, except for occasional furtive stumpings along the river-bank with George Hake, did not include much fresh air or any exercise. He dined at ten, when the Morrises were going to bed, and fell into his first drugged slumber at about three or four. " He has all sorts of ways so unsympathetic with the sweet, simple old place," wrote Morris, " that I feel his presence there is a kind of slur on it."[1] Moreover, he was impatient of the limitations of country life, and any criticism was blasphemy to Morris. The room where he worked was hung with tapestry, which caused him great annoyance ; the design of it—the story of Samson—distracted him, and he found its occasional stirrings in the draught quite insupportable.[2] " He is unromantically discontented," Morris wrote in the letter quoted above. Several of his letters contain phrases of pleasure about the charm of the house and gardens, but it is clearly their solitude for which he prizes them. He was typically Bloomsbury bred in his attitude to the country. When he tries to express his delight in some natural beauty it is nearly always by comparison with something artificial. " The river growths have continued to develop one after the other," he wrote. " The arrowhead rush puts forth eventually a most lovely staff of blossom *just like a little sceptre*. The way that the white blossom grows triple round the staff is most lovely, and *the whole might really be copied exactly in gold for a sceptre*." He liked a well-staged scene, but was entirely without that sense of reverence for " the earth and the seasons and weather, and all things that deal with them and all that grows out of them." The scenery round Kelmscott was " monotonous and uninspiring " to him, and its only real attraction for him was its

<hr />

[1] Mackail.

[2] This tapestry was not, as some people have supposed, a piece of Morris's own work from Merton Abbey, but some old tapestry found in the house when he took it.

solitude and the sense of refuge from his enemies that it seemed to support.

For some time after Morris's return from his second and final visit to Iceland the personal relations of the household showed unmistakable signs of strain, but the final rupture was caused by an incident from outside. In July 1874 Rossetti and George Hake were on one of their river-side walks when he took violent offence at some remark he overheard, or supposed that he had overheard, from a group of anglers. It is no doubt conceivable that his rather remarkable appearance may in fact have excited some impertinence from them, but whatever they may have said was quite out of proportion to the sudden onslaught of indignation and abuse with which Rossetti assaulted them. He was with difficulty got away, and Hake did his best to explain to the anglers that Rossetti was somewhat " eccentric." The incident aroused comment and animosity, and Rossetti felt that Kelmscott's one compensating quality of solitude had been violated. Much to Morris's relief, he gave up his tenancy and returned to Cheyne Walk.

2

One of Rossetti's activities at Kelmscott typical of his restlessness of mind was the feverish review of his earlier work, which has already been commented on. From now until the end of his life his patrons found it increasingly difficult to induce him to admit that any of his paintings were finished. He liked to keep them by him, continually adding and retouching, and when once he had parted with them he would make every effort to get them back again for revision. For the most part these later emendations were not improvements. *Lady Lilith* notably suffered from the practice ; *The Beloved* alone appears to have gained by it. His more astute patrons soon refused to allow him to see his work again once it had left his hands.

The great achievement of his Kelmscott period is the

long series of idealised studies of Jane Morris, culminating in *Proserpine*. They had begun immediately after the sumptuous period of his art, which, as we have seen, had attained complete expression three years before the collapse in *The Beloved* and *Monna Vanna*.

It is this series which has fixed the " Rossetti type " in the public mind, and one of the criticisms most resented by Rossetti and by his brother was the frequently repeated statement that this type was exclusively pre-eminent in his work. As we have seen, three women dominate Rossetti's life and work—Elizabeth Siddal, Fanny Schott, and Jane Morris. William Rossetti, in his biography of his brother, has been at pains to show that many other models sat to him at various times, but, whoever may have been before his eyes as he painted, it was always one or other of these three types of beauty that looks out from the canvas. In 1856 Christina wrote :

> One face looks out from all his canvases,
> One selfsame figure sits or walks or leans :
> We found her hidden just behind those screens,
> That mirror gave back all her liveliness ;
> A Queen in opal or in ruby dress,
> A nameless girl in freshest summer greens,
> A saint, an angel—every canvas means
> That one same meaning, neither more nor less.
> He feeds upon her face by day and night,
> And she with true, kind eyes looks back on him,
> Fair as the moon and joyful as the light :
> Not wan with waiting, not with sorrow dim ;
> Not as she is, but was when hope shone bright ;
> Not as she is, but as she fills his dream.

Two other faces were to appear with equal insistence, each corresponding to a part of Rossetti's life and character. As Elizabeth Siddal typifies his early simplicity and cloistral purity, and Fanny Schott breaks through coarsely and voluptuously in the rich gaiety of the " good years," so now Jane Morris, " as she fills his dream," stands for all the haunting melancholy and frustration that beset him at the close of his life.

In 1868 she first appears in *Reverie*, one of the least attractive drawings of the series. She is represented leaning on her bed in a peculiarly uncomfortable position, her two arms and neck forming an uncomfortable quadrilateral, her eyes gazing out with undue prominence and little discernible significance. A far more successful study of the same period is the large crayon drawing entitled *Aurea Catena*, a sombre half-length portrait of her, seated by a parapet, her face shadowed in hair, her hand playing with a golden chain. Then comes the first study for *Pandora*, and in 1870 a number of works in the same series of varying beauty. *La Donna della Fiamma* represents her in a slightly comic position, gazing with abstracted melancholy at a tongue of flame which is bursting from the palm of her hand and from which emerges a winged spirit form. It was most probably intended as the study for a painting. *Silence* is a far more successful drawing. It was practically finished before the collapse in 1872, and was sold, apparently without his knowledge, during his convalescence in Scotland. He bought it back, intending to use it for a painting, but never did so, and finally sold it again to Rowley of Manchester. Two versions exist of the drawing. *The Roseleaf* is a singularly beautiful little portrait, representing Mrs. Morris holding a spray of leaf and looking over her right shoulder. *The Prisoner's Daughter* and two studies for *La Donna della Finestra* belong to this year, and also the fine oil painting of *Mariana*. This had been begun two years previously for William Graham, whose son figures in the composition as the page with the lute. The only important works of this year which are not inspired by Mrs. Morris are a study of Fanny Schott called *The Lady with the Fan* and two studies for pictures, *Troy Town* and *The Death of Lady Macbeth*. Neither of these was ever executed. The latter, an elaborate work with seven figures, might have made an impressive painting ; the drawing is full of vigour and beauty.

In 1871 he painted the picture of *Pandora*, a study for

which has been mentioned above.   It is a typical three-quarter-length of Mrs. Morris, dressed in a Venetian red gown and carrying in her hands the casket from which arise fumes of spirit forms.   The sonnet which Rossetti wrote for it has been praised by Swinburne as " the most perfect and exalted of those done for his pictures," and the picture itself as " amongst the mightiest in its Godlike terror and imperial trouble of beauty."

A replica of this picture, dated 1879, shows numerous differences, notably the massive modelling of the bare shoulders, which contrasts disagreeably with the exaggerated spirituality of the face.   Two versions exist of *Water Willow*, one in chalk and the other painted in oil.   The painting includes in the background a vague study of Kelmscott.

Here the succession is again broken, this time by a work of first-rate importance—the *Dante's Dream* which many critics have held to be his finest painting.   As has been mentioned, the first study for this was done as far back as 1856 ; it was a subject peculiarly suited to the temper of his imagination, and its attraction had deepened with the years.   It is best described in the words of the *Vita Nuova* :

" A few days after this my body became afflicted with a painful infirmity . . . and I remember that in the ninth day, being overcome with intolerable pain, a thought came into my mind concerning my lady.   And, weeping, I said to myself : ' Certainly it must some time come to pass that the very gentle Beatrice will die.' Then, feeling bewildered, I closed mine eyes ; and my hair began to be in travail as the hair of one frantic, and to have such imaginations as here follow. . . . I conceived a certain friend came unto me and said : ' Hast thou not heard ?   She that was thine excellent lady has been taken out of life.' . . . Then my heart that was so full of love, said unto me : ' It is true that our lady lieth dead ' ; and it seemed to me that I went to look upon the body wherein that blessed and most noble spirit had its abiding-place.

Then Love spoke thus : ' Now all shall be made clear ;
Come and behold our lady where she lies.'
These idle phantasies
Then carried me to see my lady dead ;
And, standing at her head,
Her ladies put a white veil over her ;
And with her was such very humbleness
That all appeared to say, ' I am at peace.' "

The picture is the best known, probably, of all Rossetti's work. Reproductions of it of varying sizes can be found in almost any picture shop. Rossetti certainly regarded it as his masterpiece, as did most of his friends. It is by far his largest canvas, measuring 7 ft. 1 in. by 10 ft. 6½ in. The physical exertion of covering so large an area, though not remarkable in comparison with that habitually exhibited by most of the prominent painters of the time, taxed his strength very greatly, and no doubt contributed largely to his subsequent breakdown, both directly and in the effect it had of leading him to further indulgence in chloral and alcohol. The general plan of the composition is almost identical with that of the 1856 water-colour, but there are changes typical of the artist's development. The drawing of the figures is very much more sophisticated. In the water-colour, as in all his work of the same period, the lines of the dresses are stiff and formal. Dante's gown forms a sombre wedge, the line unbroken from shoulder to hem ; in the painting it follows a curve through neck, hand, and heel, the folds carefully built up on a solidly conceived structure. In the same way the thigh and knee break the fall of the gown of the pall-bearer on the right, while at the same time the grave and sexless face has become artificially lifted and posed. Both she and her companion are " stunners." The figure of Love curves over the bed with studied grace. Dante has been brought close to him. The clasped hands are happily expressive of reluctant fascination. Beatrice now occupies Dante's position as the centre of the picture. In the water-colour she is like a Gothic effigy on a tomb, flat and stiff, with straight dark hair, austere and lifeless as stone. In the picture she has become a swooning *première danseuse*, her pale head weighed back by the curling masses of her golden hair, her throat curving back, her chin high, her body raised up on the cushions, her hands pressed to her breast. There has been a marked loss both of " humbleness " and " peace." There is an ordered scheme of chiaroscuro, a high light breaking in from the left, picking out Dante and Beatrice and one of the attendant ladies.

The changes in detail are also interesting. The three little portholes over the bed are replaced by wreaths of flowers. The bed itself, originally high and fitted with a concealed aperture, has become a low draped couch. Love's bow and arrow have become a dart ; the two glimpses of the city have lost their Flemish character and become more Italian ; the diaper decoration has given place to a more elaborate design ; a lamp makes its appearance, and two doves. The musical instrument (?) has gone from the left-hand corner, its place being taken by a scroll bearing the *Quomodo sedet sola* inscription that had appeared in the panel of *Beata Beatrix*. The technical advance in the eleven years is gigantic, yet, even in this comparison between one of his less attractive water-colours and his most admired painting, one cannot help being struck with the inadequacy of his later work in the face of his early promise. The feeling of frustration that permeates the *House of Life* is here painfully evident ; as though the flood of his genius had been dammed, not by some obstruction thrown in its path, but from the refuse it carried down with it. There just is something *wrong* and lacking in *Dante's Dream* that, for all its crudeness, was not wrong and lacking in the earlier water-colour.

When the picture was finished it was found to be too large for William Graham's walls. For a short time it hung on his staircase, but Rossetti asked for it back, and in 1880 finished a smaller replica of it, which went to the original purchaser, the larger painting having been sold meantime to Valpy for fifteen hundred guineas ; on that gentleman's retirement to Bath, it was returned to Rossetti in 1878 and re-sold for a thousand pounds, Valpy being repaid in kind. He had thus characteristically been paid three times for the picture.

With his return to Kelmscott in 1872 the series of paintings of Mrs. Morris continued, with two or three interruptions. The affected but affecting *Veronica Veronese* was painted from Miss Wilding for Leyland at the price of eight hundred guineas, which from now onwards became the fairly regular market price of Rossetti three-quarter-length female studies. It illustrates a quotation purporting to come from Girolano Ridolfi's letters, but composed for the picture either by Rossetti himself or possibly by Swinburne. Veronica is listening to the singing of a bird, and :

" Se penchant vivement, la Veronica jeta les premières notes sur la feuille vierge. Ensuite elle prêt l'archet du violon pour realiser son rêve ; mais avant de décrocher l'instrument suspendu, elle resta quelques instants immobile en écoutant l'oiseau inspirateur, pendant que sa main gauche errait sur les cordes, cherchant le motif suprême encore éloigne. C'était le mariage des voix de la nature et de l'âme—l'âme d'une création mystique."

What is the more artificial—the honeyed quotation, itself spurious, or the lovely Miss Wilding, delicately posed in green velvet, *la feuille vierge* scored with a line of notes, the white flower beside it, the canary, the cage, the hanging fan ? But just for this reason we cannot take offence at it. It is a charming, trivial piece of work, typical of the period, executed with facility and relish. It is on an entirely lower plane than the achievement of *Beata Beatrix* or the attempt of *Dante's Dream*, but it is highly agreeable and harmonious.

La Ghirlandata is another study of Miss Wilding made at Kelmscott in 1878, representing her playing upon a garlanded harp in a forest clearing. It lacks the *verve* and *chic* of *Veronica Veronese* while attempting to achieve the same effortless soulfulness.

NR

The studies of Mrs. Morris during these years were all stages in the evolution of the lovely *Proserpine*. The history of this picture, which is the epitome of the whole Jane Morris series, is somewhat intricate. In 1871 Rossetti had made the first drawing for the subject and given it to Mrs. Morris. As soon as he took up his tenancy at Kelmscott he set to work to paint it, and made no less than four attempts on canvas during 1872. The fourth of these was finished off, probably not by Rossetti, and sold to Parsons & Howell. It remained unsold, and two years later Rossetti took it back from them. Leyland saw it in 1873, and, rather undiscriminatingly, offered his accustomed eight hundred guineas for it. Hearing, however, that Rossetti was then at work on another and much superior version of the same subject, he decided to take that instead for a higher price. Nothing more is heard of the earlier painting. The other three, meanwhile, were cut down and sold as heads, after various floral attributes had been added. The only one of these that Marillier was able to trace is called *Blanzifiore*, or sometimes more modestly *Snowdrops*. It belonged at one time to Fairfax Murray, and passed from him to Mr. Goldman.

By October 1873 the fifth version was almost complete when Rossetti found that, in lining, the face had become rucked. Accordingly he began on a sixth version, and, working with impatient application, had got it far advanced in a month, when he found that the lining of the fifth had been put right and was in every way satisfactory ; he wrote offering it to Leyland, and describing it as " completely of his best work." On its transit from the framemaker's to Kelmscott, however, the picture disappeared, and it was No. 6 that was finally sent to Leyland in December. Even now the complications were not at an end. It arrived with the glass broken and the surface of the painting seriously damaged. Back it came to Rossetti, who began on yet another version—the seventh. No. 5 is never heard of again, though probably it passed through Rossetti's hands. No. 7 went to Leyland and

No. 6 remained in his studio until 1877, when he had
the head and hands cut out and inlaid into a new canvas.
He and Dunn repainted the background and drapery
and redated it, rather misleadingly. There are thus two
finished works inscribed :

"*Dante Gabriele Rossetti ritrasse nel capo d'anno del
1874*," and "*Dante Gabriele Rossetti ritrasse nel capo d'anno
del 1877*," the second of which was, for the most part,
painted before the first. There are also probably two
others in existence, one of them of first-rate quality. The
1873–1877 version is generally regarded as the better, in
spite of the obvious haste and inferior workmanship of
the repainted portions.

This lovely composition stands to Mrs. Morris as
Beata Beatrix does to Miss Siddal and *Monna Vanna* to
Fanny Schott (and, in a slighter way altogether, *Veronica
Veronese* does to Miss Wilding)—as the apotheosis of
her beauty and her personality " as it filled Rossetti's
dream."

It is fascinating to observe how fatally everything in
Rossetti's life falls into its place. As the Oxford Union
frescoes typified the evanescent high spirits of Red Lion
Square, so *Proserpine* becomes the very embodiment of
his life at Kelmscott. The history of the picture—with
its baffled painting and repainting ; the succession of
small disasters ; the frustration and destruction and
waste ; the subject itself of the imprisoned bride of Pluto,
brooding in the cold light of the subterranean palace of
her winter exile ; Mrs. Morris, " as she filled his dream,"
torn from the clipped yew walks and sunny stones of
Kelmscott into the nether world of Rossetti's unplumbed
melancholy—reflect without any straining of allegory the
dark declivity of Rossetti's later years.

Another picture of this period which caused Rossetti
considerable worry was the elaborate and unfinished
Boat of Love. The subject is taken from Dante's sonnet
to Guido Cavalcanti, and attracted him from the earliest
time. He began a small water-colour of it in 1855, and
in 1863 Mr. Dunlop commissioned the large painting

Nothing, however, came of it, and in 1867 another water-colour of the composition was commissioned by Mr. Craven. In 1873 the work was still unexecuted, and Leyland and William Graham simultaneously commissioned it, the one on a large scale and the other a smaller version. All that survives of all this negotiating is an unfinished monochrome painting in the Birmingham Art Gallery, the beginning of Graham's version, abandoned in 1881 owing to a disagreement about the price. *The Bower Maiden* (also called *The Gardener's Daughter*, *Marigolds*, and *Fleurs de Marie*) was painted at Kelmscott from the daughter of a gardener there.

The other important works of this year are *The Damozel of the San Grail*, painted for Mr. Rae, and *The Roman Widow*. Both are quite able studies of female beauty, slightly insipid and with few noticeable features to break the monotony of the series. *The Damozel of the San Grail* compares most unfavourably with the exquisite water-colour of the same subject in the Tate Gallery, painted in 1857. The golden hair spread out like wings has become a heavy curtain of glossy chestnut; the austere face of the angel has become a typical late Victorian beauty; the Grail itself, so sacred in the water-colour, has become a modern chalice, straight from the windows of any ecclesiastical outfitter. The whole picture has an indefinable taint of ill breeding about it. *The Roman Widow* is a little more exaggerated but a little more dignified, but it is just about as classical as *The Damozel of the San Grail* is mediæval or Christian.

3

It was during his stay at Kelmscott that Rossetti first came into touch with Theodore Watts, a solicitor better known by the name of Theodore Watts-Dunton, under which he wrote and later lived. Of late years people have conspired to regard as slightly comic and undignified the devoted friendship which this gentleman accorded to men of genius whom he recognised as greater than himself

—notably to Rossetti and Swinburne.   But he was never
so regarded by the artists themselves.   There was
nothing about him of the toady or the climber.   In fact,
the whole attitude of contempt that was centred upon
him may be attributed to the one circumstance of his
home being in Putney.   There *is*, indeed, something
rather unseemly about the idea of Swinburne at " The
Pines," look at it as you will, and about the roast mutton
and the potatoes and the single little bottle of light beer.
But Rossetti was never reduced to this sort of dependence.   He had the warmest respect for Watts-Dunton's
opinion in the intricate confusion of his private affairs,
and, more than this, for his opinion upon his poetry.
His companionship was one of the few bright features
in the tartarean gloom into which he was descending.
Their friendship, that was to become such an important
part of Rossetti's life, began prosaically and disagreeably
enough over the question of a forged cheque.   The
forgery had been committed by a woman of Rossetti's
close acquaintance whom he was unwilling to prosecute.
Watts-Dunton came to Kelmscott as his legal adviser,
and settled the matter with great tact and delicacy.

In 1874 he acted for him again in a matter which was
not capable of such smooth solution.   This was the
break-up of the Morris firm, which took place immediately after Rossetti's evacuation of Kelmscott.   The
ill feeling excited during these protracted negotiations
in spite of superficial reconciliations, really dissolved the
Pre-Raphaelite Circle.   The situation was this.   The
firm was founded in 1861 as a company of unlimited
liability, owned by seven partners.   Money was to be
levied from them as occasion required.   In April 1861
there had been a call of £1 a share, and in January
1862 for a further £19 a share, making the total investment of each partner £20, though it is doubtful whether
in all cases this was ever paid up in full.   No
dividend had ever been declared, and after the first two
years Morris had taken over the entire control of the work.
Besides giving his time to it, he and his mother had again

and again advanced large sums of capital as the business grew. These were nominally loans, bearing interest at 5 per cent. By 1874 the firm had become a big business, with works at Merton Abbey and large London show-rooms ; its name was becoming known all over Europe. No one attempted to deny that this prosperity was directly due to the genius and industry of Morris, but legally the company was still owned by the seven original partners. When the money that had been lent by Morris was paid back, the capital value was still very large and out of all proportion to the original investments. Morris now saw that if the firm was ever to expand to its fullest extent it must be put on a more businesslike basis, under his own entire legal control. The partners were divided about what attitude they were to take. Madox Brown had no intention of abandoning his claims to anything he could get. He was a married man with a family to support. Watts-Dunton, acting for him also, said that he would not on any account sell his share unless he were forced to, and that in that event " the position of the several members ought to be considered as equal in respect of their claims on the assets of the firm ; and, further, that he, Mr. Brown, considered the goodwill ought to be included in the said assets." This last claim was not quite so preposterous as it sounds. It must be remem-bered that at the foundation of the firm Morris was an entirely unknown man, when Brown had a wide if not wholly enviable reputation. His name and Rossetti's had no doubt been important factors in the success of the first unstable years. It must also be remembered that the risks run by Morris were borne equally by all the partners, and that if his more ambitious ventures had failed, they would have been responsible for the firm's deficit. The discussions went on with unabated bitter-ness throughout the following winter. The Pre-Raphaelites were always a quarrelsome set, and during these months they showered unforgettable insults upon each other with unrelenting profusion. Eventually in March 1875 Brown was forced to sell, but at a handsome

price. Rossetti's attitude throughout was laudably moderate. By this time he might with all justice have
claimed that his name was the firm's most valuable asset,
but he seems to have been willing to forgo all remunera-
tion, and, when finally he was paid, with the other
partners, he put the money aside for the eventual advantage of a member of the Morris family. It is characteristic of this generous impulse, however, that by the
time of his death this sum was found to have been
heavily depleted in successive encroachments. After
the break-up of the firm he saw nothing of Morris,
though Mrs. Morris sometimes visited him in Cheyne
Walk. Brown and Morris were for a time completely
estranged, and, though later they made some show of
reconciliation, the old terms of jovial friendship were
never restored. Brown and Rossetti continued to be
nominally upon terms of cordial friendship, but they saw
less and less of each other ; the cold breath of the law,
even when directed by so sympathetic an advocate as
Watts-Dunton, seemed to have chilled them all and put
them out of ease with each other. The general ill-will
thus generated was particularly unfortunate in its coincid-
ence with Rossetti's suspicious melancholy.

It may be mentioned here that in 1874 Oliver Madox
Brown—" Nolly "—died very suddenly, poisoned, it
was found later, by the air of a subterranean stable. He
had been the centre of the hopes of all the Pre-Raphaelite
Circle, and Rossetti, with the rest of them, had prophesied
the greatest things for the boy's future. His affection-
ate memory of him was destroyed, however, with the
posthumous publication in 1876 of a novel, from which,
with his wretched sensitiveness to unintended allusions,
he " received a painful impression."

Another incident of 1874 may be worth mention as
typical of Rossetti's discordance with the peace of
Kelmscott. It is recorded in William Bell Scott's
Autobiographical Notes, and commented upon and a
little discredited in William Rossetti's *Memoir*, that
Scott received a letter at this time from Rossetti rather

diffidently asking for the loan of £200. At some inconvenience, he sent it to him by return of post, and received it again as quickly, with a grateful letter explaining that the embarrassment had already been relieved. Scott was left with the impression that the application had been made as a trial of him by his old friend, to test the sincerity of his affection. If so, he came out well from the trial, and such a suspicion is certainly typical of Rossetti's attitude of mind. William, however, thinks that the dates may have been confused, in which case it is possible that Rossetti was in need of just that sum.

During these years Rossetti's absence from London made it difficult for him to transact business with his clients. As we have seen, the negotiations for the sale of his pictures frequently got very much involved and could only be disentangled by personal discussion with his disappointed purchasers. Accordingly, he now appointed Charles Howell as his agent. The arrangement was in many ways an excellent one. Howell had very nearly as much adroitness and nerve as Rossetti himself in forcing a bargain, and in his untiring social exertions was in touch with a far wider circle of wealthy people. At first he acted with a Mr. Parsons, but later, owing to a quarrel between that gentleman and Rossetti, he abandoned the partnership. He certainly got Rossetti some of his highest prices. But there were compensating disadvantages in his service. He had a way of speculating on his own account, buying pictures for himself and reselling them at a profit, which Rossetti naturally resented. He was also singularly unscrupulous in the undertakings he gave for Rossetti. In the excitement of bringing off a big commission he would, without consulting his principal, pledge his name for future work in a way which proved exceedingly embarrassing. It was for these reasons that the connection came to an end two years after Rossetti's return to London, but he often expressed himself grateful for Howell's services, and maintained that he had gained rather than lost by them.

He never accused Howell, or, I think, seriously suspected him, of complicity in the considerable number of forgeries of his work which now began to appear in the market. The facts, however, are that Howell was himself an expert copyist, and, as such, had first attracted Ruskin's interest; moreover, he was at this time closely connected with a young woman named Rosa who had the same gift. The frequent appearance of spurious drawings, often from quite reputable sources, disturbed Rossetti deeply, but his reluctance to appear in court for any purpose whatever was insurmountable, and he never attempted to investigate the origin of these very able forgeries. If he had, the result would almost certainly have been the detection of Howell and Rosa. As it is, grave doubt attaches to many reputed Rossettis in private hands, and there is no way of proving their authenticity. As we have seen, his own work varied erratically, from the most timid and slipshod to that of the highest exaltation.

CHAPTER VIII

THE LAST PHASE, 1874–1882

London, 1874—The Grosvenor Gallery—Last paintings—Last poems—
Hall Caine—The Vale of St. John—Death.

I

TUDOR HOUSE, empty for two years, was a little more
gloomy and a little more dissolute when Rossetti returned
to it in the summer of 1874. The blue china was gone,
the animals were gone, there was a talk of his garden
being taken away from him and built over in the near
future. Chelsea was beginning to be more fashionable.
He was himself a broken man in body and mind at the
age of forty-six. The remaining eight years of his life
form a story of cumulative distress by lingering over
which little can be gained ; it falls naturally into two
parts, before and after 1877, the point of division being,
characteristically, another physical breakdown.

He spent the winter of 1874 and the spring and summer
of 1875 at Cheyne Walk, entertaining little and never
going to his friends' houses. Indeed, he seldom left
the house at all except late at night in a four-wheeled cab
with George Hake ; in this he drove to Regent's Park,
where he would descend, walk for an hour, and then
drive back to whisky, chloral, and bed. Hake, who had
been growing stout at Kelmscott, was gradually getting
on Rossetti's nerves, and finally there was a row of
some violence, after which neither he nor his father, to
whom Rossetti owed so much, had any further dealings
with him.

In the winter of 1875 Robert Buchanan, who had for
three years been subject to an unrelenting persecution

from the whole influential Pre-Raphaelite Circle, at last turned on his assailants, and sued Peter Taylor, of the *Examiner*, for libel. This suit was successful, and he was awarded £150 damages. Rossetti was alarmed that he might be called to appear in the witness-box and distressed at the revival of all the painful issues of *The Fleshly School* controversy. Accordingly, he left London and took a house at Bognor called Aldwick Lodge, where he remained until the spring of 1876, when he went on a prolonged visit to Broadlands, in Hampshire, the home of Lord and Lady Mount Temple. Here he seems to have lived very much his own life, seeing little or nothing of the other guests who came and went throughout the summer. He painted and drew in the rooms set apart for him, stumped about the garden, and wrote with the greatest enthusiasm of Lady Mount Temple's " Christ-like " character.

While he was away the builders were at work at his studio, for during the previous year he had been disturbed by the sound of music coming from the house next door to him, and, supposing that this was some malicious demonstration by his neighbours, had ordered the room to be made sound-proof. This was effected by building another wall outside the existing one and filling the intervening space with padding.

In 1877 the Grosvenor Gallery was founded, and rapidly became the centre of the new æsthetic movement which had been in the air for some time. Overtures were made to Rossetti and Madox Brown to exhibit, but, after long deliberation, they refused. It was the last concerted action of the Pre-Raphaelites. Rossetti's letter of refusal gives as his reason the consciousness of failure that was heavy upon him. He had not done what he had set out to do, and he was content with the appreciation of the limited circle who were willing to judge him by his endeavour rather than his achievement. It is a pathetic confession coming from an artist still in early middle age, and at the height of his reputation. Perhaps he had at the back of his mind the intention of one day collecting the best of his works and exhibiting them together in their proper atmosphere. William Rossetti suggests that he may have entertained some such project, but there is a ring of sincerity about his excuses. The ignorant abuse that had greeted him in 1850, joined in his mind with the malicious abuse of 1872 and his conviction of the existence of a widespread conspiracy against him, made him unduly apprehensive of the verdict of the public and of free criticism. He did not know that the leaven of Ruskin and Morris had been working steadily among the artistic public. When, after his death, the great double exhibition of his collected works was held at the Royal Academy and at the Burlington Fine Arts Club, there was scarcely a dissentient voice in the chorus of praise and admiration. Had he, during his lifetime, taken the risk and received the reward, the next years of his life might have been very different. He would certainly have exercised a decisive influence upon the temper of the Grosvenor Gallery. Without him or Madox Brown the Gallery broke, instead of carrying on, the tradition of the Pre-Raphaelites. Burne-Jones swam into instant fame, and from the first set the tone of the annual exhibitions. If the robust influence of Madox Brown and Rossetti had been given full scope, English art might easily have escaped from the "greenery-yallery" fever which has set Beardsley in such a false light and made the progress of post-impressionism so inevitable.

In the summer he had another severe attack of the uræmic trouble to which he was subject. The operation was successful, but on this occasion he rallied from it very slowly. For two months he was prostrate ; when at length he could be moved, he went with Madox Brown to a little place called Hunters Forestall, near Herne Bay. Here he was sunk in abysmal depression, and consumed, as before, with the fear that he would never be able to paint or write again. His mother and Christina—Maria Francesca had died the year before at her sisterhood—joined him, and also Watts-Dunton. For some time

they shared his despair, but in October he showed signs
of rallying, made three admirable portraits of his mother
and Christina, and, with that remarkable recuperative
power that always characterised him, he was back again
in London in November.

From then onwards his life became completely
secluded. It is doubtful whether he ever left his house
at all. The midnight walks were given up, and the only
exercise he took was an occasional prowl round his
deserted garden. Even here, he complained, the birds
had been trained by his enemies to sing insults at him.
One by one his old friends had fallen away—Hunt,
Woolner, Millais, Browning, Morris, the Hakes ; now
he quarrelled over a futile difference with his oldest and
staunchest friend, Ford Madox Brown. As in 1872,
his cessation from work reduced him to considerable
financial embarrassment, and, as an economy, Brown
suggested the dismissal of two idle and possibly dishonest
servants to whom he had taken a great dislike. Rossetti
refused to do so, and Brown said he would not come to
the house again while they were there. The result was
that he did, in fact, keep away for two years, when
Rossetti needed him more than ever before, and finally,
when they were reconciled, he was at work in Manchester,
and unable to see much of his old friend. " None but
new men were now to be seen about him," wrote William
Bell Scott. Frederick Shields and William Sharp were
frequent visitors, neither of whom had known him or his
art in its youth and strength, and occasional curious
young men, drawn by the desire to gaze on the man who
presented so romantically a picture of ruined greatness.
It was only with the utmost repugnance that he could
force himself to receive a stranger, though, when he did
so, it was with a good show of geniality. William Rossetti
and Theodore Watts-Dunton share the honour of sustain-
ing him through the next two years of his life. Watts-
Dunton was given a bedroom in the house, where he
often slept after sitting up with Rossetti until four or five
in the morning. His chloral and alcohol were increased

to still heavier doses, despite the attempts of his friends to dilute them.

2

His artistic output shows some sign of failing, but up till 1877 he still maintained a high standard of industry and taste. *La Bella Mano* is the only oil painting done in 1875, but it bears comparison with any but his most inspired work ; technically it is perhaps his happiest, if not his most ambitious, achievement. It represents a lady washing her hands, a position he had chosen more than once before. Harmonious curves predominate in the composition, the curve of the shoulders running smoothly away into the curve of her dress, which is echoed by the towel held for her by an effeminate boy angel in the right of the canvas. Another winged child of great beauty holds her rings and bracelets. The lady herself is a characteristic Rossetti type—probably taken from Mrs. Stillman (Miss Spartali), though it becomes increasingly difficult to recognise Rossetti's models in the tricks of exaggeration and stylisation that he plays with them ; her head and eyes are thrown up in a characteristic pose, her bare arms are heavily modelled but in proportion to her rather massive shoulders and breast. A view of Rossetti's own bedroom appears in the convex mirror which forms a halo round her head. The canvas, as usual, is crowded with " adjuncts," many of which are already familiar. The openwork linen cloth of *The Loving Cup* reappears, and the astonishingly ugly ewer over the basin may be recognised as having been painted years before in *Lucretia Borgia*. The pearl wheel grows like a flower from a pot in the background, also of remarkably ugly design.

The other important work of this year is the large pencil drawing called *The Question* or *The Sphinx*. For some reason this most interesting drawing has never become as well known as it deserves. It is important for several features, notably as being the only work of

Rossetti's later period in which female beauty does not play a predominant part. It is also his last " subject " picture. Rossetti himself regarded it from this point of view, and, during his last illness, talked of using it for the frontispiece of a collection of poems and tales by himself and Watts-Dunton that they were thinking of bringing out. He retained the drawing in his studio, and it was not sold until the sale after his death. An attempt has been made in another part of this book to analyse its restless but impressive composition.

The subject is one to which Rossetti attached first-rate importance ; the Sphinx, symbol of the unsolved riddle of life and death, sits upon a crag of rock over the sea. Three naked pilgrims have come to question her, representing Youth, Manhood, and Age. Youth, first to arrive, has fallen back dead, his question unanswered,[1] his spear still erect in his hand. Manhood is gazing into the Sphinx's eyes, thrusting aside the branch that bars his way. Age still toils to reach the summit. It has been said that the idea of the death of Youth on the threshold of knowledge was suggested by the death of Oliver Madox Brown. This may well be so, or perhaps, more probably, he may have had in mind the story of Chatterton, for whom he now began to evince a fantastic admiration. At any rate, the conception of frustrated promise had a peculiar poignancy for him, sharpened by the sense of the failure of his own life. This is one of the few examples of the nude in Rossetti's work. If we except *Venus Verticordia*, there are only two others, both drawings from the same model. He shows an inclination to treat the human form as he habitually treated his more substantial draperies, disposing it into curves without reference to its structure or weight. It is impossible, for instance, to reconstruct the positions through which Youth, in the foreground, attained to his present pose. Is he arrested in the act of subsidence ?

[1] This is the view taken by Marillier and most commentators. It seems to me equally probable that Rossetti intended him to have been slain by the answer.

He appears to be supported along his shoulders by a branch of the tree, but there is nothing except the exigencies of the composition to explain why he should arch from the knees instead of doubling up in the middle. Which way is he going to fall ? I spent an exceedingly ungraceful half-hour before the looking-glass attempting to get into the same position. It is one into which it is just possible to *raise* the body, but quite impossible to let it fall. Notice, too, the female curve of Manhood's thigh and the depth of recession from his left foot to his hip. These things do not necessarily make it a bad picture, but they are undoubtedly ones which he would have described as " slosh " in 1850.

The Blessed Damozel took up most of the next year, and was not finished until 1877. It is interesting to see him at this late hour attempting to recapture the simplicity and sweetness of his earliest poem. Two versions exist, each with a predella of the earthly lover. In one the background of the main picture is a paradisal landscape strewn with reunited lovers. In the other, two disembodied cherubs float over the Damozel's head. Two girl angels—" stunners "—stand with broad, bare shoulders below the golden bar. A riot of filmy drapery has taken the place of the " robe ungirt from clasp to hem." The hair falls low on the forehead ; the lips and neck are more than usually exaggerated.

Two pictures, closely allied to each in form and spirit, follow. They show Rossetti at his best when least controlled. *Mnemosyne* or *The Lamp of Memory* or *Ricordanza* was finished in 1876, *Astarte Syriaca* in 1877. They are inspired by Mrs. Morris, though probably not painted from her. His intimacy with her had continued till the last, unbroken in the breach with her husband, but her visits to Cheyne Walk were not, I think, frequent enough to allow of her sitting for an important picture. No doubt he had in his possession numerous studies made while he was at Kelmscott, and used these to paint from. An interesting sentence in a letter to Madox Brown is quoted by Marillier. Writing of a crayon study of *The Blessed Damozel*, done in 1873 for Leyland, he explains his intention of painting from it at once, as " such pictures have more unity if one does not do them from nature, but from cartoons."[1]

The history of the two pictures is as follows :

Astarte Syriaca was commissioned early in 1876 by Clarence Fry, the well-known photographer of the firm of Elliot & Fry. It was one of the last deals engineered by Howell, and the price of £2,100 was the largest Rossetti ever earned. When it was sold again, shortly before Fry's death, it fetched a very much smaller sum. It is now in the Corporation Art Gallery at Manchester. The picture was begun by June 1876, but in the same month we find Rossetti offering for sale, at the price of £500, a finished painting called *La Ricordanza*.[2] This, now known as *Mnemosyne*, is obviously a study for *Astarte Syriaca*. Oddly enough, he offered this too to Clarence Fry. It was eventually sold to Leyland in 1881. *Astarte Syriaca* was finished and sold in 1877. It is thus difficult to assign priority to either of these intimately connected paintings. *Mnemosyne* contains a single figure very heavily modelled, with a great curtain of black hair falling behind the massive shoulders. A robe of sea-green falls from them and hangs insecurely over the breast. In the right hand she holds a huge lamp ; her left arm falls in a dead weight down the side of the picture, and the hand touches a cup of exceedingly curious design, described in the couplet on the frame as the " winged chalice of the soul " ; a yellow pansy, a feather, and a sunset complete this very striking composition. The face is obviously derived from Mrs. Morris, but is dehumanised to a degree which, by comparison, classes *Proserpine* with *Veronica Veronese*.

It is, in fact, an attempt to express purely unæsthetic emotions in terms of an abstraction of facial expression. This inclination has long been apparent in Rossetti's

---

[1] No doubt the anatomical exaggerations of his later work are largely attributable to this habit.

[2] Marillier.

work, and is of doubtful legitimacy. It is nearly allied to the " close-ups " of the cinema film. There the need to express emotions—the ordinary human feelings of love, hate, fear, etc.—which is met in good drama by dramatic action and dialogue has given rise to the system of enormous enlargement of the face to such proportions that only a sophisticated observer could collect and re-group the shadows and associate them with a human face of normal dimensions; emotion is then expressed by the use of symbols—a kiss or a tear, for instance, or by appeal to the unaccountable deep-seated instinct for recognition of facial expression. *Mnemosyne*, in common with a great number of Rossetti's later pictures, raises the two questions of whether such emotions are a proper subject for art and whether such devices may legitimately be used to express them. Both the acquired and intuitive symbolism are very evident in *Mnemosyne*—the hideous little chalice and the brooding eyes.

Astarte Syriaca is a very much larger painting, including, besides a three-quarter-length study of the central figure, two full-length attendant worshippers. The head and shoulders of the Syrian Venus are almost identical with those of *Mnemosyne*; the robe, of the same colour, has been girded under the breasts and round the hips with a silver chain. This has the happy result of restraining the somewhat dishevelled effect of *Mnemosyne*. The hands touch the girdle. The moon at the back and the silhouetted hands, the sunset and the torch, the depraved faces of the worshippers, haunted by unformulated aspirations, all give the atmosphere of the solemn and obscure worship of the mystery cults. He describes the picture in the following sonnet :

> Mystery ; lo ! betwixt the sun and moon,
> Astarte of the Syrians ; Venus, Queen
> Ere Aphrodite was. In silver sheen
> Her twofold girdle clasps the infinite boon
> Of bliss whereof the heaven and earth commune :
> And from the neck's inclining flower-stem lean
> Love-freighted lips and absolute eyes that wean

The pulse of hearts to the sphere's dominant tune.
Torch bearing, her sweet ministers compel
    All thrones of light beyond the sky and sea
    The witnesses of Beauty's face to be ;
That face, of Love's all-penetrative spell
Amulet, talisman, and oracle—
    Betwixt the sun and moon a mystery.

This is one of the happiest examples of harmony between
Rossetti's painting and poetry.   There is a feeling about
the picture as though a curtain had just been drawn
revealing it, as though Astarte had been standing just a
little longer than she had expected behind the arras—a
laxness in the pose, a strain in the eyes—and there is in
the opening of the sonnet—" Mystery ; lo ! "—exactly
the same feeling, the swish of the silk and the crash of
the cymbal as the goddess is revealed ; a sense of age
" ere Aphrodite was," the " absolute eyes " expressing
the very abstraction of which we have just been speaking.
It is a very different goddess of love from the *Venus
Verticordia* or *Lady Lilith*.

Of *Sea Spell*, painted in the same year, it is kinder to
the memory of the artist to say nothing.   It is the work
of a prematurely faltering mind and hand.

There is only one important painting in 1878—
Fiammetta, a study of Mrs. Stillman as the mistress of
Boccaccio, to whom he wrote many of his sonnets.   It
actually illustrates the last but one of Rossetti's book of
translations, which opens with the lines, " Round her
red garland and her golden hair, I saw a fire about
Fiammetta's head."   Besides this, Rossetti composed
another sonnet to the picture beginning, " Beloved
Fiammetta, shown in vision here."

The painting shows great recuperation from the
terrible *Sea Spell*, and is quite fit to be classed with *The
Loving Cup*, and *The Damozel of the San Grail*, and
Rossetti's other less inspired but competent paintings.

La Donna della Finestra of 1879 is another study of
Mrs. Morris which he had long contemplated, and for
which he had made studies as far back as 1870.   It

represents the lady at the window in the *Vita Nuova* who, looking down at Dante one day, was so afflicted at the poet's grief " that the very sum of pity appeared gathered together in her," and who, whenever she saw him, " became pale and of piteous countenance, as though it had been of love." Rossetti used to fancy that this lady might be Gemma Donati, whom the poet eventually married.[1]

Another long-deferred picture of Mrs. Morris, called *The Day Dream*, occupied much of his time during the next two years. All Rossetti's failing concentration and genius was lavished upon this beautiful canvas. It was almost finished when he decided that the legs were too short, and accordingly set to work repainting the whole lower part of the picture, an operation which involved the copying on to a separate canvas of the sycamore shoots which were painted on top of the drapery, because the season of the year had passed for obtaining fresh specimens. The head was also entirely repainted more than once.[2] Mrs. Morris is represented sitting in a sycamore-tree, a book on her knees. She has fallen into a reverie. The pattern of sycamore leaves against the sky is particularly beautiful ; there is one curve of head and hands. The painting of the lower half is undistinguished but unobtrusive. It is Rossetti's last worthy painting.

Two pictures remain, about which Stephens is loyally reticent—*The Salutation of Beatrice* and *La Pia*. They were both purchased by Leyland, who appears to have liked them ; to anybody else they would have been inexpressibly painful.

La Pia ends the record of his work. It is fitting that his last months should have been occupied with the story of Pia di Tolomei, the imprisoned bride, slowly dying among the pestilent exhalations of the Maremma marshes —the end of a life's work which began with the sweet girlhood of Mary the Virgin.

---

[1] Marillier.   [2] Ibid.

In 1881 Rossetti had another volume of poems ready for publication, and he took the opportunity of reissuing his earlier book in a slightly different form.

It may be as well to give here a brief bibliographical survey of Rossetti's writing. Five volumes were published under his name during his lifetime. They are:

A. *The Early Italian poets from Ciullo d'Alcamo to Dante Alighieri* (1100–1200–1300) *in the original metres, together with Dante's "Vita Nuova," Translated by D. G. Rossetti. Part I: Poets chiefly before Dante; Part II: Dante and his Circle* (*London: Smith, Elder & Co.*, 1861).

These were the translations written by him for the most part during his Pre-Raphaelite Brotherhood period, and to the publication of which Ruskin subscribed £100.

B. *Dante and his Circle, with the Italian Poets preceding him* (1100–1200–1300). *A collection of Lyrics, edited, and translated in the original metres, by Dante Gabriel Rossetti; revised and rearranged edition. Part I: Dante's "Vita Nuova," etc., poets of Dante's Circle; Part II: Poets chiefly before Dante* (*London: Ellis & White, 29 New Bond Street,* 1874).

This is almost identical with A except in arrangement.

C. *Poems by Dante Gabriel Rossetti* (*London: F. S. Ellis*, 1870).

D. *Poems by Dante Gabriel Rossetti. A new edition* (*London: Ellis & White*, 1881).

E. *Ballads and Sonnets by Dante Gabriel Rossetti* (*London: Ellis & White*, 1881).

The relations between C, D, and E are somewhat intricate. D is for the most part a new edition of C, while E is made up of the work written by him between 1870 and 1880. But there are modifications of this scheme, the most important being the bodily transference of all the sonnets from *Sonnets and Songs, towards a work to be called "The House of Life"* from C to E. This section, considerably amplified and reorganised, thus appeared as a sonnet sequence under the title *The*

House of Life. It should be noted, however, that many of the additional sonnets were not new ones, but taken from his work written before 1870 and not included in that volume. Poems written after 1870 were inserted in D to take the place of *The House of Life.*

William Rossetti, in the collected edition of his brother's poetry which he brought out in 1887, was thus obliged to disregard C altogether and, having thirty-one previously unprinted works to include,[1] he decided upon a new and perfectly happy arrangement, which has been preserved in subsequent editions.

Nuptial Sleep, already quoted, and *On the French Liberation of Italy,* which was held to contain a " repulsive metaphor," were omitted by Gabriel from the re-issue of his work and by William from the collected edition.

Ballads and Sonnets was dedicated to Watts-Dunton. It contained, besides *The House of Life,* which was now a substantial work of a hundred and one sonnets, thirteen lyrics, eighteen miscellaneous sonnets, including *Astarte Syriaca, La Bella Mano,* and others written for pictures, and the three superb ballads *Rose Mary, The White Ship,* and *The King's Tragedy.* These last, and particularly *Rose Mary,* are held by most admirers of Rossetti's poetry to be the highest achievements of his genius.

But Rossetti, by this time, was in a state when the enthusiasms of his admirers meant little to him.

3

The story of Rossetti's last years may be told very briefly. Four years before his death he came into touch with a young man whose enthusiasm and reverence and peculiar receptiveness, that so often accompanies half-formed taste and high ambition, endeared him to the failing master with a felicity which William Bell Scott was the first to resent.

---

[1] Eight of them had appeared in various magazines.

Sir Hall Caine had not at this time begun his career
as a novelist. He was engaged upon a series of popular
lectures on contemporary literature at the Royal Institution and the Free Library at Liverpool. One of these
dealt with Rossetti, and in a fashion particularly agreeable
to his idiosyncrasies. " I thought," wrote Hall Caine,
' that Rossetti's poetry showed how possible it is . . .
to be unconsciously making for moral ends. . . . Every
thought in *Dante at Verona* and *The Last Confession*
seemed mixed with, and coloured by, a personal moral
instinct that was safe and right."

In the hope that " Rossetti himself might derive a
moment's gratification from the knowledge of the fact
that he had one ardent upholder and sincere well-wisher
hitherto unknown to him," he sent a copy of the magazine
containing the text of the lecture to Tudor House and
almost by return of post received a reply from Rossetti.
" . . . I am grateful to you," he wrote, " for you have
spoken up heartily and unfalteringly for the work you
love. I daresay you sometimes come to London. I
should be very glad to know you."

It was the autumn of 1880 before the meeting took
place, but in the meantime there flourished a correspondence of sustained vigour, on the one side patiently didactic,
on the other eagerly appreciative, numbering nearly two
hundred letters a head, and extending in scope as their
intimacy deepened from a mere interchange of opinions
on literary subjects to politics, religion, morals, and the
most minute details of health and illness.

" Correspondence with yourself," wrote Rossetti,
" is one of my best pleasures . . . you cannot write too
much or too often for *me*."

A few extracts from Rossetti's part in this correspondence—Sir Hall's, alas ! has not survived—show the
tone of easy friendship which gradually arose between
the two.

" Your swing of arm," he wrote, referring to a sonnet
sent him for criticism, " seems to me firmer and freer
in prose than in verse. I do think I see your field to

lie chiefly in the achievements of fervid and impassioned prose."

" I was truly concerned to hear of the attack of ill health. . . . I myself have had similar symptoms (though not so fully as you describe), and have spat blood at intervals for years, but now think nothing of it."

" I judge you cannot suspect *me* of thinking the apotheosis of the early Italian poets . . . of more importance than the ' unity of a great nation.' But it is in my minute power to deal successfully (I feel) with the one, while no such entity, as I am, can advance or retard the other ; and thus mine must needs be the poorer part."

It is a singular friendship. He keeps a close eye upon the evolution of Sir Hall's " fervid and impassioned " prose style, and in one letter takes him to task—surely unduly—for the use of " mythopæic " and " anthropomorphism," saying that he does not find life long enough to know the least what they mean. He declines the honour of the dedication of a lecture on the relations of politics to art, but in the most gracious terms. He advises his reading, introducing him to Chatterton and Smart's *Song of David*—the former in terms of wildly exaggerated adulation. Finally a visit was arranged.

" I will be truly glad to meet you when you come to town. You will recognise the hole-and-cornerest of all existences ; but I'll read you a ballad or two, and have Brown's report to back my certainty of liking you." . . . " Of course, when I speak of your dining with me, I mean *tête à tête*, and without ceremony of any kind. I usually dine in my studio, and in my painting coat."

Considerable " epistolary ceremony " marked the arrangements. Three letters—from two of which the foregoing extracts have been taken—arrived almost simultaneously, explaining and reaffirming the details of the engagement. A fourth arrived shortly after Hall Caine's departure, begging him to keep certain subjects about which they had corresponded out of the conversation. It was some time since Rossetti had had to meet a new acquaintance, and he found the situation unnerving.

For Hall Caine, too, the visit was rather alarming. There was nothing in Liverpool quite like the sombre old house, with its air of neglect and its bizarre furniture. Nor had he ever met anyone quite as famous in quite such a romantic way. Rossetti, however, despite his own qualms, soon put his guest at ease. He exhibited his usual hearty geniality, holding out both hands and crying " Hulloa," which was " Italian in its spontaneity but English in its manly reserve." William stood in the background, rather more austere but infinitely courteous.

The first greetings over, Rossetti lowered himself upon the sofa, and, sprawling in his characteristic pose, head low, feet high, began talking in his luminous, incisive, opulent way, first about Hall Caine's appearance, then about various topics they had recently discussed in their letters, then, with tolerant banter, about his friends. After dinner, which, contrary to expectation, was not served in the studio, he read aloud *The Ballad of the White Ship*.

The evening passed pleasantly, and it was arranged that Hall Caine should spend the night there on his return journey through London. This time the meeting was not untouched by disquiet. Very late at night Rossetti began suddenly and insistently to ply his guest with questions about some criticisms he had heard uttered about *Jenny*. He drank in the details with unnatural avidity, and then, his voice charged with emotion, said, " It was the old story, which began ten years before, and would go on until he had been hunted and hounded to the grave." " You tell me," said Hall Caine, " that you have rarely been outside these walls for some years and your brain has meanwhile been breeding a host of hallucinations like cobwebs in a dark corner. You have only to go abroad, and the fresh air will blow these things away." But he continued for some time in the same strain, bitterly quoting as his enemies three or four of his closest and most loyal friends. Then, all the wit and the charm dead within him, he lumbered off to bed. Hall Caine accompanied him to his room ;
PR

the black velvet hangings seemed to stifle their voices. " There is a skeleton in every cupboard," Rossetti said, pointing to the bottles beside his bed ; " that's mine ; it is chloral."

Next morning Rossetti did not come down. Hall Caine looked at his library, wandered for a little about the unkempt garden where Mr. Watts-Dunton was " reluctant to interfere with Nature in her clever scheme of the survival of the fittest," and left a little before luncheon without saying good-bye to his host. He had a great deal to think about in the train north. A chill had struck into the heart of the young man. Was Art quite such a noble thing as it had seemed in Liverpool ?

4

Six months later he again visited Cheyne Walk. He found Rossetti somewhat changed, his complexion brighter, his eyes duller, his movements more laboured, " as though the body unconsciously lost and then re-gained some necessary control and command at almost every step." He shambled about in this fashion, to and fro, almost incessantly. His conversation alternated between extravagant praise and extravagant abuse of his friends and contemporaries. On the evening preceding his guest's departure he pressed him to take up permanent residence with him. To this proposal Hall Caine made no reply. But the matter was not allowed to drop. Some months later, when his own health was endangered, he told Rossetti of his intention of spending some months in seclusion in the Vale of St. John in Cumberland. Rossetti now decided that he too must go to the country. Would Hall Caine take charge of him ? He would take a large house in the Vale of St. John and make his permanent home there. At any rate, he would go there for a few months. They were at last taking his garden away from him at Cheyne Row. He must leave London at once.

By the next post came a letter abandoning all intention
of leaving London. A little later another letter to say
that his housekeeper was leaving. The house he had
been looking at in Brixton was hopeless. In his bewilder-
ment he turned to his newest friend. Hall Caine must
come at once. He came intending to make only a short
visit. On his arrival he found that Rossetti had fitted
out rooms for him and was set upon his coming to live
there. In this way he drifted into his position as house-
mate. This was in July 1881. In September it became
clear that Rossetti was a very ill man, and the thoughts
of his friends again began to turn towards Cumberland.
Almost intolerable precautions were necessary before
he could be induced to set out. His indecision mani-
fested itself in every detail. At the last moment he
insisted that Fanny Schott must come too. Books,
painting materials, and clothes for a year's visit were
laboriously assembled. Through the long night journey
Rossetti sat in sleepless lassitude. At dawn they reached
Penrith and drove to Legberthwaite. Rossetti, saturated
in chloral, complained that he could not see.

A month later they returned to London after the most
hideous period in Rossetti's life. Fanny Schott, now
bereft even of her physical charm, had come to the Vale
of St. John with one purpose, to induce Rossetti to make
a will in her favour. Alternately coaxing and bullying
him and continually plying him with whisky, this fiendish
woman completed the ruin that was already so far
advanced. He returned to London a dying man.
" Thank God," he said as Hall Caine helped him over
his doorstep, " home at last, and never shall I leave it
again."

In the last months of his life he became increasingly
dependent upon his friends. He could not bear to be
left alone for an hour. Hall Caine lived in the house with
him ; Frederick Shields, W. B. Scott, Miss Boyd, with,
of course, Watts-Dunton, and the Rossetti family were
constant visitors.

Just before Christmas he was lying on his sofa talking

to Philip Bourke Marston and his father when he suddenly cried out that his arm had become paralysed, and,
on trying to rise, that his leg also had lost its power.   The
paralysis proved temporary, but a crisis had obviously
arisen, and his doctors now decided that the chloral habit
must be decisively stopped.   By the gradual substitution of morphia in successively weaker doses, this was
achieved ; his brain cleared and for a time his friends
entertained extravagant hopes of his complete recovery.
But he had not the strength to begin life over again.   By
January he was comparatively normal in mind, but utterly
worn out.   He was moved to a bungalow belonging to
J. P. Seddon at Birchington-on-Sea.   For nine weeks
he lived there, growing weaker and more weary, attended
to the last by Hall Caine.   He began writing a comic
ballad about a Dutchman and the Devil.   On Thursday,
April 6th, his speech became thick and barely intelligible.
Hall Caine wired for Watts-Dunton, William Rossetti,
and Marshall.   Rossetti sat up in bed in a kind of stupor,
crooning over to himself odd lines of poetry.   " My own
verse torments me," he said.

Next day, Good Friday, his friends arrived.   " Then
you really think I'm dying," he said.   " *At last* you
think so ; but *I* was right from the first."

On Easter Day, at nine in the evening, his friends in
the next room heard a loud scream, and, hurrying in,
found him in convulsions ; after a few seconds he died.
He was buried some days later in the churchyard at
Birchington, where visitors who wish to may, with some
difficulty, find his grave.

CHAPTER IX

WHAT IS WRONG WITH ROSSETTI ?

Subjective painting—" Literary " painting—Spiritual inadequacy—The
problem.

I

ROSSETTI has been dead for forty-six years and it is still
as difficult to form a sound estimate of his position in
European art as it was in the first burst of enthusiasm
that greeted the two public exhibitions of his work
shortly after his death. If anything, it is rather more
difficult ; there have been other exhibitions since then,
and other enthusiasms.

During his lifetime there was, as we have seen, no
such thing as an apparatus of artistic criticism ; that
is to say, there was no generally accepted and logically
defensible scale of values that would have enabled the
critic to form his opinion of new work and express it in
intelligible terms. F. G. Stephens's praise was, in its
way, just as futile and ill directed as Charles Dickens's
abuse, and, when Ruskin attempted to advance his
æsthetic system towards its logical limits, it turned out,
much to the surprise of his admirers, to have been
political economy in disguise all the time.

At the present day there is a perceptible stability
about the standards of ordinary periodical artistic
criticism, and, despite innumerable very important
dissentients, there is a method of thought that has
attained sufficient concordance to claim, without undue
self-aggrandisement, to be the modern critical attitude.

This originally took shape when the more articulate
admirers of the post-impressionist schools of painting

found themselves obliged to explain their preferences. To do this, they pointed to what was, I think, an entirely new thing which they called the " æsthetic emotion." If there had not been an æsthetic emotion they would have had to have invented one.   As it was, the argument was all their own way.   Some people's æsthetic emotion might be more easily aroused than others, but, whenever the emotion was sincerely present, there was Art.   The intensity of the emotion was the gauge by which the value of the work of art could be assessed.   Thus the initial assumption became the foundation on which modern criticism is built.

At the beginning of this book are quoted two profoundly antithetical views of the artistic impulse, the one written by Rossetti himself, and the other by Mr. Roger Fry. Even without its context the implications of Mr. Fry's statement are perfectly clear.   " I know that real art-ists," he says, " generally begin by making an elaborate study of an old pair of boots."   There is no question, of course, about representation and imitation, the bugbear, so far as they were conscious at all of the urgency of abstract speculation, of nineteenth-century critics.   It is not to be supposed that anyone will mistake the " real artist's " drawing for an actual boot and attempt to put his foot into it.   What Mr. Fry means is that the " real " artist fundamentally is someone interested in the form underlying the appearances of things.   The function of boots as protection for the feet is not his concern ; still less are any associations about the particular pair being drawn ; no acquaintance is established beyond percep-tion of form; the artist need never have seen boots before, nor need he have the smallest conception of their uses. Artistic perception begins with an appreciation of the reality of form, and becomes creative as it begins to associate forms with each other in *necessary*, and therefore agreeable, relationships ; a work of art is a statement of such relationships or of a coherent sequence of such relationships, varying from the simplest to the most complex according to the scope of the work.   That, as far as I can see, is a fair statement of the modern (I use this in the accepted sense of ten years behind "the movement") critical standpoint. It begins, it should be noted, with the observer, postulating for himself a unique and simple emotion, and from that deducing the state of mind of the artist.

Approached from this standpoint, Rossetti, with all his "temperament" and "inspiration," is nothing but a melancholy old fraud. If Art is restricted to the splendid succession of European painting and to such works of negro sculpture as may be held to have some kinship with it, Rossetti is not "a real artist" either in achievement or intention. The last thing he wished to do was to express the necessary relations of forms. At the same time he undoubtedly had a very clear impression of the importance of his work, quite apart from its commercial value. Moreover a great deal of it leaves the observer with a similar impression, and inclines him to ask the not wholly impertinent question : "Well, if these paintings are not works of art, what are they?" which is a far more difficult problem to answer than the more usual one : "If these paintings are not works of art, what are works of art?"

It seems to me that modern criticism has failed in this : that it has taken an already existing word, "art," and has fastened it upon a newly discovered "necessary relation of forms in space." No one would deny that there is this vivifying quality to be found as a common factor in most recognised works of art, from Michel Angelo to Cezanne ; if one likes one may dignify the perception of this quality by the title of "æsthetic emotion," but surely it is unjustifiable to claim this as the one vital factor and to accept anything embodying it as a work of art? The fact that primitive negro sculpture satisfies the æsthetic emotion ought to make the healthy Western critic doubt the formula rather than acclaim the barbarian.

But there is, I think, another way of approaching Rossetti's painting, which is suggested by the confession

of his earliest promptings quoted at the beginning of
Chapter I. His first impulse to pictorial expression,
he tells us, came not from the contemplation of form—
either in plaster casts or old boots—but from an emotional state of mind evoked by firelight and singing. In
a significant phrase he describes how in this mood
" shapes rose within him." That is to say, that in him
the state of mind became automatically translated into
visible forms.

Now it is to just such configurations as these that Mr.
Hubert Waley points in his brilliant essay on *The Revival
of Æsthetics*[1] as the possible essence of æsthetic expression. Just as the ordinary man has various auto-
matic rhythms and shapes of reaction to various stimuli—
the stamping of the feet in anger, twiddling of fingers in
agitation, etc.—so it may well be that the artist is the
vehicle for the translation into visible and tangible shapes
of the more complex emotions. It is not possible, in
the present state of psychology, to produce this as a
brand-new, cast-iron system of æsthetics. It has in its
present state obvious inadequacies. Suppose, for instance, that one borrows a method from Mr. E. M.
Forster,[2] and attempts to arrange in a vast sequence all
the pictorial expressions of man, beginning at each end
with the simplest forms and working up in the centre
to the most elaborate ; and suppose that at one end we
begin, as Mr. Fry would, with the simplest expressions
we can find of ideas about form, and at the other with the
simplest forms about ideas, we shall find precisely the
same forms occurring at both ends of our sequence.
The natural temptation to fold the sequence over in
one's mind and to pretend that the two halves are identical
may contain a hint of a possible fusion that will result
in a new, workable æsthetic. However, these specula-
tions are beyond the scope of this chapter, the only
purpose of which is to suggest justifications for regarding
Rossetti as a " real " artist.

[1] Hogarth Essays.   [2] *Anonymity.*

2

Besides all this, Rossetti's painting consciously makes another appeal which brings it into conflict with the accepted canons of taste. This is its allusive or so-called " literary " appeal, a taunt from which singularly few artists are immune. " Pure " painting, according to reputable standards, should concern itself solely with beauty and not with anecdote, but, more than this, it must be with its own beauty and not with the beauty of the thing represented ; a head should be looked at as so much mass of matter, so much variation of colour, so much light and shadow. Such a restriction was essentially foreign to Rossetti's habit of thought. He had little use for anecdotal painting in the sense in which Holman-Hunt employed it for the inculcation of moral precepts, but he knew no valid distinction between beauty of picture and beauty of subject.

As we have seen, the spirit of woman was his one persistent preoccupation, and at least half of his work, both in poetry and painting, is an endeavour to express it forcibly and permanently. The mystery and attraction of womanhood and the physical beauty of women were to him quintessential elements of life, and he felt nothing unworthy in his devotion of his art to their exaltation. As he lost interest after a time in physical appearances, he strove more and more to make his painting the abstraction of sex difference ; to paint the soul and the soullessness of woman as a sex, as distinct from the shapes of particular women ; thus bringing himself further than ever from the objective standards of to-day and making his work less satisfactory to the simpler minded devotees of the " excellent likeness."

It seems to me that the defence for " literary " painting, if defence is needed—and not only for Rossetti, but for the sermonising of Hunt and even the chattiness of Frith—lies in the very word used in its condemnation. Why of the Arts should literature alone be expected to be " impure " ? Why, because we are accustomed to expressing our daily wants in words, shall poetry be allowed to traffick with other emotions besides the æsthetic emotion ? If I may legitimately be frightened by *The Ancient Mariner*, why may I not also be by Wiertz ?

One day the critics will realise that by their rigid restriction of artistic scope they are making bores of all but the very greatest.   How one longs, among the undeviating nudes and still lives of a modern exhibition, for the "impure" thrill of a Jerome Bosch or of a Martineau. By no means the least of the advantages to be gained from a study of Rossetti is the stimulus it gives to one's restiveness in an era of competent stultification.

One other problem obtrudes itself into any unconsidered acceptance of Rossetti's importance ; that of the *moral* position of the artist.

To the muddled Victorian mind it seemed vaguely suitable that the artist should be melancholy, morbid, uncontrolled, and generally slightly deranged.   It was a complement of the somewhat earlier popular tradition that to be " understanding " one must be also an invalid, and to be " pure," impoverished.   This mischievous misconception found its fulfilment in the 'nineties when, in London and Paris, at any rate, most of the considerable artistic figures were in fact consumptive or perverted or epileptic or in some way enough debased to give colour to the impression that Art was the lily that flowered from the dung-heap.

In Rossetti's own day, no doubt, not a little of the adulation he aroused came from this romance of decay— a sort of spiritual coprophily characteristic of the age. Even now we are inclined to think of him with melancholy tolerance and to say, " If he had not been improvident and lethargic, how great an artist he might have been," as we say of the war poets, " If they had not been killed . . . ."   But it seems to me that there we have the root cause of Rossetti's failure.   It is not so much that as a man he was a bad man—mere lawless wickedness has frequently been a concomitant of the highest genius— but there was fatally lacking in him that *essential rectitude* that underlies the serenity of all really great art. The sort of unhappiness that beset him was not the sort of unhappiness that does beset a great artist ; all his brooding about magic and suicide are symptomatic not so much of genius as of mediocrity. There is a spiritual inadequacy, a sense of ill-organisation about all that he did.

But if he were merely a psychopathic case and nothing more, there would be no problem and no need for a book about him. The problem is that here and there in his life he seems, without ever feeling it, to have transcended this inadequacy in a fashion that admits of no glib explanation. Just as the broken arch at Glastonbury Abbey is, in its ruin, so much more moving than it can ever have been when it stood whole and part of a great building, so Rossetti's art, at fitful moments, flames into the exquisite beauty of *Beata Beatrix*. It is the sort of problem that modern æsthetics does not seem capable of coping with. It has been the object of this book to state, though, alas ! not to solve, this problem.

INDEX